HAPPY ODYSSEY

For a description of this book and some information about the author, see back of cover.

"General Carton de Wiart has won more battle awards, suffered more wounds and seen more varied campaigns than any living general officer. He writes as he fights, with dash, and damns the consequences. He is plainly a lovable man."—*Manchester Guardian.*

"One of the best accounts of pure soldiering that can ever have appeared."—*Spectator.*

"Outspoken, told in plain English superbly devoid of literary elegancies, his story swings along, revealing the freshness of a mind splendidly untroubled by introspection. Sir Adrian is not only a legendary figure of incredible bravery, but also that most lovable of characters—and now most rare—a great eccentric."— COLONEL VLADIMIR PENIAKOFF ("Popski") in *Sunday Times.*

HAPPY ODYSSEY

The Memoirs of

LIEUTENANT-GENERAL
SIR ADRIAN CARTON DE WIART
V.C. K.B.E. C.B. C.M.G. D.S.O.

With a Foreword by the Right Hon.
SIR WINSTON S. CHURCHILL
K.G. O.M. C.H.

COMPLETE AND UNABRIDGED

PAN BOOKS LTD: LONDON

First published 1950 *by Jonathan Cape, Ltd.*
This edition published 1955 *by Pan Books Ltd.*
*8 Headfort Place, London, S.W.*1

PUBLISHERS' NOTE

In his book General Carton de Wiart makes no mention of the fact that he was awarded the Victoria Cross. Because, as readers will agree, his conduct was no more than characteristic, the citation is here quoted in full.

On September 8th, 1916, the *London Gazette* announced the award of the Victoria Cross to Captain (temporary Lieutenant-Colonel) Adrian Carton de Wiart, D.S.O., Dragoon Guards :

" For most conspicuous bravery, coolness and determination during severe operations of a prolonged nature. It was owing in a great measure to his dauntless courage and inspiring example that a serious reverse was averted.

" He displayed the utmost energy and courage in forcing our attack home. After three other battalion commanders had become casualties, he controlled their commands, and ensured that the ground won was maintained at all costs.

" He frequently exposed himself in the organization of positions and of supplies, passing unflinchingly through fire barrage of the most intense nature.

" His gallantry was inspiring to all."

Printed by Wyman & Sons Ltd.
London, Reading and Fakenham

CONTENTS

FOREWORD

I AM glad that my old and valued friend, Lieutenant-General Sir Adrian Carton de Wiart, has written this book. I have known him for many years, and in the late war I felt the highest confidence in his judgment and services both in Norway and as my military representative with General Chiang Kai-shek. General Carton de Wiart has been decorated on several occasions for his valour in the field and services to his country, and in 1916 he gained the Victoria Cross. Although repeatedly wounded and suffering from grievous injuries, his whole life has been vigorous, varied and useful. He is a model of chivalry and honour, and I am sure his story will command the interest of all men and women whose hearts are uplifted by the deeds and thoughts of a high-minded and patriotic British officer.

WINSTON S. CHURCHILL

ACKNOWLEDGMENT

THE poem " The Toy Band : A Song of the Great Retreat " is reproduced by permission of the Executors of the late Sir Henry Newbolt.

PREFACE

FOR some years my friends have been suggesting that I should write the story of my life. My answer has always been, " God forbid ! " They assumed that I must have had an adventurous life. I think it has been made up of mis-adventures. That I should have survived them is to me by far the most interesting thing about it. However, a bad accident as I was leaving China, necessitating many months in bed, and the feeling that I might never walk again, made me think back on the years and try to jot down what I re-membered of them. As I have never kept a diary there may be chronological errors for which I apologize in advance. These are simply the reminiscences of a lucky life ; they have no pretensions to being either military or political history. I was much amused a little time ago to read in *Punch* that it was evident in view of the number of War memoirs that were being published that generals were prepared to sell their lives as dearly in peace time as they had been in war. Apart from that inducement, I think it was also due to those lines of Lindsay Gordon which have always appealed to me :

> One of these poets, which is it?
> Somewhere or another sings,
> That the crown of a sorrow's sorrow
> Is remembering happier things.
> What the crown of a sorrow's sorrow
> May be, I know not ; but this I know,
> It lightens the years that are now
> Sometimes to think of the years ago.

A. C. DE W.

CHAPTER I

BELGIUM, ENGLAND, OXFORD

A CHILDHOOD of shifting scene and a mixed nationality may be responsible for my useful knack of growing roots wherever I happen to find myself. I was born in Brussels, a Belgian, the son of a successful legal man, and with an Irish grandmother to produce a small quantity of British blood in my veins. My wet nurse, with her vast starched strings, must have obscured my vision of anything else, for I can remember nothing of my infant days. My first real recollection is of Alexandria, where my parents took me when I was three, and I can still see the fierce fires shooting up into the sky to signal the warning of the dread menace, cholera. Then we came to England, and I have hazy memories of a dozing Surrey countryside where I was transformed into an English child and learned to speak French with a good British accent, and finally induced my parents to exchange my pleated skirt and large sailor hat for something a little more manly.

When I was six I lost my mother, and my father decided to uproot himself from Europe, transfer to Cairo and practise international law. My father's sister and her family came to look after us, and saw to it that my French accent improved.

Suddenly my whole horizon changed, for in 1888 my father met and married an Englishwoman who was travelling abroad as companion to a Turkish princess. To my youthful eyes she appeared very pretty, but she was full of rigorous ideas accentuated by a strong will and a violent temper. My father's house was cleared of all his extraneous relations, and I was given the English child's prerogative, a little precious freedom, and encouraged in what was to be my first and lasting love, sport.

Originally I had been given a donkey to ride, usually hung round by attendants, but now I became the possessor of a pony, a polo pony, perfect in my eyes except for the living and terrible shame of a rat tail. The local photographer must have been a man of rare understanding, for when he came to take a picture of me astride my steed he sensed my shame, and thoughtfully embellished my pony with an im-promptu tail.

One other gift marked the beginning of my sporting career. It was a small breech-loading gun, a Flobert, and with it I harassed the wretched Egyptian sparrow.

By this time I was tri-lingual, for I could speak French, English and Arabic, and when an Italian governess appeared to plague me into learning Italian I thought it overdoing things and revolted. Our dislike of each other was mutual, her authority doubtful and her reign brief! I was then packed off to a day school run by French priests, memorable only because I was allowed to ride there every day on my charger.

In Egypt in those days a child's chance of survival was very small, with a perpetual battle against disease. I was continually ill and eventually had to leave my day school to be put in the hands of an inefficient tutor.

Summer brought me still more freedom, for my father took a house at Ramleh, on the sea near Alexandria, where my stepmother proved herself an inspired swimming in-structress by the simple expedient of throwing me in.

The rest of my childhood's recollections can be summed up with a miniature gymnasium erected in the garden for physical jerks, an irrepressible mania for catching frogs, a love of pageantry and all things military. It was a life too lonely and formal to be truly happy, and I knew nothing of nurseries, plump, kind nannies and buttered toast for tea.

All this time my father had been enjoying a most suc-cessful career as a lawyer, and he had become one of the leading men in the country. Later he was called to the English Bar and became a naturalized British subject. His naturalization can have been only for business reasons, as although he had been educated in England at Stonyhurst he struck me always as a foreigner, and at heart I know that he remained a Belgian. My father was tall, neat, clever and hardworking, and the soul of generosity. He had two traits at variance with his legal calling, a guileless trust in man and no discrimination in people. He was utterly helpless and incapable of even shaving himself, let alone tying his shoe-laces, and I seem to have inherited from him one very trying habit of buying everything in dozens. We were on very good terms and I admired and respected him, but we were never intimate. Our interests lay too far apart for real under-standing; he was a hard-working indoor man, while I was idle and loved the out of doors.

No doubt because of my stepmother's influence my father decided to send me to school in England, and in 1891 I was dispatched to the Oratory School at Edgbaston, near Birming-ham. With mingled feelings of pride and trepidation I set out for the unknown.

In the early nineties conditions at the average public school were pretty grim. Food was bad and discipline strict, and there was a good deal of mild bullying—bad enough for a small English boy initiated at a " prep " school, but very overwhelming for a Belgian boy who felt, and probably looked, a strange little object.

Foreigners are seldom enthusiastically received at English schools. They are regarded with grave suspicion until they have proved they can adapt themselves to traditional English ways and suffer the strange indignities which new boys are expected to endure with restraint, if not with relish. How-ever, I was fairly tough and found that I really loved English games and had a natural aptitude for them. It was an easy road to popularity, and soon my foreign extraction was for-given and in fact forgotten.

Cardinal Newman founded this school. In my time it consisted of only a hundred boys. It was too small, in my opinion—I met so few old schoolfellows in later life.

After a couple of years I began to enjoy myself. Fagging was behind me, work reduced to the irreducible minimum, and there was an endless procession of games. Eventually I became captain of the cricket and football elevens, won the racquets, tennis and billiards tournaments, and felt that the world was mine.

I am quite convinced that games play an extremely im-portant part in a boy's education, a fact ingored by most foreigners and a few Englishmen. They help him to develop his character in a number of ways, not the least being the ability to deal with and handle men in later years, surely one of the most valuable assets in life.

My holidays were distributed between my Belgian cousins and odds and ends of school friends in England.

In Belgium my relations are legion, but my nearest and dearest were, and still are, my two cousins, both my contemporaries and now men of eminence. Count Henri Carton de Wiart was formerly Prime Minister, and Baron Edmond Carton de Wiart was at one time Political Secretary to King Leopold II, and is now Director of La Société Générale de Belgique. They owned various delightful houses; my favourite was Hastières in the Ardennes, where we spent the summer on or in the river, scrambling over the hills or, like all boys in all countries, just fighting. One incident stands out in my mind with painful vividness. I was skating one Christmas on a lake on the outskirts of Brussels when I heard a shot fired in the woods surrounding the lake. I rushed in the direction of the shot and came upon a man, dead, with a revolver dropping from his hand, his coat open and the marks of the burn on his shirt where the bullet had gone through. It was the first time that I had come up against death, let alone suicide. I was haunted for many nights afterwards, and it did nothing to help to dispel my terror of the dark. It remains with me still.

By this time I had become indistinguishable from every other self-conscious British schoolboy and was invariably covered in confusion at the fervent embraces of my Continental relations. I should have got used to what was, after all, only a custom of the country, but it always made me feel a fool.

In 1897 it was decided to send me to Oxford, and in a rush of optimism I was put down for Balliol. I had overlooked the necessity for examinations and had rather an unpleasant shock when I tried and failed my first attempt at Smalls. But with the second attempt the authorities were kind and, after some delay because of a riding accident, I went up in January.

Once up at Balliol, I thought the triumph of Smalls would carry me along for a term or two, and I prayed for a successful cricket season and visualized three or four pleasant years and a possible Blue.

We lived in great comfort, had indulgent fathers, ran up exorbitant bills and developed a critical appreciation for good wine. We were unable to develop a taste for the ladies, as in those ascetic days they were barred from the universities.

We were the usual miscellaneous collection of brains and brawn, and though many of my contemporaries have become famous, illustrious in the Church, Politics and all the Arts, I then measured them by their prowess at sport or taste in Burgundy and remained unimpressed by their mental gymnastics.

My summer term was a great success as far as cricket was concerned, but scholastically it was a disaster. I was supposed to be reading Law, my father still nursing his illusions, but I failed my Law Preliminary, and realizing that my Oxford career would be brief, I felt a strong urge to join the Foreign Legion, that romantic refuge of the misfits. However, once again Balliol was lenient and I came up for the October term, when suddenly there were reverberations from South Africa and the whole problem was solved for me, most mercifully, by the outbreak of the South African War.

At that moment I knew, once and for all, that war was in my blood. I was determined to fight and I didn't mind how or what. I didn't know why the war had started, and I didn't care on which side I was to fight. If the British didn't fancy me I would offer myself to the Boers, and at least I did not endow myself with Napoleonic powers or imagine I would make the slightest difference to whichever side I fought for.

I know now that the ideal soldier is the man who fights for his country because it is fighting, and for no other reason. Causes, politics and ideologies are better left to the historians.

My personal problem was how to enlist. I knew my father would not allow it as he had set his heart on my becoming a lawyer, besides which it would have been frowned on by the family, Belgium, like the rest of the Continent, being pro-Boer, and I was liable to conscription in Belgium. From a British point of view I was ineligible, being under age and a foreigner. I decided there was only one way, to pass myself off as British and enlist under a false name and age.

It was all too easy. The recruiting office was pandemonium and only too eager for fresh young blood; in fact so much so that the next day I went up and enlisted again for a short-sighted friend who couldn't pass his medical.

Seething with enthusiasm, and under my new name of Carton, I joined Paget's Horse, a Yeomanry regiment. Most of the officers and N.C.O.s had been regulars. I was disappointed to find that the whole atmosphere was far too mild and gentlemanly for my ferocious appetite.

I wanted life in the raw, rough and tough and full of bitter experience, and I did not appreciate dangling around for two or three months being drilled, first at Chelsea and then at Colchester, and learning from my superiors that soldiers are made and not born.

However, we eventually sailed in a troopship, and over-night my longings for the rough were fully satisfied. Men were sick anywhere and everywhere and it was my delightful duty to clean up the mess, and incidentally the latrines. I was tasting experience.

It was a relief to get off that ship at Cape Town and go to the base camp at Maitland, a few miles inland. Here we were given horses and broken in to looking after them, and our N.C.O.s made full use of all opportunities of airing their views on us. They were masters of the English language and their lessons have remained indelibly imprinted on my mind.

Once I was trying to groom a particularly unpleasant horse and was proceeding rather gingerly, when I looked up to find our old sergeant-major gaping sardonically at my efforts and inquiring whether I thought I was ". . . tickling a woman ? "

We were sent down to the docks to fetch some horses just arrived from Australia, a really wild lot, and I was given four of the brutes to lead back to camp. Having engineered them through Cape Town, I got sick of them and let them all loose in the open country and arrived back empty-handed. I was luckily unnoticed in the dark. They were casual days.

More dreary weeks of training found my war fever drying in my veins and being rapidly replaced by bully beef, hard biscuits and strong tea. There was not a sight of the enemy or the sound of a bullet, and by the time we were sent up to Orange River I got fever and retired to hospital and felt my ignominy as a soldier was complete.

On emerging, rather sooner than was meant, I joined a local corps that happened to be in the neighbourhood and on trying to cross a river in full view of some Boers I received a bad stomach wound and, still worse, a bullet through my groin. A tactless interrogator asked me if there were many Boers about, and I said, " No, but the few were very good shots."

I then found myself back in the same hospital I had just left with a doctor leaning over me shaking his head gravely, and leaving me in no doubt as to my condition. The main point of interest to me was that I survived, but my identity was discovered, my parents notified and I was sent home to be invalided out of the Army.

I do not think it possible for anyone to have had a duller dose of war, and I returned bereft of glory, my spirits deflating with every mile, wondering what my father would have to say. But he rose magnificently to the occasion, decided to ignore the episode, and sent me up to Oxford again, where, because of my wounds, I was treated like a hero. It was no less pleasant because it was undeserved. But in spite of all the fuss I felt restless and unsettled and knew beyond all doubt that I was not cut out to be a lawyer. Plucking up my courage in the Christmas vacation, I went to Egypt to ask my father to let me take up soldiering as a permanent career, and he, realizing very sensibly that it was the one thing I had set my heart on, gave in, and I came to life.

Looking back on my Oxford career, I never feel that my time there was wasted. Academically I was not very much the wiser, but I had made many friends at a time of one's life when one makes them and keeps them. I had been part of a bigger, more varied world than I should have found if I had gone straight to Sandhurst from school, and I felt it had helped me to a broader if not more tolerant outlook on life.

Of my friends at Oxford, Aubrey Herbert was by far the most remarkable. Brilliant, insanely brave, nearly blind, he was the most untidy man I ever met. His tie was always round his ears and quite out of control of our stand-up collars, and he was so short-sighted that the tip of his nose was generally black from caressing the paper he was reading.

When reading at night he had a habit of using two oil-lamps, each about three inches from his ears. He loved hare-brained escapades as long as they spelt danger, and was passionately addicted to climbing from one window-ledge to another. For choice he preferred the top floor and would chant Italian love songs to his assorted and sometimes indignant listeners. He usually wore dancing pumps and reserved boots for visits from his mother. He seldom wrote more than just a weird signature; he ordered a professional typist down from London for his Final History School, in which he got a First.

Aubrey was heartbroken at not being able to get out to the South African War, and when I got back he would come and sit for hours and pump me as to my experiences. He took part in the Great War, and escaped being killed by a series of those miracles that occur to those who are not pre-destined. He had gone out to Turkey as an attaché to our embassy in Constantinople and developed an infatuation for Albania. He loved its country, its people and its problems and by some method all his own he infiltrated himself into a position as a sort of uncrowned king.

John Buchan, who was up at Oxford at the same time, took Aubrey Herbert as his model for the character Sandy Arbuthnot in *Greenmantle* and describes him in his *Memoirs* as " the most delightful and brilliant survivor from the days of chivalry."

As a Member of Parliament he enlivened the House of Commons with his pithy comments. During a debate on the antics of the Peace Conference he asked : " Is it true that rabies has spread to Paris ? " During the First World War I had the most charming letter from him in which he attri-buted to me " genius in courage." I was touched and very flattered, but unfortunately both for his friends and for England Aubrey died before his time.

Of other friends, I like best to remember Tom Connolly, an American (in those days a rarity at Oxford), Nobby Argles, our very successful Balliol cox, and Charlie Meade. Charlie was a quiet and gentle man who later developed a great liking for mountaineering. He wrote some excellent books on the subject.

Outside my circle of friends were a number of contem-poraries who made their mark. Brilliant Raymond Asquith, killed in 1918 leading his men; William Temple, a rather messy young man careless of his appearance; the present Lord Beveridge, whose lustre as an economist was not at that time discernible; Lord Henley, who with two companions walked 80 miles from Cambridge to Oxford in 23 hours 45 minutes and finished on Magdalen Bridge at 11.45 p.m. with 15 minutes to spare; the brothers Tomkinson, Charles and Jimmy. Charles rowed in the Oxford boat and Jimmy made a great name at squash racquets. At the latter he was so good that handicapping was impossible and there was no one in the world to test him. Their father, an amazing sportsman, was killed riding in a point-to-point at the age of seventy-two.

Remembering my undistinguished and interrupted career at Oxford, I was intensely flattered when, fifty years later, I was honoured with a degree and a dedication that read:

> This is the famous Balliol man who was torn from his undergraduate studies to serve against the Boers in South Africa; who was there twice wounded; and who now after fighting in more campaigns than others have even read about, and receiving nine further wounds, has been elected an Honorary Fellow of his old college.

CHAPTER II

SOME BOER WAR SKIRMISHES

My Egyptian trip was successful and, having got round my father, and with my pockets bulging, I went back to England to make my farewells. I knew I should stand more chance of action in South Africa with the Colonial Corps than if I enlisted in a British regiment, where I should be forced to train for at least a year before being sent abroad.

Thinking that a little luxury might be advisable as a prelude to things that might come, I booked myself a first-class cabin in the Union Castle line. It was a nice contrast to my last trip.

The farewells in England were intense but very expensive and by eking out my luxury voyage by some parsimonious tippings and no visits to the bar, I arrived in Cape Town with exactly one pound in my pocket. Necessity must have spurred my efforts, for the self-same day I managed to enlist in the Imperial Light Horse, which was no mean feat, as they were then at their zenith, and their riding tests were so stiff that only five per cent. of us got through. Many experienced horsemen were at first thrown out because they could not vault into the saddle without using their stirrups, though later on the tests became a farce and merely a question of bribery in the right places.

Anyway, that day in Cape Town my luck was in and I was delighted with myself and the world at large, as the Imperial Light Horse was considered the best of the Colonial Corps and had a wonderful record in the early days of the war.

There were many well-known men in the regiment, among them two Irish Rugby Internationals, Tommy Crean and Johnson. Johnson got a V.C. at Elandslaagte and everyone was full of congratulations except Tommy Crean, who merely remarked " Well ! If a B.F. like you can get a V.C. anyone can," and he got one himself some months afterwards.

By 1901 the type of man joining up had deteriorated visibly and the Colonial Corps in particular, with its high rates of pay, was attracting a very different type. A trooper in the Colonial Corps received five shillings a day, a considerable sum, whereas the private in the Regular Army or Yeomanry received a shilling.

Two of my tent mates at the base were most unsavoury specimens. Once when they returned in the early hours from one of their usual nightly marauding expeditions, they were stuffed with loot from a tobacconist's shop, and in order to guarantee my silence they insisted, rather forcibly, to put it mildly, on my sharing their plunder.

These two ruffians had been in camp for weeks. Troopers, the day before being sent to the front, drew one pound advance pay, and whenever my two drew theirs they used to desert and then join up in another of the numerous corps enlisting in Cape Town. They may be doing it still.

Not long after joining up I was promoted to the rank of corporal, but my proud state lasted only twenty-four hours ; I was demoted abruptly for threatening to hit my sergeant.

At that age I was extremely truculent and quick tempered and very resentful of being cursed or shouted at ; it always brought out the worst in me. All the same, I was lucky not to be court-martialled and still don't know by what lucky chance I escaped.

I loved my life as a trooper. I had no responsibility, but had the invaluable experience of meeting all classes of men, being forced to live with them and like it.

Some months afterwards I was given a commission in the Imperial Light Horse, and though it meant sacrificing some of my irresponsibility, inwardly I was glad and felt my foot on the first rung of the ladder.

An officer's life did not spell much in the way of comfort. Life was hard, and often weeks were spent without cover of any sort, and if occasionally a tent was available it had to be shared with a number of officers. The daily fare was very spartan : bully beef, hard biscuits and strong tea unrelieved by either milk or sugar. But there were gala occasions when we killed great numbers of sheep to stop the Boers getting hold of them first, and then we feasted on liver and kidneys cooked in our home-made ovens or roasted over the open fires, when the succulent smells hung in the still air and proved most disturbing to our tantalized digestions.

We were cut off from all our friends and our families. Mails were almost non-existent, but in some ways we were lucky, for no one tried to boost our morale with pep talks or highfalutin education, or to probe our egos with uncomfortable psychiatry. We asked and got very little, but somehow we enjoyed it, and the rough, open life hardened us physically and mentally and brought its own consolation. I still had seen very little fighting ; my life seemed to consist of trekking from one end of the country to the other, without aim or object.

War was still eluding me, and my vivid imaginings of charging Boers single-handed and dying gloriously with a couple of posthumous V.C.s were becoming a little hazy. My one opportunity of single-handed exploit had been shattered by my colonel. We had been about to attack some Boers, but were held up by a barbed-wire fence which the Boers were covering with their fire. Longing for an opportunity to show my courage, I went up and asked my colonel if I could go and try to cut the wire. The colonel left me with no illusions, told me I was a damned fool and to get back and remain with my men. The colonel may have been right, but he hurt my pride badly, and I had to swallow the disagreeable knowledge that I had made a bloody fool of myself.

As we could spend no money on trek, unless we gambled, we amassed a nice sum by the end of our six months (we enlisted for six-monthly periods) and so we would go to Durban and live in great comfort at the best hotel and surround ourselves with the smooth and easy friends who seem to pop up from the ground when one has money to burn.

When I first got my commission the Second Imperial Light Horse was commanded by Colonel Briggs of the King's Dragoon Guards, a first-rate officer who rose to be corps commander in the 1914–18 War and after that became chief of the British Military Mission to Denikin in Russia, when I was chief of the British Military Mission to Poland.

Incidentally, that was the first time I became aware of the existence, let alone the identity, of the General commanding the forces. Nowadays such ignorance would be counted a capital sin and severely punished.

Tom Bridges was a major in the regiment and my wholehearted admiration for him was curbed by a respectful distance ; I had no presentiment of how often our lives were to rub along together in the future. Even in those early days he was unforgettable, a very tall, good-looking and attractive man, with a hidden quality which commanded the respect and devotion that followed him all his life.

He had been serving in East Africa when the South African War broke out ; he managed to get ten days' shooting leave and came and joined the Imperial Light Horse as troop leader. During Buller's attempt at crossing the river Tugela, Bridges carried out a very fine reconnaissance, which entailed swimming the river in the dark, and he was recommended for the V.C.

The War Office, unaware of what had happened to him until they received this recommendation of gallantry and with their genius for anti-climax, responded magnanimously by taking him down thirty-five places in seniority, ignoring his courage.

Later in the year I was offered a regular commission, accepted it, and was gazetted to the 4th Dragoon Guards, then stationed in India. I sailed for home in November.

As a trooper I had always been well treated by the officers —with one exception, an ex-ranker from the 17th Lancers who had done everything in his power to make my life unpleasant. Imagine my delight in meeting this gentleman again in our small troopship, with a large account to settle and at least thirty days to do it in.

There were only about a dozen officers on board, all of them young, and by the time we got to Cape Town, where my ranker friend joined us, the rest of us were very good friends.

I told them of my debt and they all joined to help me pay it in full; by the time we got to England the creature had been bullied and ragged out of existence, both by night and day, and the debt turned into a large credit balance on my side.

On arriving in England my ranker reported me to the War Office, who asked me to explain my conduct, but as I never heard of this again even the War Office must have thought that he only got his deserts.

Arriving home, I applied to go to Somaliland where we were indulging in one of our frequent campaigns against the Mad Mullah, but the application was refused and I was told to join my regiment. After calling on my family in Egypt I reached Rawalpindi in March, 1902.

India, from the start, held no mysterious fascination for me. It was tawdry. It emitted revolting smells and noises and its only attraction in my eyes was that I knew it was a wonderful centre for sport. I wanted to get down to playing polo really seriously, and I worked very hard to pass my recruit's courses. It was therefore a great blow to me to be sent to Changla Gali in the Murree Hills on a musketry course far away from a polo ground. However, I got through the course and had the luck to be sent with the advance party of the regiment to Muttra, the regiment having just taken part in the Delhi Durbar.

Muttra was the ideal station. There was only one cavalry regiment there and no other troops—and best of all, no generals. This added enormously to its charm in my opinion. The shooting was good and the pig-sticking excellent.

There had been no troops in Muttra during the South African War and pig were plentiful, and I transferred my keenness on polo to pig-sticking, which I found the finest and most exciting sport in the world.

> Over the nullah, over the level,
> Thro' the dark jungle we'll ride like the devil,
> There's a nullah in front and a boar as well,
> So sit down in your saddle and ride like hell!

The lines are from a pig-sticking song with a rhythm which captured the tempo of the sport. It is carried on at top speed, full out, a great deal over blind country and with a fighting animal to deal with. Falls are inevitable and numerous, but we never thought about them and seldom got seriously damaged.

My start was inauspicious and was in the company of the only other British officer then in Muttra. He was also a novice, but equally anxious to get going. We started out full of suppressed excitement and duly found and rode a boar, but almost immediately my companion took a fall; his horse fell on the spear which transfixed and killed the poor beast. That was the end of that.

The second time I went out a big boar crossed sixty or seventy yards in front of me, both of us going as hard as we could, and I succeeded in cutting him off with the triumphant result that all three of us, horse, rider and boar, were laid out flat on the ground. Happily the boar alone was dead.

Of the many boar I killed since then I never remember killing another with only one spear.

The third time I went out alone on a very hard-pulling polo pony, inaptly named Dear Boy. I rode a boar who proceeded to jump over a mud wall. Dear Boy, who was certainly no jumper, shot me out of the saddle, but at least we both landed on the far side of the wall. I remounted and tore after the boar, who perversely jumped the wall again. Having by that time no control over my pony, I followed suit, fell again and this time damaged my shoulder badly. Having lost the boar and feeling extremely sore, I did not relish the idea of hacking home some twelve miles.

Suddenly I spied a goose alighting behind a nearby bank, and never having shot a goose I felt the omission should be remedied there and then. Taking my gun from the syce, I stalked it, pain forgotten, and popped it in the bag. It was a most consoling prize, but never shall I forget the agony when I let off my gun.

The only other time I hurt myself badly when following a boar I was cantering slowly on very bad ground. My horse fell, rolled on me, cracked several of my ribs and damaged one of my ankles.

Once I bought a horse for my colonel, who thought he would start pig-sticking, but my purchase was very tactless and deposited the colonel in a cactus bush. He was not a very persevering man and tried no more. Perhaps that is one of the reasons why I always considered youth an essential to pig-sticking, but as I never had an opportunity to pig-stick after the age of twenty-four, I was never allowed the privilege of changing my mind.

About this time I very nearly lost my commission in India. I was convalescing after my cracked ribs accident and shooting in the Murree Hills. One of the coolies annoyed me and I threw some stones at him. He got himself out of range of the stones, turned round, and laughed at me. This was too much for my temper and I promptly put up my gun and peppered him in his tail, no doubt inconvenient for him but certainly not dangerous. However, he ran to the nearest cantonment magistrate's office and reported me, and I was put under arrest next morning. I had to pay a heavy fine, but I saved my commission.

Lord Curzon, who was Viceroy at the time, dealt very severely with officers who ill-treated natives and did not recognize the climate as an excuse for fiery tempers.

By this time I had got to know and love the regiment and had made many friends. The older officers were very much of the heavy dragoon type, but the younger ones were a fine lot, as was proved in 1914, but at that time in India they were full of the joys of spring and the most inveterate raggers. Chief delinquent was Bobbie Oppenheim, a most charming and attractive person, bubbling over with humour. One night he and Harry Gurney, also in the regiment, were staying at some hotel and came in very late. The lift-boy who took them up to their floor was rather cheeky, so Bobbie emptied one of the fire buckets into the lift to help it on its way down. They then went to their rooms and undressed. Up came the manager, burst into Bobbie's room protesting loudly, found him completely stark, and requested him to leave the hotel at once. Bobbie put on his top hat, grasped his cane and proceeded to saunter down the passages of the hotel in his birthday suit. Within a few seconds a perspiring manager was at his heels, begging him to change his mind and stay for ever. Reluctantly, but very graciously, Bobbie allowed himself to be led back to his room.

Harry Gurney also afforded us endless amusement. One night, having dined too well and not too wisely, he had gone to bed. Bobbie Oppenheim, who had the next room, was woken up by the most awful groans coming from Gurney's room. He went in to find out what was the matter, and Gurney said he could not feel one of his legs and knew it was paralysed. Bobbie pulled back the bed-clothes and found Harry had put both his legs into one leg of his pyjamas.

Butcha Hornby and Bob Ogilby were and still are two of my best friends. " Butcha," Hindustani for " Little One " because he looked so young, had the courage of a lion and a heart of gold. He was a very hard rider after pig and a fine polo player, but he never allowed himself to drift into semi-professionalism as did so many officers.

Bob Ogilby was a character from his early youth. He liked to give a false impression of himself and could be extremely cynical and cutting, but if you needed a friend he was there, and his real value cannot be assessed in words.

When we were in India his father died and he had to return home and attend to the estate. He left the regiment and joined the 2nd Life Guards, and I missed him badly. He left me his polo ponies in India to ride that season, and I was never so well mounted.

One of the few things that did interest me in India was the attitude of the Hindoos to animals. Although I knew it was against their religion to kill them, I had not realized to what extent they held them sacred. Only a few miles from Muttra on the river Jumna lay the Holy City of Bindraban from where the natives would go down to the banks of the river to throw food to the animals waiting to devour it. I have seen monkeys jump on to a turtle or crocodile's back, snatch at a handful of grain that had been thrown into the river, and leap ashore again, often getting their tails bitten off in the act!

The dead bodies of the Hindoos were thrown into the river Jumna after the funeral rites had been performed, and once I was treated to the gruesome spectacle of a crocodile, a turtle and a pi-dog all feeding off a corpse at one and the same time, each pulling in a different direction.

There were hundreds of crocodiles lying along the river banks in those days and we often used to shoot them. After one had been shot the vultures would arrive while the shikari was skinning it, and settle down within a few yards to wait until the removal of the skin. Then they would launch themselves upon the remains of the crocodile and in a mere matter of minutes there would be nothing left but the bones.

The Hindoo pilgrims walked hundreds of miles to bathe themselves in this sacred river, and after bathing they would fill a bottle with water from the Jumna, place it carefully in an enormous basket filled with straw, and walk back, uplifted and content, to wherever they had come from.

All the time I had been in India I had dreaded snakes, but had never seen one until just before I was due to leave Muttra, when I killed three in a week. I got my first victim when I was shooting quail and my shikari was beating out a bush. A cobra shot up suddenly, rearing its head and ready to strike; the beater let out a yell of terror and disappeared in a flash. I just managed to lift my gun and shoot it at a range of about eight feet. My second I got when I was riding home from parade. I saw a cobra disappearing down a hole in front of my horse, and, leaping off, I seized it by its tail and broke its back with my sword. It was an extremely foolish thing to do, but I was young. I got another in rather the same way when I was riding across the grass farm. A cobra slithered along in front of my horse, and I was able to bend down and break his back with my sword.

This had proved a very gruesome week, for one morning we found a pony dead from an obvious snake-bite. We tried a local snake-charmer to lure it to its doom, and this he did most successfully. Then he offered to clear up the compound and rapidly found three more. Turning to an officer, he suggested trying his bungalow, and the officer replied that he could if he liked, but it was rather a waste of time as he had seen no signs of any snakes. But such was the magic of the snake-man's music that he produced no less than seven cobras from within that man's bungalow. He shook us all to the core.

Manœuvres, although no doubt of serious importance to generals, were in those care-free days very much the lighter side of soldiering to the rest of us. India had a faculty for wonderfully organized camp life. We were as self-contained as a snail and lived most comfortably on the march.

One night, during Lord Kitchener's big manœuvres in 1902, Bobbie Oppenheim, having somehow got to hear that we intended to pull his tent down that night, went and changed his name-plate with the colonel's. When we went to carry out our attack and started to loosen the tent-ropes, we were met with a volley of abuse in the colonel's voice. We retired in disorder, very crestfallen, and had to chalk up a victory for Bobbie.

On the same manœuvres Bobbie and the redoubtable Gurney were returning one night from dining with a neighbouring regiment, when they ran into an infantry brigade marching to a rendezvous. This was too much temptation for our hilarious pair, and as Gurney had rather an impressive corpulent senior officer's appearance, Bobbie galloped up to the brigadier and told him that the general (Gurney) wished to see him. The brigadier having arrived in the presence, Gurney proceeded to tell him off for being there, with the greatest fluency, and without allowing the unfortunate brigadier to utter a single word. He then ordered him to march his brigade back to camp immediately, thereby disorganizing the entire manœuvres.

In the cold light of a reasoned dawn poor Bobbie and Harry shook in terror over their misdoings and took days to recover, waiting for the axe to fall.

In 1904 we received orders to go to South Africa, and although we had had a good time and plenty of sport, I for one was not sorry. My first impression held good. India for me was a glittering sham coated with dust and I hoped I should never see her again.

CHAPTER III

HEYDAY

OUR destination was Middelburg, Cape Colony, centre of dust storms and renowned as the worst station in South Africa. The 16th Lancers, whom we were relieving, made no attempt at disguising their joy in leaving it. A day or two after arriving in Middelburg, Butcha Hornby and I were given leave home and we sailed at once from Cape Town.

I spent most of that winter in Egypt in the ease and luxury of my father's house, and when I think of the youth of to-day with its ceaseless and ageing struggle for existence I realize how lucky I was to have been born so soon.

I was in full agreement with George Borrow, who decided :

Life is very sweet, brother; who would wish to die ?

My soldiering was without ambition and I was solely concerned with the present. I wanted to be fit, to be efficient, to have good ponies, good shooting, a good time and good friends. Some would find fault with my philosophy, but I was in no way unique. Life played into our hands for those few short years. We had everything, we accepted it and at any rate we enjoyed it.

I was very keen on racing and in Cairo was offered a mount in a hurdle race, but it entailed my taking off seven pounds of weight in twenty-four hours. Turkish baths were inadequate, so I wrapped myself up in countless sweaters, topped by an overcoat, practically ran the six or seven miles to the Pyramids, climbed them and staggered back again. Alas, although I lost the required seven pounds, I reduced myself to such a state of collapse that I had a bad fall in the race, severe concussion, and did not ride again that winter.

Bob Ogilby had come out to stay with me, and after my accident my father, kind as ever, gave me almost the first car in Egypt, an Oldsmobile with a phaeton body. Our drives to the Pyramids were hazardous in the extreme. Progress was a series of short, sharp jerks at a maximum speed of ten m.p.h. and we were often overtaken by a camel. But we were the cynosure of envious and astonished eyes and I was very reluctant to leave my mechanical toy behind when my leave was up and I had to return to Middelburg.

After my return General Hickman, who was commanding there at that time, took me on as his galloper. He was a great sportsman, loved racing and shooting, and took me wherever he went.

Ever since being so badly wounded in South Africa I had been possessed of a mania for physical fitness. Good health, like most things in life, has to be lost before it is properly appreciated, and now I went to almost any lengths to get it and keep it. I ran, I did physical jerks, I played every game, I was out all and every day, but my most ingrained habit that has clung to me all my life was to get up very early in the morning. To me it is essential and imperative, but in later years it has probably been anathema to those of my staff who like their last five minutes in bed.

One morning I was out at dawn exercising the horses, and on riding past the railway station I saw a private railway coach on the siding. Distinguished visitors in private coaches were so rare in Middelburg that my curiosity was aroused. On making inquiries I found the visitor was none other than Sir Henry Hildyard, Commander-in-Chief of the Forces in South Africa. Realizing that someone must have blundered and fearing that the fury of the Commander-in-Chief might descend upon us all, I galloped back to warn General Hickman, who at once went down to the station to meet the Commander-in-Chief, with all due ceremony. Inspection was carried out, and as the Commander-in-Chief was on the point of leaving he asked me if I would care to come to Pretoria as one of his A.D.C.s. I accepted with alacrity and counted the day as one of the luckiest of my life.

Sir Henry was the most charming man I have ever met, and it was my greatest privilege to serve him. He was tall and exceptionally good looking, a highly educated soldier, a brilliant judge of men, tolerant, broad-minded and gentle and with the perfect manners that are so seldom met with in many high places. I felt nearer to him than I did to my own father, and I owe much to his wonderful influence at a very impressionable time of my life.

The other A.D.C. was Reggie Hildyard, a son of Sir Henry's. He had a very good head for business and administration and ran the whole establishment with great efficiency, doing all the serious indoor work and leaving me in my element to accompany Sir Henry on most of his expeditions throughout South Africa.

Lady Hildyard was a most charming hostess but an inveterate gambler, and South Africa, with its fortunes won and lost overnight, was a dangerous centre for the unstable. One day she came to me in great distress. She had gambled and lost an enormous sum, practically all Sir Henry's capital, and what should she do? I advised her to confess at once. All Sir Henry said was : " Never mind, my dear, I might have done much worse myself."

I was always a reluctant card-player, but bridge was considered an essential part of an A.D.C.'s equipment. One night Lady Hildyard, who was my partner, had committed what I considered to be several enormities and as she got up to leave the room at the end of our game I shook my fist after her retreating back. Sir Henry entered the room at that unfortunate moment, and I thought I was for home. Instead he turned to Major Winwood, the military secretary, and said : " De Wiart's a very patient man, isn't he ? "

We travelled extremely comfortably in those days, for Sir Henry had been presented with Kruger's railway coach. We lived in this while reviewing troops all over South Africa. During this time I came in contact with many of the great ones and had the thrill of seeing those two distinguished military leaders, Generals Smuts and Botha. They were universally respected by both friend and ex-foe. I was only able to revere and admire at a distance, and little knew that I should take over a command from General Botha twenty odd years later.

The Boers were amiable to us and some of them even friendly, especially the farmers, but there was an undercurrent of feeling throughout the whole country which could be sensed, though difficult to describe in words.

Lord Milner, who had been succeeded by Lord Selborne,

had a most unusual faith in the combination of youth plus brains and had surrounded himself with young men, only recently left college, and known throughout even official circles as " The Kindergarten." But his faith seemed justified by the following extract from *The Times History of the South African War* :

> Their sheer ability, their enthusiasm and their unselfish devotion to duty far outweighed all minor defects . . . most of them remained in the country and have continued to work for it in Milner's spirit of creative effort. . . .

Certainly, Lord Milner was an inspired chooser. Those of the Kindergarten who remained on in my day included Philip Kerr, who as Lord Lothian was to prove one of our most successful British ambassadors to the United States in the early part of the late war, and whose efforts were defeated only by an untimely death ; Geoffrey Dawson, later editor of *The Times* ; Lionel Curtis, who held innumerable and important posts in South Africa and was well known in the literary world ; Patrick Duncan, who became Governor-General of South Africa.

Life at Roberts Heights was delightful and a very gay affair. The Bays and Camerons were stationed there, and guest nights were wonderful, rowdy and very destructive.

Parlour tricks were compulsory and my ability to tear a pack of cards in half was most remunerative and earned me a steady income, but the Almighty must have resented my ill-gotten gains, for, later, he removed one of my hands. Another rather showy trick of mine was to dive over four men and be caught the other side by a couple of fielders. This trick was inadvertently made much more showy when one night the fielders forgot their jobs and I landed on my shoulder without hurting myself. I continued ever after to perform this trick unaided.

The third trick which has lasted me well, until last year when I fractured my spine, was to straddle a chair and fall over backwards. Simple but impressive and inspired very regularly by a liquid dinner. Beyond one occasion when an officer's spur finished its course up another officer's nose, I cannot recollect any real disasters.

One day I was told that there were two small girls coming

to stay at Headquarters House. I was not very pleased, as I knew it would be my doubtful pleasure to take them out riding. They turned out to be the two eldest daughters of Sir George Farrar, a financial magnate actively concerned in the East Rand goldfields. My fury soon evaporated and I became devoted to the two little girls. I loved taking them out, and it gave me the entrée afterwards to their charming home at Bedford Farm about thirty miles from Pretoria, and to the open hospitality of their parents who became my great friends.

Bedford Farm and the Commander-in-Chief's house had both been designed and built by Baker, the architect who was responsible with Lutyens for the planning of New Delhi. South Africa abounded in what were known as "Baker Houses." These were built in the Dutch style and on two floors with spacious modern comfort and complete with bath-rooms and accommodation for English servants.

Whilst with Sir Henry Hildyard I could indulge my exer-cise mania to the full, but Sir Henry warned me that I was storing up a miserable old age for myself. I should become muscle-bound and riddled with rheumatism. But for once I think Sir Henry was wrong, and I know it was entirely through being so fit that I managed to overcome my many misadventures.

I thought nothing of riding to Johannesburg and back, seventy-two miles, to ride my racehorses. One night after dining with a regiment at Pretoria someone bet me I would not walk to Johannesburg that night in ten hours. I took the bet and won it with forty minutes to spare; but the climate was so stimulating and perfect fitness so easy to attain that the effort was not really remarkable.

Jo'burg was full of snares for the unwary, and I was not always a good chooser of friends. I met a man who had served with me in the South African War, a good deal older than myself, who entertained me with flattering enthusiasm. One night he told me that he knew of a really good thing if I had any money to invest. Having that very morning re-ceived a cheque from my father I fell for it hook, line and sinker, and told my plausible friend I would send him a cheque. At that Rand Club I ran into a brother officer who said, " I've just seen you with X—watch him ! " But I was too excited over my embryonic million and did not listen. I sent my cheque and the shares rose rapidly, and I wired, " Sell now ". X wired back he had sold and having more than doubled my money I felt quite smart and ran up a few bills in celebration. But X disappeared with my money and I am looking for him still !

The racing in Jo'burg was hot, to put it mildly, and once I backed thirty-two consecutive losers. I have never had a bet since and count that experience cheap at the price.

I had a very good mare called Piccaninny which I ran very successfully in hurdle races. One day a friend asked me casually if I expected to win, and I said " Yes ". After the race a hilarious figure staggered up to me, thanked me, and said he had put £800 on my mare. If I'd known it beforehand I should most certainly have fallen off.

In 1906 I had to go home to be operated on for an old wound. After the operation, as games were forbidden me, I went to Vienna for the first time. It was then in its heyday of light-hearted gaiety, and the Austrians have never been surpassed in the art of froth-blowing. They are as gay and unmaterialistic as the French are witty and grasping, and as much as I could love any city I loved Vienna.

Money seemed as cheap as in South Africa and I realized that gambling must be a universal disease, for one night at the Jockey Club Count X lost £100,000 at écarté in four hands. His opponent offered to play a fifth hand double or quits, but the Count was not to be drawn and refused.

My several weeks of recuperation and worldlinesses made me thankful to get back to Pretoria to the Hildyards and also to my horses. I returned to find another addition to the Hildyard family circle, Kathleen Hildyard, a niece of Sir Henry's. There can never have been a more kindly and courageous woman. She had that gay spirit, unmalicious humour and calm certainty that springs only from an inward peace. It gave the impression that she was on most excellent terms with her Maker, and quite regardless of the material fortunes that had not come her way. She was the friend and confidante of all of us and added much to the already delightful atmosphere created by all the members of that unique family.

34

Sir Henry had been commandant of the Staff College before the South African War, and I once asked him who had been his best pupil. He answered, without one moment's hesitation, Douglas Haig. It was just another instance of his shrewd and penetrating judgment as, though Haig was at that time Inspector-General of Cavalry in India and had been Lord French's chief staff officer throughout the South African War, he was by no means then at the top of the tree.

The polo in South Africa was first class, and as I was deprived of pig-sticking, polo was second on my list.

We won the inter-regimental twice whilst we were in South Africa with Oldrey playing No. 1, myself No. 2, Lamont No. 3 and Butcha Hornby back. The 9th Lancers, 4th Hussars, 5th Dragoon Guards, the Bays and the 6th Mounted Infantry all had good teams, including Noel Edwards and Ritson, who both played for England, and Reggie Hoare and Sadler Jackson also in the first flight.

In 1908 my chief was due for retirement. It was a great wrench to break up my long and happy association with him and return to the life of an ordinary, more conventional, soldier.

I had a few months with the regiment and then went home on leave and rejoined the regiment at Brighton. If change is good for the soul then Brighton should have been a real refresher course to mine, as one could hardly imagine a bigger contrast to Middelburg, Cape Colony. There was one similarity only: I was equally free of corroding generals and I was able to spend most of my time racing and keeping a couple of chasers at Findon, where I motored out in the early morning to ride work.

Polo in England had become very professional and lost its charm for me and temporarily I had given it up, when suddenly I was forced into the open again when Oldrey went sick and I had to play for the regiment in the inter-regimental. We won the cup, but I cannot say that I enjoyed the tournament, knowing that the onus would be on me should anything go wrong. In the round before the semi-final I was badly bumped and my leg was extremely painful. I managed to last out the tournament, but on having it X-rayed afterwards my leg was found to be broken, but already mending.

Soldiering in England was not an exciting profession. There was no pressure of work, leave was easily come by and I took advantage of the leisurely pace to get better acquainted with the Continent.

I was drawn chiefly towards Austria, Hungary, Bavaria and Bohemia, all renowned for their excellent shooting, which ranged from red deer, roe deer and chamois to pheasants and partridges.

The shoots were delightful, sport a great bond, and the guns were pleasantly international and unflavoured by politics.

I was once on my way to Bavaria and I stopped for a few hours in Paris to change into another train to take me on to Augsburg. On arrival at the German frontier I got out of my carriage for the customs examination, and as I stepped on to the platform a German in plain clothes advanced on me and said, " Are you an officer? " On my replying that I was he told me to come along with him, and I foresaw the delightful prospect of being locked up. Walking down the platform, my escort said, " You are a French officer?" and when I disclaimed that and said, "No! I am English," his attitude changed completely. He became most friendly, did all he could to get me through the customs and finished up by showing me his police dogs. On thinking the incident over afterwards I imagined that a German agent must have marked me down in Paris, jumped to the conclusion that my name was a French one, and wired information to his people on the frontier. This was in 1910, and it showed how closely the frontier was being watched by the Germans, how deep was their animosity towards the French, and how elaborate their precautions.

It was at a shoot in Bohemia with Prince Colloredo that I met Colonel Bob Sandeman. He was the Colonel of the Royal Gloucestershire Hussars, a fine sportsman and a natural soldier, and my delight must have been plainly visible when he offered me his adjutancy. Loath as I was to soldier in England, I knew the life of a yeomanry adjutant was an enviable lot and renownedly pleasant both militarily and socially, and Gloucestershire the heart of good hunting country.

In such a county first things came first and the training of the Yeomanry was most carefully timed not to interfere with the May-fly season and to finish before the hunting, but during our weeks of training the enthusiasm and keenness of the officers and men were really stimulating. We put them through a gruelling training and still they asked for more, and would have been extremely disappointed if they had not got it. The nights were hilarious and rowdy and produced the casualties we had not suffered by day.

In the early autumn when there was no training, no fishing and no hunting, I found a delightful system whereby I conducted my adjutancy from the Continent by a correspondence course. I had all the papers sent out to me to sign and return, and occasionally and regretfully resorted to the expense of a wire. All this showed the lack of national crises and the high degree of efficiency and smartness of the Royal Gloucestershire Hussars, who were undoubtedly the pick of the Yeomanry and quite capable of entirely running their own show.

During my first winter I had a flat in Cirencester, and after that a house in Brinkworth, on the edge of the Duke of Beaufort's country. The Duke was a wonderful man to hounds and had that enviable knack of always being in the right place at the right moment. The power of anticipation plays an important part in nearly all sport and games, but in hunting and in the M.F.H. it adds enormously to the enjoyment of the entire field.

The Duke weighed twenty stone and rode colossal horses. He never jumped a fence, but opened a gate with such dexterity that he shot through quicker than anyone else could jump the nearby fence. Later, when he had to give up riding, he hunted in a Ford and still managed always to be on the spot, and he can have had no superior as a fox-hunter.

His huntsman George Walters and his first whip Tom Newman gave us excellent sport, and there were always a great many soldiers out with the Duke's : Jumbo Wilson, now Field-Marshal Lord Wilson, Ellington who became marshal in the R.A.F., John Vaughan, who commanded a cavalry division, Noel Edwards, Maurice de Tuyll, Oldrey, all fine horsemen. Nearly all of the young ones, alas, were to be killed in the 1914–18 War.

An amusing character was hunting there at that time—a horse coper named Arthur Rich. He pestered me continually to buy a horse off him, and one day he was riding an animal I liked and I asked him the price. He named some ridiculous figure. I told him it was far too high, and I hadn't any money, anyhow. He merely said, "Oh! I thought you 'ad," and never came near me again.

Another time Rich was trying to sell a horse to a local peer whose reputation was distinctly lurid; he had played the leading man in several scandals. The peer told Rich to leave him alone, adding : " Your name stinks in people's nostrils." Whereupon Rich retorted : " Yours ain't exactly all violets, m'Lord."

I had a couple of chasers at the time and one of them, Quinton, was second in the Grand Military Gold Cup, but as I had had another accident he was ridden by Crawley de Crespigny, a well-known gentleman rider and son of that adventurous tiger Sir Claude de Crespigny, whose exploits are legendary.

The whole world must have been gathering itself to a crescendo, but before that final disaster my own private and special world started to disintegrate.

On January 3rd, 1914, I received a letter from my father with the bald facts that he had crashed financially through the slump in Egypt and over-trust of his fellow-men and he could no longer afford to give me an allowance. Money I had looked upon as a most useful commodity, appearing with the regularity of breakfast, and as important as my morning shave, but it was by no means a god. Momentarily my father's disaster gave me a shock and I wondered how I should acclimatize myself to poverty. My second reaction found me almost glad, for it opened out the whole wide world again to me ; it meant I could not afford to soldier in England, could sever my ties, begin a new life and possibly see active service abroad.

I was faced with the prospect of having to settle my accounts, and one of my few assets were my horses. They were good horses, but had done a good deal of work and received some hard knocks. I approached Drage, one of the biggest horse dealers of the day, asked him to come and look at them, and asked him eight hundred pounds for the four. He thought this was too high a price, and I sent them up to be auctioned at Tattersall's and got twelve hundred guineas for them. As I had never paid more than a hundred and fifty for a horse, and usually considerably less, I felt this was a good start.

Before leaving for Somaliland I had to go up for my examination for promotion to major. I failed gloriously, achieving a record in obtaining 8 marks out of a possible 200 in Military Law. How lucky that wars wash out examinations and I have never been asked to do another since.

Having arranged my affairs as best I could, I sailed for Somaliland on July 23rd, 1914.

CHAPTER IV

FIGHTING THE MAD MULLAH

IT seems extraordinary to think of my utter ignorance of world affairs, but at that, even then, pregnant moment I fondly imagined I should be one of the few people to see a shot fired in anger, and I could hardly believe my ears when at Brindisi or Malta we heard that Germany and Russia were at war. And my cup of misery overflowed when on arrival at Aden I learned that England also had declared war on Germany.

Our only idea was to get back to England by fair means or foul, but our efforts were fruitless and we arrived next morning in Berbera, thousands of miles from the main battlefield, *en route* for a secondary little affair; it felt like playing in a village cricket match instead of in the Test.

The Mad Mullah was still in command of the Dervishes and had held that position for years by the sheer force of a magnetic personality. He had started life as a stoker, but had shaken off the dust to become a colourful and romantic figure, always fighting superior odds, but managing to inspire the Dervishes with that degree of fanaticism that makes death a privilege. In spite of many expeditions against him he had evaded capture, and when he was finally defeated by aeroplanes I felt a sense of real personal loss. He was a godsend to officers with an urge to fight and a shaky or non-existent bank balance.

When I first arrived in Somaliland the *kharif* was still blowing, a hot, labouring wind heavy with sand, and the climate of Berbera at sea-level was singularly unpleasant. We left at once for Burao, some 1,500 feet up, where, in spite of the tail end of the *kharif*, the climate was very delightful. I knew at once that I loved Somaliland.

The country seemed to consist of endless sand adorned with extremely thorny bushes, but it exhaled a friendliness towards me that made me forget my personal worries and imbued me with a *joie de vivre* that I had not felt in my palmy days in England.

The Somali is a Mohammedan, but his prayers are spasmodic and indulged in, with feverish energy, only when in the near neighbourhood of a Dervish.

I can still see the evening I arrived in Burao. It was towards the end of the Mohammedan fast of Ramadan when the fast is broken by the first sight of the new moon. There were hundreds of Somalis silhouetted against the darkening sky, gaping with rapacious eyes at the relentless dust clouds and with their empty bellies rattling. Suddenly the clouds parted, the new moon winked a second and was gone ; a yell went up from hungry souls, and the fast was over.

The Somalis were a fine-looking bunch and very smart in the uniform we gave them. It consisted of a sweater, shorts, puttees and a khaki cummerbund and puggaree. They were cheerful soldiers, of rather excitable natures, but capable of greatness.

One officer who had been in a very hard fight with the Dervishes told me that the Somalis had formed square and were being heavily attacked. One of his men, having fired all his ammunition, quite simply put his rifle across his shoulders and walked into the Dervishes. These are the gestures that sound so useless on paper but are so gripping in fact and give to war the touch of the sublime.

The Somalis were Fuzzy-wuzzys ; one of my orderlies had a particularly luxuriant head of hair. I had dismissed him after morning parade and told him to report for next parade in about two hours' time. He duly turned up, but with his entire head shaved, and when I asked him why he merely remarked he had a headache.

Once we had a Somali sergeant very badly wounded, and as our doctor thought his case was hopeless he told him he might go home. Two or three weeks later the man turned up, right as rain, and when asked how he managed to recover he said he had had a camel dung poultice applied to his wound. He was ahead of his time, as it was only in this last war that our doctors discovered that wounds should be allowed to putrefy and heal themselves—a nauseating but extremely satisfactory cure.

All the officers in the Camel Corps were British, seconded from British or Indian regiments. We were a mixed crowd, and I suppose our only common denominator was that we were all short of cash, a fact quite unnoticeable in Somaliland which was about the one and only place on earth where one could not use it.

The week after my arrival Colonel Tom Cubitt arrived to take over command of all the troops in the country, consisting of ourselves and an Indian Infantry contingent. Colonel Cubitt was a first-class soldier and a fine leader of men.

The essentials of the art of leadership have been argued and probed since time immemorial, but to me it rests simply in the quality of the man. He either has it or he hasn't. Tom Cubitt had it and the troops felt it and responded immediately. In appearance he reminded me of Tom Bridges, tall and attractive and full of a genial *bonhomie* and all the human frailties that made one love a man instead of just admiring him. His flow of language was unrivalled; he never bothered with spades being spades—they were always " bloody shovels."

" Pug " Ismay, now Lord Ismay, became his staff officer and did very fine work in Somaliland, but by his thoroughness, soundness and utter dependability he made himself indispensable to that theatre of war and was never allowed to get back to Europe. What was Somaliland's gain was certainly a dead loss to the other arenas.

Paddy Howard, John Hornby (brother of Butcha and the toughest officer I ever met) and Boomer Colquhoun were all good hard men who made the best of a bad job.

In Burao we started training in real earnest, and having every confidence in Colonel Cubitt we knew he would attack the Dervishes immediately it was possible. We could shoot only around the camp, but we managed to keep our larder well stocked, and whiled away in between hours playing polo and hockey.

Lawrence, who commanded the Camel Corps, had an attractive tame cheetah, a charming pet when it was not feeding, but a dangerous one when it was. One day it dashed out at some goats, and the old woman herding them lifted and drove her spear straight through it, thinking it a wild cheetah—a tragic end, but all the same she was a very brave old woman.

On November 14th Colonel Cubitt received permission from the authorities to attack. The Dervishes were known to have established themselves in some blockhouses at Shimber Berris, and on the 17th we marched, hoping to attack on the 18th.

Until then our troops had always waited for the Dervishes to attack, then formed square and killed as many as they could. This time the methods were to be new, and we managed to march to Shimber Berris and arrive unmolested and within four or five hundred yards of the Dervishes. Here we waited while our O.C. decided how and when to tackle them.

The blockhouse facing us was about fourteen feet square, made of stone, and with the solidity of a minor fortress—a most unpleasant and formidable objective.

Colonel Cubitt was in doubt as to which troops to use; he favoured the Indian contingent, but as I was very anxious for him to use my Somali company, he allowed me to prevail upon him. I had been warned that Somalis in the early stages of a fight were liable to turn their backs on the proceedings, but I felt full of confidence in my men and my faith in them was justified.

Waiting for the decision was distinctly amusing, for the Dervishes kept popping up and hurling insults at us, all querying our legitimacy, and as they jumped we took pot-shots at them. Although we did no damage and they never fired at us in return, it relieved the tedium of waiting for zero hour and saved us from any anticipatory cold feet.

At last the word came to attack, and we charged over the bare intervening ground. Our gathering impetus must have rendered the fire of the Dervishes extremely inaccurate, as we achieved the blockhouse without a casualty. Then, and only then, I realized what a tough proposition this block-house was going to be. The only entrance was a door, but to get to that door we had to jump three feet to the threshhold which was covered by the loopholes above it.

I was in shirtsleeves and the first shot fired at me passed through my rolled-up sleeve and did no damage, but as the muzzle of the Dervish's rifle could not have been more than a yard away from me the blast blew me backwards and I wondered what to do next. Some of our men were being hit and the wounds were bad, as the bullets were heavy and soft, but luckily the Dervish, for economy's sake, used a small charge of powder.

By this time I was seething with excitement. I got a glancing blow in my eye but I was too wound up to stop— I had to go on trying to get in.

The next hit was in my elbow, and I plucked a large but not too damaging splinter from it. But the following shot split my ear, and as the doctor was standing conveniently near he stitched it up there and then, looking meanwhile at my eye, which was feeling pretty painful. It seemed to be beyond immediate repair.

While I was being sewn up Lieutenant Simmons made an attempt on the threshold, but he had the back of his head blown off by one of these soft bullets and was killed instantly.

Patched up, and still wound up, I tried again to storm this blockhouse, but a ricochet from a bullet went through the same damaged eye. We were so near the Dervishes that I could touch their rifles with my stick which was only a couple of feet long.

Our Somalis were having heavy casualties, and Tom Cubitt decided to let the Indian contingent have their try. But they fared no better, and as the light was beginning to fail we withdrew to camp not far away to take stock of the situation and lick our wounds. Rather magnanimously, we offered the Dervishes their lives if they would surrender, but our generous gesture brought forth a still brighter volley of rudery as to our parentage.

It had all been most exhilarating fun and the pace too hot for anyone to have had any other sensation but thrill, primitive and devouring. But by the time I got back to camp I was in bad shape, my eye very painful, and I was practically blind.

Next day I had to be taken up on a stretcher behind the

43

attacking troops; I could not be left in camp, as had the Dervishes attacked it my fate would have been most unpleasant. On arriving again at the blockhouse it was a considerable relief for us to find it had been evacuated and there were no signs of our enemy.

Next day I was sent down to Berbera, eighty miles away, on a camel. I sat in front with my orderly behind holding me up. Even at Berbera there were none of the requisite instruments, although all that kindness could do was done for me by Captain de Cologan. So on I was sent across to Aden to a hospital run by nuns, and the missionary eye surgeon was called in. But he also could do nothing.

A P. & O. steamer was coming through at that moment and the authorities requested me a passage, but although the boat was half empty the P. & O. had an aversion to wounded officers and at first refused, eventually being prevailed upon to drop me in Egypt. There the eye specialist did not mince matters; he said my eye must be removed at once. I refused point-blank to allow it, as I knew that this was my one and only chance of getting sent to England with maybe a possibility of the war in Europe, eye or no eye.

By great efforts of persuasion I succeeded in being sent home, but the journey was nothing less than a nightmare. I was practically blind, physically and morally the world was black, and I was sick at heart.

Paradoxically and mercifully time passed very quickly. It may be only a personal kink, but I have found, whenever I have been very ill or badly wounded, that though the hours crawl, the days and weeks flash by with their monotonous impersonality, each indistinguishable from the other.

My old chief Sir Henry Hildyard had very kindly arranged for me to go to King Edward's Hospital run by that wonderful character Miss Agnes Keyser, but I felt little inclined for the regimentation of a large hospital, and managed to get myself into a taxi and drive straight to Sir Douglas Shields' Nursing Home at 17 Park Lane, an address that was to mean much to me in the coming years, and a real home to all wounded officers in every sense of the word.

Soon after arriving I was examined by Sir Arnold Lawson, who corroborated the Cairo verdict and said my eye must come out. Although I had feared it, and inwardly known it, the decision shook me and I wondered how the loss of an eye would affect my future.

The eye was taken out on January 3rd, 1915, the first anniversary of the news of my father's financial crash. From that moment on I have become more and more superstitious, and though I have tried to persuade myself that it is a sign of weakness and slightly ridiculous, I have never risen above it. Each year I dread January 3rd and long for it to be free of misfortune. I dislike any new undertaking on a Sunday (I have been six times wounded on a Sunday) and as for seeing the new moon through glass, I go to almost any lengths to avoid it; the two occasions on which I failed were followed by deaths.

When the eye had been removed a piece of metal, which must have gone through it, was found behind the eyeball.

Number 17 Park Lane was the acme of comfort and the care and treatment I received far above praise. When I became one of their most regular customers they always gave me the same room on the top floor, open to the skies and looking over the park; even silk pyjamas with my name on were reserved for me. We came to regard it as our unofficial club; the only subscription demanded of us was to be sick and in need of help, and help they gave in full.

On this occasion I was in the home for three or four weeks and then was given sick leave. On my appearing before the Medical Board they seemed rather shocked at my desire to go to France. We argued, and they produced the astonishing solution that if I found I could wear a satisfactory glass eye they would consider me. I imagine they did not wish the Germans to think that we were reduced to sending out one-eyed officers.

At my next board I appeared with a startling, excessively uncomfortable, glass eye. I was passed fit for general service. On emerging I called a taxi, threw my glass eye out of the window, put on my black patch, and have never worn a glass eye since.

CHAPTER V

A CAVALRYMAN LOSES HIS SPURS

FEBRUARY, 1915, found me on a Southampton steamer bound for France. From all sides I had heard how well the regiment had done, and I felt a great pride in belonging to it, though very much of an outsider, and I wanted a chance to justify my existence.

Tom Bridges and Butcha Hornby had been helping to make history, and as I lay in my cabin I thought of them both, and wondered what life might hold for me.

We had been one of the first regiments to land in France after the declaration of war, and soon after landing, Tom Bridges was sent to reconnoitre with his squadron. He questioned all the villagers and collected every piece of available information, and, together with his French liaison officer, came to the conclusion that there were many thousands of Germans coming towards the British force. Tom Bridges immediately sent in his report, which was passed on to G.H.Q. The report was ignored, no action was taken, and the Germans advanced to open the 1914 campaign.

Early in the war an exhausted infantry battalion had arrived at the town of St. Quentin. They were met by the Mayor, who implored them not to fight as he wished to save the town from wanton destruction, and spare the lives of the inhabitants.

The colonel of the infantry battalion, too tired to withstand the appeal, wrote what amounted to a surrender, to be handed to the advancing Germans.

At that psychological moment up rode Tom Bridges at the head of his squadron, took one look at the situation and without a moment's hesitation proceeded to retrieve it. He collected all the musical instruments out of a little toy shop in the town, formed a band, and with the penny whistles blowing he put new heart into that footsore dispirited battalion, and marched them out under the nose of the Germans.

This epic was made memorable by Sir Henry Newbolt in a poem, "The Toy Band: A Song of the Great Retreat":

Dreary lay the long road, dreary lay the town,
Lights out and never a glint o' the moon:
Weary lay the stragglers, half a thousand down,
Sad sighed the weary big Dragoon.
"Oh! if I'd a drum here to make them take the road again,
"Oh! if I'd a fife to wheedle, come, boys, come!
"You that mean to fight it out, wake and take your load again,
"Fall in! Fall in! Follow the fife and drum!"

"Hey, but here's a toy shop, here's a drum for me,
"Penny whistles too to play a tune!
"Half a thousand dead men soon shall hear and see
"We've a band!" said the weary big Dragoon.
"Rubadub! Rubadub! Wake and take the road again,
"Wheedle-deedle-deedle-dee, come, boys, come!
"You that mean to fight it out, wake and take your load again,
"Fall in! Fall in! Follow the fife and drum!"

Cheerly goes the dark road, cheerly goes the night,
Cheerly goes the blood to keep the beat:
Half a thousand dead men marching on to fight
With a little penny drum to lift their feet.
"Rubadub! Rubadub! Wake and take the road again,
"Wheedle-deedle-deedle-dee, come, boys, come!
"You that mean to fight it out, wake and take your load again,
"Fall in! Fall in! Follow the fife and drum!"

As long as there's an Englishman to ask a tale of me,
As long as I can tell the tale aright,
We'll not forget the penny whistle's wheedle-deedle-dee,
And the big Dragoon abeating down the night,
"Rubadub! Rubadub! Wake and take the road again,
"Wheedle-deedle-deedle-dee, come, boys, come!
"You that mean to fight it out, wake and take your load again,
"Fall in! Fall in! Follow the fife and drum!"

There was no doubt that Tom Bridges was the finest type of fighting commander, for he had the first essential quality —complete command over himself; and his quick grasp of a situation, coupled with his calmness in a tight corner, made him a great leader.

Butcha Hornby had had the distinction of being the first British officer to kill a German with his own hand. He was pursuing a German patrol, and catching up with them, he hesitated, wondering whether he should put his sword through the nearest Hun. The Hun had no such hesitation, but attempted to drive his lance into Hornby, who then killed him with his sword.

He rode back with his patrol through several villages held by Germans, got through unscathed and was awarded the D.S.O.

A few days later Butcha received a severe wound in the spine, and was never able to soldier again. It was a tragedy for the regiment and a real loss to the Army, for if ever a man had been marked out for success it was Butcha. In my opinion, out of a wonderful lot of officers in the regiment, Butcha was the most outstanding of them all. He had a tremendous sense of duty, and was that rare thing in a man, completely unselfish. His career as a soldier finished, he brought to his mental and physical suffering all the remarkable courage he had shown in his active life—without a tinge of self-pity, or a word of complaint.

I thought also of Hardress Lloyd and Horace Sewell. Horace Sewell was second in command of the regiment, and destined to command the 1st Cavalry Brigade, and Hardress Lloyd, who had rejoined the regiment in 1914, was now A.D.C. to General de Lisle. Hardress was a world-famed polo player who had captained England against America, and had proved to be a first-class soldier with an exceptionally charming personality.

Arrival at Le Havre interrupted my thoughts, and I found my cousin Henri Carton de Wiart waiting to meet me. He was a member of the Belgian Government which, since being forced to leave Belgium, had made their Headquarters at Le Havre.

That same night I left for the front. I was to join my regiment as a squadron leader at Mont des Cats in Flanders, and found them leading a comparatively dull life within sound of the guns of Ypres.

Colonel R. L. Mullens had taken the regiment to France, and his training and enthusiasm had brought it to a high pitch of efficiency. By the time I arrived he had been given command of the 2nd Cavalry Brigade, and was succeeded by Colonel Solly Flood.

I found two of my oldest and best friends at Mont des Cats, Bob Ogilby and Foxy Aylmer; they had been in it all

48

from the beginning. They had seen the Retreat from Mons and its annihilating casualties, and the battles of the Marne and the Aisne with our first advance. By the time they had told me of the first Battle of Ypres, I felt that my small war in Somaliland had been light sparring compared to France's heavy punching.

It was a grim tale of losses and unequal odds, but in spite of it the living conditions in France seemed to me to be elegant compared to Somaliland. We had billets, a bed to sleep on, plenty of food, letters and papers arrived daily, and half the contents of Fortnum & Mason as well. At that moment I had not sampled the trenches and found how hard and pathetically short life could be. To me, then, far and away the worst part was the scene of utter desolation. Mile upon mile of nothing except an occasional weird cluster of amputated tree trunks blown bare and standing like eyeless effigies surveying destruction. I suppose we got used to it day in, day out, but if ever I went away from it, on my return it hit me anew with its despairing emptiness.

The scales of war were still weighted heavily against us. We had hardly any aeroplanes, few guns, little ammunition and fewer bombs. In those early days our field guns were rationed to half a dozen rounds a day, and if they managed to fire less they were praised for their economy by the High Command.

Everywhere I found great respect for the German soldier, but still greater for his ammunition. The German sniper was a particular bugbear; he was so well trained, armed and employed, and we suffered heavily at his hands, especially among our officers. Although later on we made great progress and trained our snipers to be as good as the enemy's, in my opinion we never used them as well.

The war may not have been going very well for us, but we had two great assets which the Germans could not emulate—the unconquerable spirit of the Britisher, who is at his best when he is losing, and that unfailing sense of humour which can rise above everything.

My friends in the regiment were full of stories of the lighter side of battle, for war manages to be a universal provider of funny situations, no doubt ordained to preserve a proper balance with intensity.

One of our officers was holding up the Germans from a barricade at the end of a cobbled village street. The brigadier came up to him and said : " This is no time to shoot at Germans, Mr. X. You will charge them." Mr. X, having no choice in the matter, endeavoured to carry out the order, but, luckily for him, his horse slithered on the cobbles, slipped up, and put an end to his charge.

A Prussian guardsman complete with beard was seen coming down a hill on a bicycle, and one of our men, instead of shooting him, merely shoved his rifle through the spokes of the bicycle. The bearded Prussian turned a complete somersault, and on rising to his feet cursed our man loud and long. Wounded dignity cancelled out any gratitude for sparing his life !

One of my friends who was a liaison officer with the French told me about a small force of French reservists who held a sector of the line. They evacuated the line every night so as to enjoy the greater comfort of the nearest inn. In the morning they would form up and charge their positions, which, luckily, the less imaginative and more disciplined Hun never thought of occupying.

One day the same friend on going up to the line met a French reservist coming away from it. On asking him where he was going, the French reservist pointed over his shoulder and answered : " *Les cochons, ils tirent à balle* " (the swine are firing live ammunition). This was quite enough for what must have been the equivalent of our " Ole Bill ", and he was off !

On the other hand, after the war, several German officers told me that when French troops were cut off they were far more difficult to deal with than the British. The French are very good soldiers, but they are a race of individualists, less amenable to discipline, and much less responsive to the herd instinct.

I was very anxious to see the line. Soon after my arrival Bob Ogilby and I hacked up one day to Ypres, ate an excellent lunch in a restaurant, and rode on to the Infantry Brigade Headquarters. There we were given a most chilly reception, as two mounted officers were almost bound to attract the attention of the Hun artillery. Sure enough we did, and returned far quicker than we had gone up, but in our hurry we got caught up on telephone wires strewn across the road, and arrived back with our horses festooned in them.

Soon after this we were ordered to take part in the second Battle of Ypres.

Our horses were left behind with just enough men to look after them, and we synchronized our arrival with the first gas attack.

Gas is the most abominable form of warfare, and affects people to a varying degree. We were issued with little gauze and cotton pads which, firstly, we had to soak in some primitive and home-made liquid, before placing them over our mouths.

I found the gas was not affecting me much, but the shelling was terrific and would have been exhilarating if only a little of it had been coming from our side. I was standing next my second-in-command wondering what to do, when he said : " I wish you'd duck when those shells come." I was on the point of telling him that I was a fatalist and believed in the appointed hour when we heard another shell coming and he ducked. The shell burst quite near us and I was thrown some distance. I picked myself up and started to move my men, when I noticed a hand on the ground. The hand was encased in a special kind of leather glove, which I recognized instantly as that worn by my second-in-command. His body was thirty or forty yards away.

We were up for a very short time, sent back to our billets at Mont des Cats, but called up again soon after, for the fighting had become much heavier.

Our first night at Ypres we were ordered to go and relieve some infantry, and were told that a staff officer from the Infantry Brigade would meet us on the Menin Road and guide us to the line.

Colonel Horace Sewell was commanding the regiment and leading it up the road, with Gallaher the Adjutant and myself walking with him. There was no one on the road to meet us, let alone to guide us, and as we passed some dead Germans an ominous feeling began to creep over me that we were going too far, as I knew the Germans had not broken our line. Suddenly the silence was split by a cry of " Halt " in obvious German, and we were fired on at the same moment. I had stopped instantly on hearing the first shout, hoping to locate the German, but the next second I found myself sprawling on the ground with a damaged hand. I caught hold of it, but it seemed to be a gory mess. I could not hear or see either Sewell or Gallaher, but I could make out the outline of some Germans a short distance away. I picked myself up, and though they went on firing at me they did not hit me again. On the way up the road I had taken a woolly scarf off a dead German as the night was cold, and now I wrapped this scarf round my wrist, holding the ends between my teeth, and started walking back. The pain had ceased and was succeeded by numbness. Gallaher had run back a short distance and, seeing the shadow of someone coming, he thought I was an advancing German, so picked up a rifle and took a shot at me. Then he ran farther back and told the regiment the Germans were coming down the road. By this time I was beginning to feel very weak, called out, and luckily my voice was recognized. Some men came out to pick me up, and took me to the dressing station.

My hand was a ghastly sight; two of the fingers were hanging by a bit of skin, all the palm was shot away and most of the wrist. For the first time, and certainly the last, I had been wearing a wrist-watch, and it had been blown into the remains of my wrist. I asked the doctor to take my fingers off; he refused, so I pulled them off myself and felt absolutely no pain in doing it.

I was sent to a hospital at Hazebrouck, as far as I can remember, literally packed with patients. It had a pathetically inadequate and harassed staff unable to cope with such an overwhelming situation. It was another patient who really looked after me, an officer in the 3rd Dragoon Guards, and I never knew his name until three years later, when I recognized him at the Armistice in Brussels. I learned that he was Brigadier-General Alfred Burt, and I was so glad to have an opportunity at last of thanking him for all he had done for me, and founded a friendship which lasted until he died very recently.

From Hazebrouck I was taken to Boulogne and put under the care of Sir George Makins, who had looked after me in South Africa. He feared the hand might light up at any minute, and advised my being sent straight back to England. In a few days I found myself back in number 17 Park Lane, and for a long, long session.

I was too ill and exhausted from pain to know or care whether I was to live or die, and for a whole week, my nurse told me afterwards, she had never expected to find me alive in the morning.

The regiment had had heavy casualties, and I heard that the same night that I had been wounded Harold Gibb had been blinded. He had been in holy orders before the war, and after his blindness he resumed his normal life undeterred by his affliction.

For the rest of 1915 life crawled by. I had innumerable operations, and each time another bit of my hand was chopped off until the very sight of it filled me with such a nausea that my only idea was to have it taken off. The surgeons thought differently, believed in miracles, and endeavoured to save the horrible remains.

Whilst I was lying there I heard that my father had died in Cairo. I had seen him in December on my way back from Somaliland and realized then that his brain had begun to fail and that the end could not be far off. Although I had been prepared for his death it did not lessen the blow, for he was my only real tie in the world, the one solid piece of background as well as the most kind and generous of fathers. My stepmother was left to battle with the dreary trappings of death as well as with the winding up of my father's financial affairs. There had been a slump in Egypt and it needed all my stepmother's clear-headed determination to bring any order to the chaos that was left.

By December, 1915, my patience was running out. My hand showed no sign of healing, I could stand it no longer, and I insisted that it should come off. As I detest anæsthetics and am a very bad subject, the surgeon said he would amputate simply with gas. The whole entertainment was no worse than having a tooth out, and an hour afterwards I was sitting up eating a meal, when the door opened and into the room walked Tom Bridges.

Tom said he was leaving the next day to command the 19th Division and he offered me a job in it. The effect of this offer was magical, my health improved by leaps and bounds, and within three weeks I was out of hospital and had every intention of returning to France.

At the back of my mind, for some time, I had wanted to

53

go to the infantry, as it was obvious that the cavalry was not suited to the modern trend of warfare. They were outstaying their usefulness and did not seem likely to have much to do in the future. Originally the idea had been put in my head by Ferdie Cavendish-Bentinck, who, owing to the appalling casualties among infantry officers, had foreseen the dire need for cavalry officers in the infantry.

People imagine the loss of a hand to be far more serious than the loss of an eye, but having tried both I can say sincerely that it is not my experience. It is rather my private conceit that I can do most things a two-handed man can do, and almost as quickly, but I do not think a single day has passed when I have not missed my eye. There is an old Indian proverb which says : " Never trust a one-eyed man, as he sees everything." In a way it is true, as the loss of an eye makes one very observant, but there are many irritating drawbacks that are apt to get on one's nerves. Anyone standing on my blind side makes me feel I have my back to them, and I have never really enjoyed playing a ball game since I lost my eye.

As for my hand, I found several more uses for my teeth other than just eating, and had great fun learning to master my tie and my shoe laces. My greatest triumph came when I left hospital and went to stay with Ralph Sneyd for his dry-fly fishing on the Test, where I discovered to my joy that I could still tie on a fly.

Fishing was an accomplishment, but I knew it would not hold much sway with the Medical Board, and I prepared myself for a hostile reception. In the middle of the inquisition I was visited by an inspiration, and said that since leaving hospital I had been hunting and shooting, and if I was able to do that successfully, surely I could be some use in France. My one eye must have been wearing an honest look, for the board seemed duly impressed and again I was passed for general service.

I rejoined the regiment near Boulogne, where they were stationed in great comfort, but soon after I was posted as second-in-command of the Loyal North Lancs in Tom Bridges's 19th Division. Up till now I felt that I had seen little fighting, and sad as I was to leave the 4th Dragoon Guards, I knew everyone understood the reason of my going and did not resent it.

Life with the infantry was a very different business from anything I had ever experienced. In comparison with a cavalryman, the infantryman seemed to have very little to do, for he had far less equipment to clean, no horses to care for, and too much time on his hands.

The infantryman had the hardest of all lessons to learn—endurance; and he endured danger, hourly and daily, until it became monotonous; discomfort, noise, long spells of the line, fatigues and carrying parties; and he was dog-tired and he looked it. He was well clothed and fed, and supposed to be able to draw so many changes of shirts and socks that he never bothered to wash them. He had little to cheer him but his own unfailing spirit and superb sense of humour.

By this time—March, 1916—our ammunition supplies were improving enormously, and our Artillery and Machine-Gun Corps were developing quickly and effectively, having received a hard lesson from the Hun.

The German machine-gunners were outstanding, almost invariably very brave men and the pick of the German Army. One day on the Somme we were held up for a considerable time by a German machine-gun. Finally we silenced it and were able to advance, and found the whole crew dead, but all of them bandaged, having been wounded several times before being killed.

Another time we found a young German lying dead beside a machine-gun, and the villagers told us that all the Germans had retired except this one boy who had remained firing his gun until he was killed.

Bombs were never much in my line because, firstly, I felt that I might blow myself up with them, and, secondly, they made it possible for the men to sit at the bottom of a trench and lob them over the top, without even looking to see what was going on outside.

My first spell in the line was in a quiet sector at Neuve Chapelle, where our chief anxiety lay in being mined. Monty Hill commanded the North Lancs when I went to them. He grounded me in infantry work, and having been adjutant in the Scots Guards, he was the ideal mentor. It was Monty Hill who gave me the most invaluable lesson on running an officers' mess, impressing me with the importance of keeping the highest possible standard whether in the line or out of it. Trench life is apt to be demoralizing and officers get casual and sloppy in their appearance and habits, but the effect of a really first-class mess had a high disciplinary and moral value, as well as a more appealing approach to the stomach.

There were several excellent officers with the North Lancs, one of whom, Captain M. H. Maule, I took to Poland with me in 1919, knowing that I was taking both a good companion and a most efficient officer. He had an unsurpassed energy, and a zest for living under trying conditions which enabled him to overcome the very serious wounds he received later on the Somme.

In April or May, 1916, we were taken out of the line and sent to the Amiens country to be fattened up for the Battle of the Somme.

I had had no opportunity of meeting the high and the great ones in my subordinate rank, but while we were training for the Somme I was introduced to Lord Haig, the Commander-in-Chief of the British Forces. He was a man of striking appearance, but without any charm of manner and no Churchillian gift of words. He mumbled at me, saying that I had given a good example by coming out to France in spite of my disabilities, but the tone of his voice and his unsmiling face made it as uninspiring as if he had said : " It is a wet day."

Just before the start of the Somme offensive I was given command of the 8th Gloucesters, and I could never wish to meet a nicer lot of officers or men. They were a fine battalion and in wonderful training after their rest and preparation, like the whole of the division. Captain Parkes was my adjutant ; he later commanded the regiment, receiving both the D.S.O. and M.C., which he richly deserved.

When I took over I received another goodly inheritance in the shape of my predecessor's servant, Holmes. He was a delightful scoundrel and provided me with endless amusement besides giving me some very devoted service. One day Holmes annoyed me considerably by letting off his rifle in my ear at some passing plane, and I thereupon seized his rifle and from that day forward he was armed only with my blanket and my primus stove. I never carried a revolver, being afraid that if I lost my temper I might use it against my own people, so my only weapon was a walking-stick.

Holmes and I must have been a quaint-looking couple advancing into battle !

We marched up to the Somme in easy stages and when the battle started on July 1st we were in reserve. We were told that our first task in the battle was to capture La Boisselle.

We were allowed only twenty officers in an attack, which meant careful choosing and elimination, and countless heartbreaks for those who had to be left behind. Lieutenant James prevailed on me to let him take part, and I regretted my weakness, as he was very badly wounded in the leg, but he recovered. Later in the war he was awarded the V.C.

The spirit of the men was amazing, for though they knew that they were going to have a bad time and that casualties would be heavy, they seemed not to have a care in the world, and spent their free time playing games and behaving like schoolboys on a half-holiday.

We moved up the night of July 2nd–3rd to attack in the morning.

La Boisselle was one of the strongest positions the Germans held on the Somme, and there had already been two unsuccessful attacks. No-man's-land presented a ghastly sight, for it was strewn with British corpses in those grotesque attitudes peculiar to the dead on a battlefield.

In this attack my battalion, the 8th Gloucesters, were in support. The battalion we were supporting soon advanced into a heavy German barrage, and in the noise and confusion imagined they had received the order to retire. This battalion were retiring through my men, and as retirement is the most infectious disease there was a desperate moment of chaos, when the issue hung in the balance. The officers of the 8th Gloucesters were truly magnificent, and the men rallied and responded to them. They advanced regardless of their appalling casualties until they had fulfilled their appointed task and captured La Boisselle.

During that engagement I was compelled to use some bombs for the first and last time, and found a new use for my teeth, pulling the pins out; I was thankful that my teeth were my own.

I had tried to impress on my battalion the importance of correct timing, telling them that often a dozen men at the right moment were more effective than a hundred at the wrong.

This lesson was soon proved, for after our taking over of La Boisselle the Germans counter-attacked and I saw them advancing rapidly down a trench. At that moment one of my sergeants turned up with six or seven stragglers, and I sent him at once to stop the attack and drive the Germans back. It was the right moment, for there and then that handful of men which were all I had left drove the Germans back and they never regained a footing in our line.

In trench warfare there is no way of finding out what is happening except by going to look, and in my opinion a battalion commander has no time during a battle to sit about in the dug-out provided for him. He should cover as much ground as possible as fast as he can, for the telephones are usually the first things to be blown up and messages take a long time to arrive. When the shelling is heavy the men need a spur on from time to time, and an invisible commander in a dug-out cannot be a great source of inspiration. In a case like La Boisselle my men were untried troops, and they had to get out of the comparative safety of the trenches, advance over blown-up wire and piled-up corpses and pitch-fork themselves into battle.

I was looking round our trenches when I saw a man who was certainly not going forward. I asked him the reason for his dawdling, and he replied that he had been wounded three or four times already, and simply couldn't face it. I told him that I had been hit oftener than he had but still had to face it, and to give a little point to my argument I gave him a push in the right direction, and on he went. Later one of my cousins went to see King George V, who repeated that story to him. I had never mentioned the incident to anyone, so the man in the trench must have told that tale against himself . . . not an easy thing to do.

Until we occupied the German trenches I had no idea how comfortably the Hun lived in his deep dug-outs. We had nothing to compare with them, and in fact we had no deep dug-outs at all until after the Battle of the Somme. Personally, I did not like them, for it was difficult to get the men out of them, and both the Germans and ourselves lost many thousands of prisoners because of them.

La Boisselle was a truly bloody scene. The casualties had been appalling; there were dead everywhere, not a house standing, and the ground as flattened as if the very soul had been blasted out of the earth and turned into a void. At one moment I sat down on a waterproof sheet to write some orders, only to find when I got up that I had been sitting on a dead body.

The day was hot, and we were tired and thirsty and waiting with our tongues hanging out for the water to follow us up. When it did appear it was in petrol cans, and they had not been rinsed first.

Parkes, my Adjutant, had been badly wounded and nearly all my officers were casualties. That evening General Tom Bridges came up to see the remains of us. One could count on him to come when things were lively, and this was an invaluable visit from both the men's point of view and from mine. We were discussing the situation and I told him that if only I had some more officers and men I could advance still further. His response was immediate, he gave me another battalion and we gained valuable ground. Tom had a wonderful knack of giving a man confidence in himself, and bringing out the best in him by trusting his judgment and backing him to the end. It was on another occasion like this that Tom lost a leg. He had gone up to see one of his brigade commanders to congratulate him on his achievements, and on his return was hit by a shell.

On the morning of the 4th we were taken out of the line and put in reserve, but the very same day we were sent up again to La Boisselle; and although under a heavy barrage the battalion were splendid and took little notice of it.

Soon after we returned, a German officer suddenly walked into our trenches and said he had been lying out in no-man's-land for a couple of days. I asked what had brought him in now. He replied : " Because it's raining ! " Impervious to shells, but a drop of rain moved him like lightning.

All the next day we were heavily shelled, suffered awful casualties, but we kept the Hun out, and the following night we were relieved and the remnants of us marched to Albert for a rest and refit.

The effect on the battalion of this successful attack was quite extraordinary and their already high morale rose still higher ; one felt that they could never admit defeat. They had every reason to be pleased with themselves, for if they had not pushed through to their objective when the leading battalion gave up the advance of the whole of that sector of the front would have been jeopardized.

When the war was over I received an account of these operations from the War Office asking for my criticisms. As I could find no mention of the 8th Gloucesters in the entire report, I simply wrote and said that I had been under the impression that my battalion had taken La Boisselle, but that evidently I was wrong. So much for official history.

After coming out of the line, Tom Bridges took me for a day or two's rest to La Panne, where the King of the Belgians had his headquarters. I had the honour of meeting the King and found him a man of quiet charm and distinguished good looks, but he struck me as being most painfully shy, and he had very few words for me.

Tom Bridges was an ideal companion for a few days' leave, for he combined soldiering with a vivid and imaginative mind. He was artistic, musical and a man of letters, and to be with him was an entertainment as varied as the delightful anthology he compiled for the Army which he called *Word from England*.

My battalion had a short rest at Albert, and during that time Brigadier George Jeffreys, who had been wounded, returned to duty to command the brigade. He was the pattern of what a Guards' officer should be, and he taught me the value of drill and how it is infallibly bound up with discipline, for the man who responds mechanically to an order on a parade-ground is more likely to respond automatically in battle.

My first lesson from General Jeffreys was rather humiliating. We were at church parade and my battalion was not in the right place, and the General told me to move it. I had to admit that I did not know how to, and felt exactly like the Bateman picture of " The Guardsman who Dropped his Rifle on Parade." The general spared my outraged feelings, and benevolently suggested that next time I went on leave I might go to Chelsea Barracks and learn my drill.

From Albert we were sent up to Bazentin le Petit to take part in one of the innumerable attacks on High Wood, which was one of the many strong-points on the Somme—a most unhealthy spot and a magnet for shells of every size. I went up the line the day before we were to go in, taking one of my surviving officers. He was killed on the way up. It was easy enough to be callous when one went to a new battalion, but when one knew and liked them all and had been through so much together it was a difficult matter, and I found that I felt losses more and more as the time went on.

Our orders were to try and get High Wood in a night attack.

On my way up to the line I stepped on a man in the dark, thought he was wounded and asked him where he had been hit. His answer was that he had not been hit! Turning to my adjutant who was following, I asked him for his revolver, but before I had time to use it the man had dived straight over the parapet!

We were still moving up when suddenly I found myself flat on my face, with the sensation that the whole of the back of my head had been blown off. I was feeling around gingerly in an endeavour to find out what bits of my anatomy remained and which of my limbs were still functioning, when the faithful Holmes (as usual on my heels with the primus and blanket) pulled me into a shell-hole. He sat with me for the next few hours with shells dropping all around us, Holmes soliloquizing over the charms of shells versus machine-gun bullets. He ended up with the classical comment of, " How my missus would laugh if she could see me now," which I feel sure did Mrs. Holmes a grave injustice ! Hours later Holmes managed to get me down to the dressing station, and I know that I owe my survival entirely to his loyalty.

At the dressing station I heard the bad news that we had had no success in the attack and again awful casualties. An infantry officer's span of life at the front in those days averaged a fortnight, but at High Wood I had received eight new officers the afternoon before the attack and I lost them all that night. There was no time or room even for my superstitions ; momentarily they were suspended in the face of reality.

The doctor at the dressing station had no means of judging whether my skull was damaged or not, but to avoid shaking me unnecessarily he sent me down to Corbie in a barge, though by this time I was feeling no pain at all. Soon I was back in Park Lane in the same room with the same pyjamas and the same welcome.

After an examination the surgeon pronounced my skull intact, ordered me a bottle of champagne and told me that by a miracle a machine-gun bullet had gone straight through the back of my head without touching a vital part. The only after effect of this wound was that whenever I had a hair cut the back of my head tickled.

In Park Lane, and in every hospital, kindnesses were showered on the wounded and we were almost buried under flowers, fruit and books Theatres opened their doors wide to us, a fleet of cars took us for drives, lovely ladies upset our temperatures, and delightful country houses were put at our disposal.

For my convalescence I generally used to go to Brighton to the charming and comfortable home of Mr. and Mrs. Wagg, who spoiled me to death, and to whom I am eternally grateful.

Three weeks in England found my head completely mended. I returned to France to the 8th Gloucesters and had a spell at Messines before going back to the Somme.

One day I happened to be near High Wood and out of curiosity went to try to find the place where I had been wounded Not only did I find the spot but I found my walking-stick too, probably where I had fallen. I felt I was becoming an individual target for the Hun, because at Grandcourt I stopped another fragment of shell, this time in my ankle, and was sent back again to England and naturally to Park Lane.

When I had nearly recovered I went along to White's one afternoon, and a member known to me by sight came up and asked me if I would do him a favour. I answered cautiously that I would if it was not a financial transaction, as no good seems to come out of borrowing or lending money. He then told me there was a man paying undue attention to a lady he knew and he wanted to fight him and asked me to second him in a duel ! I agreed at once, as I think duelling a most excellent solution in matters of the heart, and saw that my man was a tremendous fire-eater with only one object in view —to kill his opponent. It was a lively change from the sick bed. I went off to see his opponent, whom I knew ; true to form, he found the whole idea quite ridiculous. I assured him that my friend was adamant and determined to fight with any suggested weapon, but preferably with pistols at the range of a few feet. It took some time to penetrate into the gentleman's mind that this was serious, and with a great deal of reluctance he appointed the seconds. As a last resort our opponent produced what he considered a telling argument, which was that if this episode was found out we should all get into serious trouble, and still more serious trouble if someone was either hurt or killed. My reply to that was that the war was on, everyone too busy to be interested, and that it would be simple to go to some secluded spot like Ashdown Forest with a can of petrol and cremate the remains of whichever was killed. This suggestion finished him off; the mere thought of his ashes scattered to the four winds unhonoured and unsung, was too much for him He promptly sat down and wrote an affidavit not to see the lady again. It was a tame end : it seemed to me that as he did not like the lady enough to fight for her, he needed a thrashing.

CHAPTER VI

PASSCHENDAELE AND PARK LANE

My sick leave up, I went back to France and was given command of the 8th North Staffordshires. We went into the line at Hebuterne.

The division had a great misfortune in losing one of its brigade commanders—the only officer to be killed in that tour of the trenches. He was Toby Long of the Scots Greys, a fine soldier and a great sportsman.

We were in the line when the news came to me that I had been given a brigade, the 12th of the 4th Division.

I shall always look back on this particular year as one of the luckiest of my life, and I blessed the day when Tom Bridges had walked into my sick-room and offered me a job when my spirits were at zero and the bottom had dropped out of my world. In less than a year I had risen from a captain to a brigadier-general, and at that moment I believe I was the youngest brigadier-general in the Allied armies. My luck had been in, but of course there was the inevitable shadow, for the two men who had put their faith in me were both dead, my father and Sir Henry Hildyard. These two had backed me and stood by me in all the doubtful times, they had helped me by their example and their understanding, and I should have liked them to know that, in part, perhaps I had justified their faith.

The 4th Division was commanded by General Billy Lambton, a charming man, though unapproachable in the early morning ! This division had had a hard time ; it had lost its spirit and gone stale with weariness, and General Lambton was given a new set of brigade commanders to pull it together. It was our unenviable duty to get rid of a number of officers, who out of sheer exhaustion were unable to produce the required initiative and energy for battle.

On taking over the brigade I soon had a visit from the corps commander, General Johnny du Cane. He asked me to take a learner on my staff. I must admit to feeling very reluctant and dubious, and wondered what on earth the learner imagined I could teach him. He arrived and turned out to be Captain Tony Rothschild, and as he remains one of my best friends he must have weathered my teaching. He says that my first lesson to him was remarkable, for I departed immediately to Paris, leaving him in sole charge of Brigade Headquarters.

The weather played a most important part in the war. Mud was our enemy number one and succeeded in sapping the vitality of the soldier as nothing else did, especially in the winter. Frost was our friend ; it built up crumbling trenches and the men's morale in a matter of hours.

My first tour of the trenches as a brigade commander was a lucky one, blessed by frost, but the very day I came out the thaw set in, and within twenty-four hours the whole place was a sea of mud with the men caked in it and nearly drowned.

After my tour we went into hard training for the Battle of Arras.

General Allenby was our Army commander, and he conceived and was responsible for the working out of the plan of the battle. General Allenby had a breadth of vision that inspired one with confidence, and a clarity of thought and speech to impress it on others. He was a big man, both physically and mentally, with a brusque and dictatorial manner, a faculty for knowing what he wanted and seeing that he got it.

I had several meetings with General Allenby, and at one of them the French Commander-in-Chief, General Nivelle, was present. My brigade had been given what I considered to be a very ambitious objective, and I was expressing my doubts as to reaching it when General Nivelle remarked : " If the first objective is taken, you will have no difficulty in taking yours." His remark remained in my mind ; he proved absolutely right and I learned a lesson in psychology.

The day before the battle I had gone up to the line and managed to get my ear split by a bit of shell. I was very alarmed in case I should be done out of the battle, but I was sewn up quickly and not detained in hospital.

In the early morning of April 9th, 1917, we reached our assembly point, where some bright staff officer in a rush of zeal had chosen to have a trench dug adorned with a large notice, " Reserved for the English dead." I hoped it was not ominous !

When the Battle of Arras opened it was the most impressive I had ever witnessed, with a bombardment that was a symphony in our ears, for it was all coming from our side. Our preparations and our counter-battery work had been so thorough and effective that every German gun was silenced, and not a shot was heard from the other side for hours.

Soon after zero hour the German prisoners started pouring in, the morale of our troops rose every minute, and any idea of failure was banished. We reached our objective, having suffered about two hundred casualties, which in those days was comparatively light. We could have taken many more prisoners and much valuable ground if only cavalry had been available, but as it was we could see the guns being driven away into the distance, to be used against us, another day.

Snow had started to fall that evening, my men were dead-beat and I could not move them further. I went up to see my front-line troops and took one of my staff officers, and on returning to headquarters I turned to speak to him, but found, to my astonishment, that he was not there. On going back to look for him I met a most bedraggled apparition : he had fallen into a big shell-hole full of snow and had had great difficulty in getting out !

The following morning the situation had entirely changed; the Germans had taken up fresh positions, brought up considerable artillery and were shelling us all the time. Our cavalry arrived eventually, but it was too late to make any use of them.

The morning after the battle I went up to see my troops at Fampoux and took Tony Rothschild. We had one of the most unpleasant walks imaginable, with shells dropping all around us and hardly another soul on the road. It is a most curious thing how often since then I have met officers who say to me: " Do you remember our meeting on the Fampoux Road on April 10th ? " Extraordinary how Tony and I never saw them.

My headquarters were in a cellar, and that day various general officers came to lunch with us. We had a remarkable feast which I have never forgotten. A large game *pâté* had just arrived from Fortnum's. We finished off with a bottle of port and sent our visitors off with a warm sensation of well-nourished confidence. I am sure they thought the brigade must be as good as the lunch.

King George V came over to see the troops and I had the honour to be invited to meet him at luncheon. After lunch I was called in to speak to him and he asked me various questions. Having answered them all, I volunteered the remark that I thought it was rather amusing that I had in fact served some ten years in the Army without being a British subject. His Majesty was not in the least amused; he showed extreme displeasure and said he hoped I had rectified the situation. In 1910 my father had reminded me that I had never been naturalized, otherwise it would never have occurred to me, imagining that having served and fought in the British Army would *ipso facto* have made me a British subject.

The Germans were holding a very strong position at the chemical works, and it took us three weeks and thousands of casualties to capture it. One day, looking out from some high ground, I suddenly saw the Germans come out of their trenches to attack us. My artillery liaison officer was with me, and he at once got in touch with the artillery, and they turned on everything they could against the advancing Germans. They had no success, and I was beginning to feel very anxious as the Huns were almost in our trenches, when at last a salvo hit them fair and square and the survivors turned and fled.

We were given orders to relieve General Maxwell's brigade. The normal routine for a relief was to take over at night, but the roads and communications in front of the chemical works were being subjected to such heavy shelling as to make movement impossible without suffering heavy losses. General Maxwell, a V.C. and a most gallant leader who was afterwards killed, suggested that our brigade should change the routine and attempt the relief by day. It seemed a hazardous undertaking, but Maxwell's reasoning was so sound that I agreed to it. We dribbled the men up in pairs, casually and at short intervals, without arousing the suspicions of the Hun, and not only did we carry out the relief successfully, but we never lost a single man. It was a good instance of the boldest plan being the safest, though it might not have succeeded a second time.

One day one of my men saw something moving in a shell-hole behind the line. On crawling out to investigate he found a German soldier who had been lying out there since the last attack two or three days before. He was starving, and on being taken into our trenches devoured six tins of bully beef and eleven glasses of soda-water—and survived it.

The division were taken out of the line for another training and fattening process, this time for Passchendaele. We were relieved by the 51st Division, one of the best fighting divisions in France. The Germans attacked them the very first night and got into their lines; but not one of them came out.

Just at this time we had the misfortune to lose General Lambton. He had a fall while hacking and broke his neck, and though he survived he was never able to soldier again. He had made a magnificent job of the division and raised its morale to the highest degree. Another Guardsman, General Matheson, succeeded him in time to command us at Passchendaele.

Passchendaele was a hard battle fought under the most gruelling conditions of the war. It was late October, but the month had been stark and pitiless, and the whole country was a vast sea of malignant mud and water. Trenches collapsed and men floundered and drowned in mud. The enemy was showing the toughest resistance, and their defences were strengthened by concrete pillboxes bristling with machine guns fatal to attacking infantry.

After our attack we were badly battered. The remnants of two battalions were taken out, and I was given the unpleasant task of carrying out another attack with a brigade made up of odd battalions.

My servant, Holmes, followed me later to the line, and when he arrived I saw that for the first time Holmes seemed very shaken. It turned out that a shell had burst near him, and he had sustained the terrible loss of both my primus and my blanket.

During the battle a German officer was brought in to me. He was accused by my men of shooting the wounded. On telling him of what he was accused, I was much impressed by his simple dignity and calm manner. When he told me that he was incapable of such a despicable act I was convinced that he was speaking the truth. I asked him several pertinent questions, some of which he answered, and then I suggested that his people were having a bad time. His reaction pleased me, for he answered : " Just the same as yours are, sir." There was nothing much in this interview, and yet I have always remembered this young German, for he had a quality and sincerity which rang through him. After he had gone I spoke to my men and told them that if they had seen him shooting the wounded they should have killed him there and then. I am sure that they would have done so had there been any truth in their accusation.

In the middle of the battle one of my men charged a machine gun which was holding us up, and upon reaching it killed every man who was serving it. Having recommended him for a V.C. which he was awarded, and richly deserved, I asked him about his action. To my amazement I found that he remembered nothing whatsoever about it.

In spite of our improvised brigade we had quite a successful battle, and on coming out of the line we met the army commander, General Sir Hubert Gough, who congratulated us. I had a great admiration for him, and I fancy the Hun must have had, too, though well spiced with hate, for " Goughie " never gave them any peace. He was bounding with energy, and vitality oozed out of every pore, and though invariably he gave us hard battles I felt that he always gave us a good run for our money.

Preparations for Cambrai were in progress, and we were sent back to the Arras front at Monchy le Preux with orders to divert the enemy's attention from the Cambrai area and be offensive on our front. Unfortunately we seemed to be too offensive and earned ourselves heavy retaliation.

One morning I was going up to the line when the enemy suddenly put down a very heavy barrage, and I stopped and hesitated, wondering whether to go on or go back. In the end I went on, thinking I might not gather the courage later, and I got round the front-line trenches without being hit, although everything was being blown up in all directions. Returning, I was within a few yards of Battalion Head-quarters when I thought someone behind had hit me, and putting my hand to my hip I found that I was bleeding profusely. I was carried to the dressing station, sent on to hospital and operated on immediately. On coming round from the anæsthetic I felt so worried about the heavy barrage the Hun had put down that I asked someone to ring up the division and find out if my brigade had been attacked and had heavy losses. The answer came back, there had been no attack and that I had been the only casualty

The next morning I heard that my headquarters had been hit and several people killed, so perhaps my wound had been a lucky one. It did not seem lucky at the time, as part of my clothes had been blown into my hip by the shell, turning it very septic and keeping me in hospital for three endless months.

Holmes, as usual, was following closely in my wake, but we suffered a severe rebuff from the embarkation officer, who refused me permission to take him home with me. I bade him a sad farewell, but half-way across the Channel my cabin door opened and there was the inevitable Holmes ! I told him to disappear quickly and to turn up at 17 Park Lane. He did, of course, but I never inquired into his methods.

The three months in hospital dragged on their weary way, and at the end of the time I was again passed fit for general service, but found General Headquarters singularly reluctant to have me back in France. I appealed to General Gough to use his influence to get me back again, and I still have the letter that I received from him by return. It was dated March 19th, 1918, and was very reassuring, telling me that the chief was only trying to nursemaid me, and ending: "We are expecting an attack any day now, in fact to-morrow is supposed to be the day, after ten hours' bombardment. We shall see. Please God we shall slay an awful lot of Huns, and inflict a bloody defeat on them as well."

It was on March 21st that the flag fell and the Germans launched their big offensive. The weight of the attack fell on General Gough's front, where he had not the troops to resist it. His Army made a heroic effort, but everything, including the weather, was against them and they failed to hold their ground. Someone had to be sacrificed and the axe fell on General Gough and he lost his command. War may be a beast, but it is not always a just beast. . . .

G.H.Q. having agreed to my going back, I was posted to the Bantam Division, but my stay was disagreeably short, for I nearly lost my leg, and again retired to a bed in number 17. On Dover station I was lying on a stretcher feeling extremely bad-tempered and disgusted with my last brief stay in France, when a well-meaning clergyman came up to me. Seeing the disgruntled expression on my face and my one eye, he told me to cheer up, as it might have been much worse; he said he had had such a cheerful fellow through his hands a few months earlier, a man who had lost both an eye and an arm. I asked him the man's name, and he said, "General Carton de Wiart," and seemed quite hurt when I lost interest in the conversation.

It was October before I scraped back to France again, just in time to see the finish of the war. I was given command of a brigade in the 61st Division, a division I was to command in the next war.

The Armistice brought a momentary thrill of victory which soon faded. I think it is only the civilians who get any real joy out of the end of a war, and the release from the strain of eternal waiting.

After the Armistice I was given a brigade in the 38th Division, which was commanded by General Tom Cubitt, under whom I had started in 1914. I noticed that one of the officers attached to divisional staff took the greatest pains to avoid me, and showed visible nervousness if he was forced into speaking to me. Eventually I asked someone about this man's curious behaviour, and he replied : " Oh, don't you know? He's the officer who should have met you that night on the Menin Road, when you lost your hand ! " His fears about me were quite unfounded, as I had never thought of him again.

I was lucky enough to be given a few days' leave in Brussels, which I found bounding in *joie de vivre* at being free at last from the hated German domination.

Several of my relations had spent the whole war there, and Count Henri Carton de Wiart's wife had had a particularly difficult time. Count Henri having gone to Le Havre with the Belgian Government, his wife had remained on in Brussels with her six children. The Germans installed a hundred men in the house to keep the family under constant supervision. The Countess armed herself with an insolent politeness, never losing an opportunity of annoying the Germans. The German Governor came to call on her, and she ordered the footman to keep him on the doorstep, where she would interview him. She was followed whenever she left the house, and one day she took her eldest child and some concealed food and tramped the forest for twenty-five kilometres, and emerged late in the evening shadowed by an exhausted Hun who had had no picnic.

A German officer demanded to see her one day to give her the news that her cousin, Adrian Carton de Wiart, had been wounded at Ypres—I suppose to show the accuracy of their information.

In the end the Countess was arrested, accused of passing letters from Belgium to the soldiers at the front, and for clandestinely helping Belgian soldiers across the frontier to join the Belgian Army. At her trial she was asked if she had anything to say in her defence, but she said " No " and that she did not want any preferential treatment as the wife of a member of the Government. She was deported to Berlin, condemned to prison in the criminal section, and was not heard of and could not herself send news until after the liberation.

After my leave was up I went back to the 38th Division and found the officers and men suffering from a bad dose of anti-climax. For months, for years, we had fought and longed for the end of the war, and now that it had come we felt flat and out of a job; training seemed useless, the men discontented and only longing to get home.

Frankly, I had enjoyed the war; it had given me many bad moments, lots of good ones, plenty of excitement, and with everything found for us. Now I had ample time for retrospection; and, thinking of the troops, it seemed to me that the Guards stood out by themselves for discipline and turn-out, and I had found that the most successful commanders based their training on the Guards' system. The English county regiments topped the list for all-round work and steadiness; but for dash and daring the bloodthirsty Scots, Australians and Canadians led the way, with the impetuous Irish close behind.

The Australians, to my mind, were the most aggressive, and managed to keep their form in spite of their questionable discipline. Out of the line they were undoubtedly difficult to handle, but once in it they loved a fight; they had come to fight and the enemy were made to know it.

They were a curious mixture of toughness and sentimentality, for when I was in hospital some Australians arrived, with a corpse on a stretcher, having carried it about two miles. The medical officer was furious, thinking they had done it to get out of the line, but one of them explained that " X " had been a religious sort of chap, and they thought he would have liked a decent burial.

General Birdwood, who commanded the Australians, passed an Australian soldier who took no notice of him. An officer with the General stopped and asked the soldier if he was aware of the General's identity. The soldier replied that he was not aware of it, and implied that he didn't much care who he was, so the officer told him it was his G.O.C., General Birdwood. This elicited the reply, " Well, why the —— —— doesn't he wear a feather in his tail like any other bloody bird would ? "

I had known very little of the happenings on the other sectors of the front, and as for technical inventions I knew nothing and was never in the least interested.

Tanks had no doubt been the greatest invention of the war, but I had never been lucky with those allotted to me, for they had invariably produced a defect at the wrong moment and failed in their appointed task.

The German Air Force had been a sore point with our troops, and I was interested to find after the war, from German officers, that they had exactly the same feelings about our Air Force, and in fact about nearly all the things in which we thought we were the underdogs.

Far and away the most interesting and important lesson that I had learned was on man. War is a great leveller : it shows the man as he really is, not as he would like to be, nor as he would like you to think he is. It shows him stripped, with his greatness mixed with his pathetic fears and weaknesses, and although there were disappointments they were more than cancelled out by pleasant surprises of the little men who, suddenly, became larger than life.

I have a creed, borne out by war, which is—never to give a man a second chance. It may sound hard, but I have found that the man who lets you down once will, infallibly, do so again.

My worst memory of the war was the stench of putrefying bodies, for I could smell them still, and though death may be sublime on a battlefield, it certainly is not beautiful.

In the midst of wondering which way lay my future, a wire arrived, summoning me to the War Office. I had had a telegram before calling me back to a War Office Board, held to reorganize the Army, where I had made many suggestions, not one of which had been adopted. This time I did not count on anything, but thought a trip home a nice diversion from the monotony of France.

CHAPTER VII

HEAD OF THE BRITISH MILITARY MISSION TO POLAND

THE War Office succeeded in delivering one of its rare surprises, for, to my astonishment, they asked me if I would go to Poland as second in command to General Botha, who was to lead the British Military Mission. My geography being a little shaky, I had only a hazy idea as to the whereabouts of Poland, but I knew that it was somewhere near Russia and that the Bolsheviks were fighting there. I could not think of any adequate reason why I had been chosen for this inviting job, and I accepted it with alacrity before anyone had time to change his mind. Then I proceeded to find out all I could about the situation there.

Poland had just emerged independent from the Treaty of Versailles, having in the last hundred and fifty years suffered three partitions of her territory—at the hands of Russia, Prussia and Austria. In 1868 she had wallowed in the lowest degradation by being incorporated into Russia, with even her language forbidden her. This last privation had proved the bitterest of all blows to the Poles, for they had managed to retain a fierce national feeling even without one piece of land to sustain it. The Poles hated the Russians, with a hatred born of unwilling submission, for all the hardship and cruel treatment they had suffered at their hands.

I learnt that Poland was engaged in five wars : they were fighting the Germans, the Bolsheviks, the Ukrainians, the Lithuanians and the Czechs. So it looked as if we were going to be busy ! I chose Major King as my G.S.O.1 and Captain Maule as my G.S.O.2, and we were sent to Paris, there to join General Botha and be put in the picture.

South Africa has a faculty for producing great men, and General Botha was one of her most remarkable. I remembered seeing him when I was with Sir Henry Hildyard as A.D.C. and feeling instinctively that I was in the presence of greatness, and when I met him again in Paris it did not take me long to realize his qualities. Within a week Fate played one of her tricks, General Botha fell ill, and it was placed on my head to lead the British Military Mission into the maelstrom of Poland.

Our diplomatic side was headed by Sir Esme Howard, later Lord Howard, a most charming man to work for. First of all I had found Sir Esme looking at me rather warily: I heard afterwards that the duelling story had come to his ears, and made him think I might be a highly undesirable character to be let loose among the Slavs.

In Paris I learnt that Poland had been earmarked as the French sphere, and the French did not allow us to forget the fact for one single instant.

After spending a few weeks of luxury in the Majestic Hotel in Paris, we left in a special train for Warsaw via Switzerland, Vienna and Prague. Our short stay in Vienna was heartbreaking, for we found no vestige of its former gaiety, no food, no fuel, no transport, and everyone reduced to a state of utter misery. Only the foreign missions, in the usual manner of foreign missions, were revelling in luxury !

At Prague we stayed a few hours for the purpose of calling on President Masaryk. The President did not impress me at all, and I was bored with the conversation as it was entirely political. I did not understand the implications, and little did I realize how soon I was going to learn them. I was glad when we resumed our unheated, hungry journey to Warsaw.

We arrived in Warsaw on the night of February 12th, 1919, and were met by Paderewski, the Minister of Foreign Affairs. I shall never forget my first startled sight of Paderewski with his intense face in an enormous frame of hair and, perched precariously on top of it, a diminutive bowler hat !

Paderewski was an international figure of renown. He had found his way into people's hearts with his music, and remained there determinedly for his political ends. He was unquestionably a patriot, and had spent the whole of the war in America devoting his entire time and his private fortune to furthering the Polish cause, refusing to touch a piano whilst his country was in the toils of war. No sacrifice was too great for him to make for Poland, but to deny himself music must have been a form of crucifixion. At the Peace Conference he gained many points for Poland, by his personality and his eloquence, which could never have been gained by a lesser man. He had been brought to Danzig, only a few weeks earlier than our meeting, by a British cruiser and had been immediately appointed Minister of Foreign Affairs.

Paderewski had a charming and devoted wife to whom he was greatly attached. Madame Paderewski had a delightful vagueness, and when a very important telegram came one day for her husband, with a feminine disregard for the impersonal, she felt he should not be disturbed, put it in her bag and forgot all about it.

75

After the ceremonial speeches at the station, our mission drove through the town to the lodgings arranged for us. There were crowds lining the streets in most flattering numbers, and I shall never forget their enthusiasm. They must have expected great things from the inter-allied missions, but I am afraid they did not get much.

Sir Esme Howard and I were given a charming flat together, and were both made members of the Klub Mysliwiski, where we took all our meals. The Klub was a centre of the *élite* of Poland, of which all members of foreign missions were invited to become honorary members.

The day after our arrival we went to pay our respects to the Chief of State, General Pilsudski. Since those days it has been my destiny to meet many of the great men of the world, but Pilsudski ranks high among them—in fact, for political sense, almost at the top. His appearance was striking to a degree, and his air that of the conspirator. He had deep-set eyes of searching penetration, heavy brows and a drooping moustache which was peculiarly characteristic.

Pilsudski had had a remarkable career. As a young man his sympathies had leaned too much towards the left, and he had been deported to Siberia. Later he joined the newly-formed Polish Socialist Party, whose chief object was to free Poland from its oppressor, Russia. Again he was imprisoned, but his partisans, with a high degree of courage and ingenuity, engineered his escape. They disguised themselves as Russian officers, went to the prison armed with forged papers and walked out with Pilsudski. Early in 1914 he was pledged to fight with his Legion on the side of Germany, but the Germans were afraid of him, thought he wielded too much power, and in their turn imprisoned him. In 1918, as the symbol and soul of Polish opposition, Pilsudski was appointed Chief of State, and inspired his friends and followers with blind faith and supreme confidence.

I was lucky enough to make friends with Pilsudski straight away, which made my position very much easier, and I was one of the few foreigners to achieve such a relationship.

There was great opposition to him from the Polish aristocracy; they staged a *coup d'état* which he foiled, and it says much for his statesmanship that many of the aristocrats afterwards became his firmest supporters, realizing that he was the only man fit to lead Poland.

Unfortunately, Pilsudski had the *défauts de ses qualités*, for he was a very jealous man, brooked no opposition, and when anyone rose higher than it suited him he got rid of him. His ruthless dismissal of Paderewski, Sikorski and Korfanty were instances of his jealousy, and he lost these three great patriots, two of whom, Paderewski and Sikorski, stood high in the eyes of the world.

Meddling in politics taught me the bitter lesson that they invariably walk hand in hand with ingratitude, and when Padereswki was dismissed, although he had many friends and few enemies, his friends let him go without a murmur. Their memories were fickle as well as short.

Early in my relations with Pilsudski he said to me that I could believe implicitly anything that he told me. On the other hand, he said that if he told me nothing I must not be surprised at anything that might happen. He stuck to his word, and only failed once to tell me his intentions. He warned me of his designs on Kieff, telling me that he would take it with Ukrainian troops under Petlura. I went back to England to report, and on returning found that he had taken Kieff, but with Polish forces instead, as he had been unable to get the Ukrainians to attack in time.

Pilsudski was a very superstitious man, and having taken Kieff he admitted to feeling uneasy, for he told me that every commander who had attempted to take the Ukraine had come to grief. Later, when he had been forced to retire from Kieff, I asked why he had attempted to take it against his superstitions. His answer was that he felt that his luck stood so high that he thought he could risk it, but he added: " You see, I was wrong ! "

He hated the Russians with intensity, and though he had no particular liking for the Germans, he felt it wiser to be on good terms with them, and during his lifetime relations remained good to all appearances. He had a great admiration for England and for all the British institutions, but at times he was justifiably bitter about our attitude towards Poland. Invariably we opposed Poland in each and every crisis, and there were many. Even Paderewski was moved to say to me : " We cannot be wrong in every case."

77

Pilsudski had no liking for the French, and resented being in the French sphere and made to feel a dependant. There was constant friction between him and the French military and diplomatic representatives. The French were hardly tactful and did not like any assistance to be given to Poland except through French channels, regarding any gesture from another country as a sign of meddling. Their attitude added considerably to our difficulties.

Pilsudski was a Lithuanian by birth and obstinacy is one of their most marked traits. One day I was trying, quite ineffectively, to persuade him to some action, when he volunteered the remark : " I'm a Lithuanian and we are an obstinate people." My answer to that was, " So I see ! " and we both laughed, but I have often wondered since if there has ever been a great man who was not obstinate.

My staff had gathered another invaluable member, a naval officer, Lieutenant-Commander H. B. (now Admiral Sir Bernard) Rawlings, who had found his way to Poland in the cruiser that had brought Paderewski over. Rawlings had outrageous powers of persuasion and had convinced the captain of his cruiser of the desperate need for one Naval representative in Warsaw, and I was lucky enough to get him. He provided us with a lot of gaiety, could see the funny side of every situation, and squeezed himself out of all dilemmas.

When our state visits were over and with our relationships firmly established, we turned our attention to the little wars going on all round us. They all seemed very light and inconsequential after France, resembling the campign in South Africa.

My first task was to see if anything could be done to settle affairs peacefully between the Poles and the Ukrainians, and I set off for Lemberg, now called Lwow, with the French and Italian representatives. We had a most peaceful journey to the old fortress town of Przemysl. During the Great War, Przemysl had suffered many sieges, changing hands often between the Russian and Austro-German forces. I expected to see it devastated and was amazed to find not a single house destroyed.

We were told that we could proceed no further, as the battle was raging between Przemysl and Lwow. After hanging about Przemysl for several hours I insisted that we should be sent on to Lwow. We arrived at Lwow without having heard one shot fired or seen even the flicker of an enemy's hind quarters, to be received with fervent congratulations at having crossed the battlefield in safety! Nothing I could say made the slightest difference to the Polish estimate of the situation and we submitted gracefully to being heroes and surviving a thrilling and dangerous journey! My servant, Holmes, produced the best description of our feelings by remarking : " The Poles seem to make the 'ell of a fuss about this 'ere war of theirs ! "

The guard of honour was drawn up at the station, and while inspecting it I found, to my confusion, it was composed of women soldiers. I believe they had fought heroically in the defence of Lwow and suffered heavy casualties, but I found them an unnerving ordeal, like all women in uniform.

The reception over, we were given a sumptuous banquet. There was supposed to be no food in town and the people were hungry and miserable. However, in critical times in most countries officials find ways and means of getting fat at the expense of their less fortunate compatriots, but this banquet shocked us all considerably.

The Ukrainians were surrounding the town, but their military activity was of the feeblest, and we were only subjected to a little light shelling to show we were at war ; they did not stop communications and every train managed to get through.

The political situation was far more complicated, but I was finding out fast that in Poland there is always a political crisis on tap. I have a great love and admiration for the Poles, but I cannot deny that they thrive on crises and produce them with unfailing punctuality and without any provocation !

Lwow was seething with opposing elements, for there were many Ukrainians living there and a large population of Jews. The Jewish question seemed unanswerable and the repercussions were already being felt in Europe and the U.S.A. Progroms were rumoured to be taking place, but I considered the rumours to have been grossly exaggerated, for there were no ocular proofs of the massacre of thousands of Jews.

The Ukrainian forces outside Lwow were commanded by

79

General Pavlenko, and he sent word inviting us to a conference at his headquarters about twenty miles away.

We went by train escorted first by a Polish guard and handed over later to a Ukrainian guard. The French general with me felt a little uncertain as to the warmth of the welcome awaiting him, so to hide his red kepi he wrapped his head up in a muffler.

On arrival at headquarters we found Pavlenko, a Cossack, very simple and friendly ; also Petlura, who was Hetman and Chief of State, a very different type of man. He had been a journalist by profession, was very churlish and unforthcoming, and though he must have had a strong personality to have attained his position, it was certainly not apparent. We talked for some time at cross purposes, and I did not think we had made much headway, but finally he consented to send a mission to Lwow to discuss peace terms with us.

A few days later this so-called mission arrived in Lwow, but it was obvious they had come for the sole purpose of wasting our time. They made it impossible for us to come to any terms with them, and finally I flew into a rage and called them *un tas de cochons*, and they returned whence they came ! I had told them that I should return to Warsaw immediately, taking only my staff, and I should expect them to let me through peacefully. I left Lieutenant-Colonel King behind to help the Poles to the best of his ability, and he did excellent work.

We departed in a special train draped in Allied flags, and reached the first station unmolested. There some Polish officers begged us to give them a lift as far as Przemsyl, but, of course, I refused. Two of them did scramble on to the train somehow, and when on the next stage of our journey we were machine-gunned, the two Polish officers were killed, though no one else was touched.

A year later, when Petlura had been driven out of the Ukraine, he came to me in Warsaw to beg my help. He greeted me as a long-lost friend, and I had to remind him that at our previous contact he, or his people, had tried to shoot me up in a train. I helped him to get to Paris, where later he was assassinated.

On reaching Warsaw I found that the rest of the mission

had gone to Posen. Posen was the capital of the province of Posnania, recently returned to Poland under the Peace Treaty by Germany, who had occupied it for the last one hundred years. I went on to Posen to give in my report, and found myself subjected to conferences by day and dinners and dances by night, and I was thankful when I was told to take on my report to Paris. I was given a special train which made me feel very important, for it is a luxury in a category all its own.

I arrived in Paris in time to have dinner with Mr. Lloyd George and Sir Henry Wilson and I gave them my report verbally during dinner.

It was the first time that I had met Mr. Lloyd George, and I felt that he listened to my tale with rather a superficial interest, but he was very agreeable and told Sir Henry that I was to have everything that I had asked for.

Sir Henry Wilson was a delightful man, with all the Irishman's love of politics as well as his love of fighting, and he was about our only high-ranking soldier capable of competing in the same field as the politicians or " Frocks," as he always called them. He loved to describe himself as purely a simple soldier, but he could play all the political games as well as the best of them, and he served our country well in his dual *rôle*. He was a great personal friend of Marshal Foch, and England and France owed much to their close relationship.

At the dinner I emphasized my chief point, which was the necessity of sending an Allied general (naturally French) of high military reputation to act as chief of staff to Pilsudski.

The next day Sir Henry took me to see Marshal Foch, and Foch asked me if the Poles had asked for any particular general. Before leaving for Paris I had discussed the matter with Paderewski, and knew that they wanted General Gouraud who, as a very heroic figure, would have appealed to the fighting qualities of the Poles. The Marshal regretted that General Gouraud could not be spared, but told me to return later, when, having given the matter his close attention, he would have decided on the appointment. On my return Foch told me that he had appointed General Henrys, and he added that I could go back to Warsaw "*et faites son plus grand éloge*", for he had proved himself a most successful

81

commander. Coming from the Marshal, this was praise indeed.

General Henrys was a comparatively young man, of a smart military appearance, but he was a failure in Poland. His task was a difficult one, and made more difficult by Pilsudski's dislike of the French. The French Mission consisted of some fifteen hundred French officers, who were responsible for the training, equipment and general needs cf the Polish Army. They were under the direct orders cf Henrys and needed close supervision and very firm handling, which they did not get. Instead they indulged themselves in easy and pleasant living not at all conducive to successful military training, and found plenty of time and opportunity to meddle in trade on a big scale, but failed to further the Polish cause.

CHAPTER VIII

FIVE SIMULTANEOUS WARS

THE five wars continued on their way throughout 1919 without any great change, but early in 1920 there were signs of the Bolsheviks starting a new offensive, and in May or June a considerable force advanced from the south-east. This Bolshevik force was commanded by General Budieny and was largely composed of Cossacks. Cossacks are the most disappointing cavalry soldiers, for they have neither enough training nor enough discipline to make them efficient in modern warfare. What they lack in skill they try to make up in brutality and murder, and their treatment of prisoners was too horrible to describe.

During the Bolshevik advance I went down to Rowno to see how the campaign was progressing, and on arrival I asked if I could visit the front. I was given permission by the Polish general, who excused himself from accompanying me, saying that he had been up all night. Rawlings and my batman, James, were with me, and we had not gone very far when I saw some Cossacks moving on the road ahead of us. I returned quickly to report the news to the Polish general, but he remained quite unmoved and tried to be very reassuring. However, the Cossacks looked too near for my taste, and I informed the Polish general that I was leaving.

My railway coach was standing in the station, and I went to see if there was any possibility of a train leaving to which I could attach it. The stationmaster said there was a refugee train due, to which I could be attached if I liked. As I knew it could only be a matter of a few hours before the Cossacks arrived, I was anxious to leave as soon as possible, and would have hitched myself on to anything on wheels.

While we were waiting on the platform a few bombs were dropped on the station, the first I had seen in Poland, but, alas! not the last.

The train crept in and was of great length and infinite variety and drawn by two engines. We attached our coach, and were speeding at the breakneck rate of eight or nine miles an hour, when we discovered that we were affording the Cossacks excellent and continuous target practice. There seemed to be Cossacks everywhere, and presently I saw a couple of light field guns in a meadow a few hundred yards from the railway line. We were the target of their dreams, and the first shot hit one of our engines and slowed us down considerably. Then there was a lull, and it struck me that they had spotted our unusual coach and were about to give us their undivided attention. Rawlings had acquired the coach on a trip to Budapest, and it was a very smart type of *wagon-lit*, quite unknown to this part of the world. I was giving Rawlings my opinion of our situation when a shell hit us, luckily rather low, and the carriage dropped on its wheels.

The last few minutes had been pregnant with national behaviour. I had been sitting thinking that our trip to Rowno had been a mistake, Rawlings was obviously highly amused, the Hungarian coach attendant was trying to get under the carpet, and my batman, James, was quietly and methodically packing my things.

When our smart coach dropped on its wheels we bundled out and ran along the length of the train to find more attractive accommodation. We reached a bogey truck and Rawlings jumped on to it, and gave me his hand to help pull me up. The day was hot, the events still hotter, and, needless to say, my hand slipped and I fell along the railway line. I can only have been on the ground for a few seconds, but it was amazing the amount of thinking I got through, like the proverbial recollections of a drowning man. Before abandoning the coach I had looked at my revolver and found that there were only two rounds in it, and I wondered whether to waste one on a Cossack before using the other on myself. I was not going to risk being taken prisoner. Getting myself up, I found the Cossacks were showing no signs of closing in on us, and seemed to be amusing themselves by charging around at a safe distance. I ran along the still crawling train and rejoined Rawlings and saw to it that I did not slip again. Our coach was acting as such a strong brake to the train that it had to be detached; we left it for the Cossacks to play with and returned gratefully to Warsaw.

Before its inglorious end Rawlings had been very proud of his acquisition of the *wagon-lit*, which he had purloined when I sent him with an Australian called Picton, to try and get war materials for the Poles from Hungary. Picton had been Master of the Horse at the famous stables of Lancut, spoke several languages, and had helped my mission on many occasions. Rawlings and Picton reached Budapest, where they scrounged the war material and started back, and all went well until they got to Prague. The Czechs, being at war with the Poles, were not over-pleased at the idea of this war material going through their country; not unnaturally they held up Rawlings. Rawlings went straight to Masaryk's palace, woke him from his sleep, and extracted the permission to proceed. Any further difficulties *en route* he settled with judicious gifts of whisky and brought the whole cargo safely through.

By this time I had seen a great deal of the Polish Army on all their fronts, and I could not imagine how they would be able to resist a really determined advance by the Bolsheviks. There was very little cohesion in the Polish Army, for not only were the German, Russian and Austrian elements trained on different lines and armed with different weapons, but there was a great deal of jealousy and political friction between the commanders.

I had a hunch that Warsaw would soon be seriously threatened, but as there were no facts to support my convictions, I was chary of reporting them to the War Office.

To give force to my report, I asked the British Ambassador, Sir Horace Rumbold, if he would back it. He thought there might be grounds for my reasoning, but he would not support me officially and refused. General Bartholomew, the A.D.M.I., arrived in Warsaw, and as he had invariably helped me before, I told him my views, and he advised me to report to the War Office at once.

The Bolsheviks started their advance, which met with little resistance, and finally Western Europe grew gravely alarmed and sent an inter-Allied mission of the highest level to Poland to see what could be done to help the Poles.

The British were represented by Lord d'Abernon, General P. de B. Radcliffe and Sir Maurice Hankey. Sir Maurice was the secretary to the War Cabinet, wielded enormous power and held great sway with Mr. Lloyd George.

The French sent M. Jusserand, a former ambassador to Washington, and General Weygand, who was an outstanding military personality and Foch's chief of staff.

By the time the mission had arrived the Bolsheviks had reached Brest-Litovsk in their advance from the north-east, and were a mere hundred and thirty miles from Warsaw.

A meeting was held at once, and General Weygand produced a map marking the various places where, he estimated, the Poles could check the enemy's advance. Then Weygand turned to me to ask me for my opinion. It was a case of fools rushing in where angels fear to tread, for, contrary to the general opinion, I insisted that nothing would stop the Polish retreat until they reached Warsaw, where in a strong national effort they might whip up their enthusiasm into defending their capital. I felt that we had got beyond the stage when maps were of any use, and that the issue had become entirely psychological.

I was seeing Pilsudski daily, and once when I asked him what he thought of the situation, he shrugged his shoulders and said that it was in the hands of the Almighty. It was the only time that I ever saw him shaken out of his almost oriental calmness, but he was not so shaken that he could not plan a masterly counter-attack, which brought him victory in three weeks.

The Bolshevik advance from the north-east continued steadily, until they were only fourteen miles from Warsaw, when the Poles counter-attacked. The Bolsheviks were exhausted, and as soon as they saw the Poles stand and prepare to fight they retreated and continued to retreat until they sued for peace.

The battle near Warsaw has been called " The Miracle of the Vistula," and never was a miracle more timely, for the issues at stake were tremendous. Had Warsaw fallen, there can be no doubt that Poland, a great part of Germany and Czechoslovakia would have become Communist.

Life for me had been full of interest and exceedingly pleasant as well. Every morning I went off to the front, spent the day there and came back to bath and then dine at the Klub, and felt exactly like a black-coated worker playing at war !

Rawlings claimed to have started the Bolshevik retreat and turned the tide of war, for he had gone to the front and so inspired a Polish general with a bottle of whisky that he had ordered his troops to attack at once !

Meanwhile the civil population of Warsaw, which included the Diplomatic Corps, had become very nervous at the rapid advance of the enemy, and Cardinal Ratti, who later became Pope, came to ask me daily if it were time for the Diplomatic Corps to clear out. When the battle had gone in favour of the Poles I rushed back to Warsaw to tell the Diplomatic Corps they could relax, and think no more of retreat, only to find that they had already departed for Posen. The British Embassy had left behind Sir Percy Loraine and no one could have proved more helpful, for he was a fine diplomat and later became one of our most able ambassadors.

One of the inner difficulties in organizing resistance to the Bolshevik advance was caused by the intrigues of the Polish Army in Posnania. They were German trained, looked down on the Austrian and Russian-trained troops, and would have welcomed the fall of Warsaw so that they, later on and alone, might have had the honour of defeating the Bolsheviks. There were two Posnanian divisions fighting, and there is no doubt that they were far better trained and superior altogether to the Russian and Austrian-trained divisions.

During this period the British Minister, Sir Horace Rumbold, asked me if I would take him to the front. I agreed, and drove him myself in my car, followed by another car belonging to the Naval Mission armed with a machine gun. We went in the direction of the north-west towards Mlawa. On getting near the front we met a very scared-looking Polish soldier who told us he had just escaped from the Bolsheviks, and he pointed to a village that we could see about a mile away.

I turned to the Naval Mission and said that we would go on but that they must follow close behind and be ready to shoot when I gave them the signal.

We arrived at the village and found the population looking terrified, and it was clear that the Bolsheviks could not be far away. We went through, and on the other side of the village I saw a Cossack right on top of a telegraph pole busy cutting the wires. At the foot of the pole he had an admiring audience of half a dozen mounted Cossacks busy holding his horse. They were a lovely target, and I signalled the Naval car to come up and shoot. Either the Naval Mission were too slow or the Cossacks too fast, but all the Cossacks galloped away unhurt, and getting cover behind a ridge about six hundred yards off, turned their fire on us. Sir Horace was enjoying every moment of his outing, it being the first time he had been under fire, and I believe he even enjoyed the last few minutes when I had to turn my large car round in a very narrow road. Personally I was relieved to return him intact. The Naval Mission were under Captain Wharton, R.N., and were always prepared to be helpful and useful to us. One of the Mission, Lieutenant Buchanan, became a great friend.

General P. de B. Radcliffe also came as a passenger in my car to the front. On returning, after an uneventful trip, we passed a Polish sentry who took no notice of us until we had passed him, when he fired at us. I was furious, stopped my car, got out and walked up to him, and having taken the precaution to remove his rifle, I boxed his ears and threw him into a ditch full of water. The most amusing part of this incident was General Radcliffe's expression. He was not expecting these antics in such a crucial moment of the war.

Another day I had gone up to the front and left Holmes, my servant, to look after the car. While I was away a Polish soldier had come up to Holmes and told him that he remembered me at Arras, adding: "Your general had his head bandaged." Apparently he had been in the German Army then, and we had taken him a prisoner.

About this time I went up to Riga, the capital of Latvia, where we had a mission under General Alfred Burt, the kind man who had looked after me when I lost my hand. General Burt was having a most difficult time, for the Letts were fighting both the Germans and the Bolsheviks. Among the officers serving under him was Colonel Alexander, now Field-Marshal Lord Alexander, and as he also served in Poland I can claim with justifiable pride that I had him under my orders. The Letts were very tough fighters and kept their end up with great courage, considerably helped by General Burt.

I had been flown up to Riga by a French pilot and owing to bad weather we were flying very low. Looking out from the side of the plane I saw a German gazing upwards; he put up his rifle and took a shot at us. I imagined that I felt something, but as the pilot did not appear to be very interested I thought no more about it. On getting out of the plane at Riga, I looked around and discovered a fresh bullet-hole six inches from my seat. A good shot and a lucky miss for me.

My old commander, General Sir Hubert Gough, was in Riga, and he told me that he was planning a large-scale attack on the Bolsheviks and wanted the Poles to take part, but it never came off.

Returning in the same plane, we had engine trouble and made a forced landing, being lucky enough to find a gap in the forest. We took off again, but the trouble was not cured and we made another forced landing. I went off to see if I could find some help, and found a Lithuanian post some distance away. On my telling them what I wanted, they made the senseless suggestion that either the Russians or Germans might help us, as they were quite near. Thanking them, I said that I preferred my chances with them, and eventually I was put into a country cart and bumped back under escort to a railway station thirty-five miles away, and sent on to the Lithuanian capital of Kovno. After a good deal of palaver I was allowed to return home, and the plane was recovered a week later.

Flying does not seem to be my luckiest mode of transport, for, when flying to Kieff when the Poles were occupying it, I had another forced landing and my plane turned turtle. The pilot managed to extricate himself, but I was tied in and jammed in by some cases of provisions we were taking to Kieff, and he could not get me out for some time. There were some workmen within a few hundred yards of our crash, but they took not the slightest notice of us, and never attempted to help. It was lucky for us that the plane had run out of petrol ; it saved us from the danger of fire.

The war against the Czechs proceeded equably, and more or less on a domestic basis. The Poles have a natural aversion to the Czechs, partly because they are neighbours and therefore prone to quarrelling, and partly because the Poles look down on the Czechs for being, like the British, " a nation of shopkeepers." To the agrarian Pole, commerce is a despised occupation to be left to the Jew, and they had great contempt for the Czechs who thought otherwise. Their chief bone of contention were the coal mines at Teschen, but there was never any serious fighting between the two nations, and we could cross the Czech line more or less at will.

CHAPTER IX

POLISH POLITICS

POLITICAL feeling ran high upon the question of Eastern Galicia, for both the Poles and the Ukrainians aspired to it. Britain with her usual anti-Polish policy was definitely opposed to giving it to the Poles. I went to Paris to see Mr. Lloyd George on the matter, and to try and persuade him either to give Eastern Galicia outright to the Poles, or at any rate to use his influence to that end. He refused point-blank, and he never spoke to me again.

Poles are very childish over their disappointment, and stupidly allow their public happenings to overflow into their private and social lives. Soon after my rebuff from Lloyd George when relationships were tricky, Sir Horace Rumbold gave a ball at the Legation and the whole of Polish society flocked to it. The band started playing, and to everyone's amazement not one Pole got up to dance. Lady Rumbold naturally was very upset, and came to ask me what was the matter. I went up to one of the leading Poles to demand an explanation, and his answer was, how could the Poles dance when we were taking Eastern Galicia away from them ?

This gentleman was the President of the Anglo-Polish Friendly Society, and I suggested to him that it was about time that he resigned his job, and added that if he and his friends were unable to dance at the ball, it would have been better to stay away. During this little chat other Poles surged up, voices were raised, feeling ran high and everyone started to take sides.

Finally a pro-British Pole challenged an anti-British Pole to a duel ! The pro-British Pole turned to ask me to second him, and I agreed with great pleasure, and then he turned to General Mannerheim—who was staying with him—to ask him to be the other second. The General consented, but said he was far from delighted.

General Mannerheim, although born a Finn, had been a great figure at the Russian court in Tsarist days. He had commanded a Russian cavalry division in the Great War, but after the Bolshevik revolution he returned to the land of his birth, Finland, and became its first President. He was a good-looking, romantic figure, straight as a die and a great favourite.

The morning after the ball General Mannerheim and I went along to arrange matters for the duel with our principal's opponent, only to find that the bird had flown hurriedly to Vienna.

I was expecting to be called out myself after my free speech the evening before, and when Captain Maule, one of my staff officers, told me there was a queue of seconds lined up outside the house, I believed him, but he was only pulling my leg, and no one came to challenge me. Having insulted most of the members of the Klub Mysliwiski, I decided not to take my meals there any more. A Pole asked me why I had not been seen there lately, and when I had explained the reason he said that he would try and get the matter settled. His idea of a settlement did not appeal to me, for he suggested that I should apologize, which I flatly refused to do. His next suggestion was that seconds should be appointed to arrange a peaceful settlement. I agreed to the seconds, but not to the peaceful settlement, and insisted that the seconds should arrange the time and place for us to fight. They thought me most unreasonable, told my opponent that I was a dangerous lunatic, the affair was patched up, and again I was done out of my duel.

The next time that I was embroiled in bloodless battle was soon after the murder of Monsieur Narutowicz, the Polish Prime Minister. A diplomat holding a very important post in Warsaw was discussing the murder with a member of the Klub, and made the pointed and tactless remark that he considered the members of the Klub responsible for the murder. This news spread like a flame to the rest of the members, one of whom telephoned to the diplomat demanding instant satisfaction. The diplomat took to his bed at once, rang me up, and told me to come round and help him out. I told him there was no way out of the mess except by fighting or apologizing, and I was not very surprised when he discreetly chose apology as the better part.

I was asked, through our legation, to go and report on the Polish-Lithuanian position for the League of Nations, and the Polish Government were also keen for me to go. Heavy fighting was rumoured to be taking place ; it was mid-winter and icy cold, and I suggested that my journey should be made as comfortable as possible. We were to proceed to Vilna, where we were to be given a special train.

Unless one had lived in Poland or Lithuania, it was impossible to realize the depth of feeling that lay between those two countries over the town of Vilna on national and religious grounds. To the Poles it was a holy city, and they were ready to sell their lives to defend it. They had been forced to hand it over to the Lithuanians owing to the Bolshevik advance, but after the Bolsheviks were driven back the Poles demanded that Vilna should be returned to them. The Lithuanians, with their usual obstinacy, refused, said that Vilna would only be taken over their dead bodies. The Poles attacked, the Lithuanians forgot to shed their blood, for they suffered one solitary casualty, and he was run over by a lorry.

We set off from Vilna, now in Polish hands. I was accompanied by one of my own staff officers and a Polish staff officer who was unfortunately the head of the Polish counter-espionage bureau. I felt that he might prove an embarrassment as he was extremely well known to the Lithuanians.

Before long our train came to a full stop at a blown-up bridge, and we could go no farther. The Polish officer managed to find some sledges and we set off for the nearest Polish headquarters.

The officer in charge of headquarters assured us that there had been no fighting in his area, but he believed that we would get evidence of heavy fighting if we went a few miles farther on. We drove on a short way and saw a small house on a hill with a sentry outside. We approached the sentry, and noticed that he appeared to be in some difficulty with his rifle. I imagined he was attempting to present arms, but the foresight of his rifle got caught up in his woolly muffler, and I told the Polish officer to tell him to be more careful. Just as the Pole was about to translate my remark he turned round to me and said : " By God, sir, he's a Lithuanian ! " At that moment out from the house rushed some soldiers, shooting at us wildly at a range of fifteen yards, though I never even heard the bullets. They were in a feverish state of excitement, bobbing about and yelling, and I realized the only thing to do was to sit still and say and do nothing ! I had the greatest difficulty in persuading my companions to inactivity, but when we had succeeded in looking unconcerned I told the soldiers to fetch an officer.

When the officer arrived I had to admit rather shame-facedly that I had come to investigate the situation on behalf of the League of Nations. I may as well state at this juncture that I had never had any respect or confidence in that institution, and by a strange coincidence the Lithuanian officer seemed to share my views ! I told him I was quite satisfied with all that I had seen, and now I should like to go back. He was most polite, but said he must first report to his senior officer and invited us to come into the house. With a temperature of 20° below zero we agreed with alacrity.

We were in a very unpleasant situation, and made much more unpleasant by having this suspect Polish officer with me. He had very compromising papers on him, which luckily he managed to pass to me unnoticed, and I was never searched nor was I asked for any paper authorizing my presence.

All the next senior officers refused to release me, and at last a message came from Lithuanian Headquarters to say that I was to be taken to Kovno by force if necessary. By now they had discovered the identity of the Pole and were taking very little interest in me, allowing me to go outside unescorted, but they watched the Pole like a hawk. The first Lithuanian officer was still most courteous and told me how lucky I was to have been taken by his regiment, for if we had been captured by neighbouring units in all probability I should have been murdered for my clothes. It turned out that I knew several of his relatives in Poland, and he must have thrown in his lot with the Lithuanians because he had property in the country.

When it was time for me to proceed to Kovno I insisted on taking my officers with me and after a good deal of argument this was agreed to. I told the Lithuanian officer that he must inform the British Minister that I was a prisoner in their hands, and to mention I had a Polish officer with me.

We were sent by car to Kovno, under the closest guard, and could not wash our hands without an escort armed to the teeth. On arrival, the Minister of Foreign Affairs came to interrogate me, and tried to find out the whys and wherefores of my crossing the frontier into Lithuania. I assured him that I had only arrived by accident, and I hoped sincerely that I should never set foot in his country again. I answered no questions, but asked if the British Minister had been informed of my capture. Of course he had not been.

Some hours later I was freed, and an official came and told me that the Lithuanian Prime Minister wished to come and apologize for what had happened I replied that I had no desire to see him, and that my arrest was a matter which concerned my Government. I was taken to the British Legation and returned to Poland via Königsberg and Danzig, but forbidden to go through Vilna. The Polish officer was released a few days later.

When I got back I heard that after I had been missing from my railway coach for a couple of days I had been presumed killed, and I was shown a most touching and flattering obituary notice written *in memoriam* and published by the Wolff Agency in Berlin. My servant, James, confident I should return, was still waiting for me in the railway coach by the demolished bridge, and would not allow anyone near it.

I left Major Mockett of the 4th Hussars as my representative at Vilna and he probed every bit of information possible and kept me absolutely *au courant* of the situation.

Shortly after my return Pilsudski sent for me and after chaffing me over my capture, he thanked me sincerely for the great service I had rendered Poland. I asked him what he meant. He answered that now perhaps the British would know what sort of people the Lithuanians were. Until then our sympathies had been very pro-Lithuanian, but after this episode our attitude changed, so in a small way I may have helped Poland.

I made a great friend of the U.S. Ambassador to Poland, Mr. Hugh Gibson. He was a pleasant mixture of diplomatic guile and good common sense, and as he always talked most openly to me it helped me considerably to hear his views. There were many other shrewd diplomats in Warsaw, but though at times they were anxious to know what I thought, they showed no great anxiety to share their views—which in the main were unpractical—with me.

General Sir Richard Haking, who commanded our troops in Danzig, was another helpful person with sound judgment and great moral courage.

General Briggs, who had been my commanding officer in the Imperial Light Horse, came to see me in Warsaw. He was chief of the British Military Mission to Denikin who commanded the White Russian troops. Denikin had started a big offensive against the Bolsheviks, and he was advancing so fast that it looked as if he would reach Moscow. Briggs had been sent to ask me to persuade Pilsudski to join in the offensive. I took Briggs to see Pilsudski and explain the situation, and to ask him personally for his co-operation. During the interview I could see that Pilsudski was not in the least impressed by what Briggs was telling him, and when Briggs had left Pilsudski said that Denikin would fail to get to Moscow, and, worse still, that he would soon be back in the Black Sea. In view of Denikin's rapid advance this seemed a fantastic statement to make, but Pilsudski's judgment rarely failed, and I had such confidence in him that I reported this at once to the War Office.

I returned home to report, and Mr. Winston Churchill, who was then at the War Office, asked me to lunch. Mrs. Winston Churchill and Jack Scott, his secretary, were the only other people at the lunch. It was the first time that I had met Mr. Churchill. I was immensely flattered by the idea of discussing with so great a man what was at that moment an important situation. Mr. Churchill wished me to get the Poles to join in Denikin's offensive, but I repeated Pilsudski's warning, and I remember Mrs. Winston Churchill saying : " You had much better listen to General de Wiart." I hastened to point out that it was not my opinion that I was giving, but Pilsudski's, and that he had never put me wrong.

Within a very few weeks Pilsudski had proved a good prophet, for Denikin was back in the Black Sea.

Pilsudski had only once kept silent with me. He had been planning to retake Vilna from the Lithuanians, and knowing that I should have to inform my Government, who would have done everything in their power to stop him from succeeding, he could not tell me of his plan.

I cannot remember our Government agreeing with the Poles over any question, and there were many : Danzig, that first nail in Poland's coffin ; Vilna ; Eastern Galicia ; Teschen ; the demarcation of the Russian-Polish frontier ; and Upper Silesia.

The Russian-Polish frontier had been drawn by the Curzon Line, which meant roughly that the Poles would not go east of Brest-Litovsk. Pilsudski insisted on the absolute necessity of a natural obstacle as boundary line, and wished to extend to the Prypet Marshes.

Upper Silesia had caused so much friction that an inter-national mission had to be called in to settle the conflict. Finally a plebiscite was held, and the Poles got all they wanted. Our own mission in Upper Silesia was so pro-German that I kept away from them, knowing that we could never agree. I kept myself very well informed on the situation there, and for the accuracy of his reports my thanks are due to Captain H. L. Farquhar, who had come out to Upper Silesia as cor-respondent of the *Morning Post* whilst waiting for an exami-nation for the Diplomatic Service. Harold Farquhar had an extraordinary gift for portraying vivid verbal pictures, and after he had reported to me I felt that I knew as much as if I had been there myself. Now he is our Ambassador to Sweden.

By 1924 the five wars that Poland had been engaged in had all ended, leaving the Poles with everything they had set out to get. There was nothing more to keep a military mission occupied, and the work was taken over by Colonel Clayton, the Military Attaché, who had been with me and had made a great success in his post.

It was amusing to think that when I was sent to Poland I could not imagine why I had been chosen. When firmly in the saddle, I asked a friend of mine if he knew the reason. His reply was enlightening. " We thought you were the sort of man who would know that country." How lucky for me they did not ask me if I did !

When I went I must admit I had the greatest doubts as to my fitness for the post, for I knew nothing of Poland, its geography, its history, or its politics. Afterwards I found my ignorance to be my greatest asset, for I was free from prejudice, tackled situations as they turned up, and knowing no history I could not assume it would repeat itself. It may do so, but not invariably, and it is safer not to count on such an assumption.

Many thought Danzig must lead to future war, but if it had not been Danzig, Hitler would have found another reason, possibly Upper Silesia.

Our military mission had had a most interesting and happy time. We had assisted at the birth of the new Poland, and had seen a nation emerge alive, strong and kicking. The joy of the Poles was infectious, and we share their feelings. The rest of my staff were spared assisting at the death of Poland as I did in 1939.

CHAPTER X

I AM GIVEN THE EARTH

WHEN the Military Mission had finished I had a difference of opinion with the War Office, and resigned my commission. It seemed a momentous decision to make in those days, though of very little importance now, but naturally I was very sorry to go, and felt lost and disorientated. As events were to turn out, I was lucky; had I stayed on I should have been too senior to serve in this last war except in a higher rank than I considered myself fitted for, having never been to staff college and knowing my limitations only too well.

One of my staff told me that I had always said soldiering was a boring business between wars, but I cannot claim boredom as my reason for resigning. However, I have found life to be very well balanced, and what she takes away from you with one hand she often gives you back with the other. The Army was lost to me, but in its place I found what was for me the perfect life, with everything that I had ever desired since I was a small boy.

My last Polish A.D.C. had been Prince Charles Radziwill, and whilst he was with me he had inherited a property from an uncle, who had been killed by the Bolsheviks.

Prince Charles told me that the property was some 500,000 acres situated in the Prypet Marshes on the borders of Russia, and he kindly asked me to go down and inspect it with him. We went by train to Luniniec, where we were met by country carts which bumped us the thirty miles to his new property of Mankiewicze. The land was just beginning to recover from the years of incessant conflict, and although we found the house of Mankiewicze standing, it was only a shell. Although not destroyed by gunfire, it had been left in a dilapidated condition by occupying troops, neglect and the general toll of war.

The country had a wild, flat beauty all its own, with limitless forests, lakes and rivers stretching into the distance. It was the home of every variety of wildfowl, and obviously a sportsman's idea of paradise, and I fell in love with it at once. Casually I remarked to Prince Charles that if there was ever any place suitable I would love to take it.

A few months later he sent me word that he had found something which might suit me, and I wasted no time in going to look at it.

This time it was no country cart that met me, but a carriage drawn by four or five Lippizana greys. The Lippizanas had been bred only by the Emperor of Austria before the 1914–18 War, and they were of part-Arab blood. Occasionally, as an imperial gesture, the Emperor had given one to a most favoured relative; Prince Charles's brother-in-law had been one of the lucky ones and had received some. It was interesting to me to see how little fuss the coachman made about driving a four- or five-in-hand. Horses were put straight into harness, and off they went, and though possibly not conforming to our more orthodox ideas it was most effective.

Mankiewicze was in the process of being transformed into a lovely house of perfect comfort, and meanwhile we stayed in the agent's charming little wooden house in the park.

When Prince Charles told me that my proposed eastate was forty miles away and could be approached only by water, I was already fascinated by the sound of it. It took us nearly a whole day to get there, with four men paddling the boat, and we arrived to find another little wooden house sitting quite alone on a small island, surrounded by water and forest.

My mind was made up at once, I knew it was exactly what I wanted, and I asked Prince Charles what rent he was asking. He seemed very hurt by my question, and said that if I liked the place it was mine . . . for nothing. He refused to listen to any argument, and there and then I became the tenant of Prostyn, and knew that destiny was playing on my side. To ease my mind under my burden of gratitude, I made as many improvements as I could think of, and built on another house for the servants.

The Polish landlords still lived in feudal splendour, in a luxury unsuspected by western Europeans, and quite unaffected by the growling of their eastern neighbours. There were no staff difficulties; servants came with the hope of serving their lifetime in the great houses, and were not concerned with their evenings off and labour-saving gadgets. Instead of Frigidaires, great blocks of ice were cut from the frozen rivers in winter and placed in the ice-house, which would then be flooded and the door left open. The whole mass would freeze into one block of solid ice which lasted a whole year.

Polish culture is French by adoption, and in all the great houses one found French furniture, French pictures and tapestries, but with all their beautiful ornateness mixed with a delightful feeling of comfort, so rarely found in France.

The Poles understand warmth, and guests are never found huddling round the one inadequate fire, which makes a visit to an English country house like a trip to Sparta. They are great gourmets, the food excellent, and the chef a most honoured and important member of the household. Mankiewicze had a particularly charming custom ; every evening, after dinner, the chef used to appear in full regalia to receive compliments on his cooking, and each guest had a say in ordering the meals for the next day.

The Poles are among the most hospitable people in the world, and the big houses are nearly always afflicted with a species of permanent guest, or less politely known as a hanger-on. He may be a relation, a friend, or merely an acquaintance, and he comes to stay for a night or week-end and proceeds to settle himself down for the rest of his life. Once when I was staying with some friends they received a wire from an acquaintance asking for a bed, and with their usual open-armed hospitality they wired back " Delighted." The guest arrived, stayed seven or eight years. After the second year he came to his host, very worried as he had the feeling that people thought he was sponging. His solution was very simple : it was that if his host would give him a salary the world would then assume he was earning his keep. His host gave it to him. Most other permanent guests were less ambitious, and seemed politely satisfied with mere board and lodging. Luckily the houses were generally built on a palatial scale, and it was possible to lose people, so the institution of the permanent guest was not as painful as it might have been in a smaller setting.

After a whole day out in the air, shooting or riding, I always looked forward to a very pleasant pre-dinner interlude. All the guests gathered in the great halls where bright fires were burning, to be served with a kind of exaggerated *hors d'œuvre*, known as *zakuszka*. They consisted of an infinite variety of exotic dishes washed down by smooth gulps of vodka with a feel of satin fire. Vodka burns delightfully when it arrives at its destination, and makes conversation very easy. Perhaps that explains why the Poles are such brilliant talkers.

Poles are very vivacious and gay, especially the women, but they all seemed possessed by a racial sadness that knows little of joy or even of contentment. Though they have humour, they are apt to take themselves too seriously, and are naturally indignant when the rest of the world does not follow suit. Their strength is their courage, their faith, their loyalty and their patriotism, and from the highest to the lowest, with or without education, they can sacrifice themselves to an idea—and that idea was always Poland, even when it existed only in their imagination.

Poles are inclined to be psychic, but I am much too superstitious to allow anyone to practise his art on me. Occasionally I was a witness of curious things. I was staying with friends and my hostess kept noticing that money was missing from her writing-table drawer. A famous medium, who was a great friend of theirs, was staying in the neighbourhood, and they asked him for his help. He arrived, sat at the desk from which the money had been taken and described in minute detail the man who had taken it. No one could make out the description, as it fitted nobody in the house. The next day was Sunday; the household, guests and the medium went to mass in the chapel, but still the medium could not spot the culprit, and he left directly afterwards with the mystery still unsolved. A week or two later, during lunch, the hostess sent her twelve-year-old daughter to fetch a handkerchief from her room. A few minutes later the child ran back brimming over with excitement, for she had found the carpenter of the estate in her mother's room. He fitted the description exactly and was proved the thief. I believe that this particular medium was so famous that he had even been called in by the Berlin and Paris police to help them unravel some mysteries.

Of all the lovely country houses, Lancut was outstanding. It had survived the war by a miracle, and was of a splendour that will never be seen again. It was the home of Count Alfred Potocki. His mother, Countess Betka, acted as hostess. Countess Betka was a unique hostess and a remarkable character of world-wide renown: she made Lancut one of the most sought-after centres of society in Europe. It combined everything, from excellent shooting to first-class English hunters, lovely gardens and famous hothouses. At tennis parties the footmen acted as ball-boys, and were rumoured to produce the balls on silver salvers. There were about six different dining-rooms, and each evening a different one was chosen for dinner, our host leading the way, with the passages flanked by footmen. In spite of her years Countess Betka seemed the youngest of us all, and every morning when we went out riding, galloping over the country and jumping all the fences, she was invariably the leader.

Many of the other country houses were equally comfortable, but they had not the same grandeur as Lancut.

Amusing stories had been reaching me about a man named Niemojeski, and I was very keen to see him. He was a country squire and sounded like a cross between d'Artagnan and Robin Hood. I was staying with one of his neighbours and we were out walking when I saw a very nice horse galloping towards us, and heard a voice saying : " Here comes Niemojeski." I looked up and saw a stumpy little man in pince-nez, dressed in a fur coat and a bowler hat with a revolver strapped to his belt. Except for the horse, it was a strange and rather disappointing apparition. He came and stayed the night, and then asked us back to stay with him. He led us over at a gallop, which apparently was the only pace he knew, and I was surprised to find a charming property, most comfortable house and a great many servants, all reputed to be of his own breeding. He was very conservative. Apart from this, his energies were directed entirely to running his property and breeding beautiful horses and greyhounds for which he often paid vast sums. His method of calling a servant was original, if a trifle disconcerting. There was a big log set in the middle of the room into which he fired his revolver whenever he wished to summon a slave. Luckily he was a good shot, but he was not a rest-cure.

Niemojeski was an excellent host, and filled us with good food and a great deal to drink, and regaled us with bawdy stories until it was time for bed. Shortly after I had reached my room my Polish A.D.C. knocked at the door, and shuffled in looking rather sheepish and embarrassed. Niemojeski had sent him to inquire if I would like a sleeping companion. No further proof of Polish hospitality can be required. In the 1914–18 War when the Germans had come to requisition his beloved horses, he had their names put over their stalls, and four of them read : " VA..T'EN..SAL..PRUSSIEN," but the Germans never saw the point. Poor Niemojeski, he is dead now, but when he had a life to enjoy he made the most of it, and will not be left regretting the things he had not done.

This, then, was the world I was choosing to live in, and I realized my luck in having such an opportunity.

Just before my resignation from the Army, I toured Poland with Lord Cavan the C.I.G.S. who wished to be shown the country, and after the tour I motored back to England and had a most unpleasant journey. The feeling against the Allies was very strong, and the Germans had quite recovered from their cringing attitude of 1919, when they were defeated, starved and pitiful, and the whole population seemed to consist of old men, miserable women and sick children. Now they were truculent, and when my car got a puncture going through a town in the Ruhr, it was immediately surrounded by a surging crowd, and the situation began to look ugly. An allied officer dropping into their midst was an easy means of reprisal for pent-up resentment, and it was only when they were discovered that I was British and not French that their attitude softened and I was allowed to go on undamaged.

In 1920 or 1921 I had been motoring through Berlin when I found the whole of the allied missions had changed into plain clothes, and I was taken to task by a senior officer for being in uniform. The Germans had announced that they would strip any allied officer that they saw in uniform. I told the senior officer that if I was stripped, I presumed my Government would take action. I never went to Germany except in uniform, and I never had any trouble. I was polite to them, and they were to me.

A few months in London made me long for my Polish marshland and little wooden house, but I had first to go to Egypt, where my stepmother, still in Cairo, had had a stroke and was now a complete invalid. I hoped to settle her affairs satisfactorily and send her back to England.

I arrived in Cairo on a day pregnant with happening. The Sirdar, Sir Lee Stack, was murdered by some Egyptians. It was one of these tragedies which occur when political feelings rise to fever-point, and the Egyptians themselves were the greatest losers by this crime. Sir Lee Stack had been their firmest and staunchest friend, and had often been accused by his own country of being too pro-Egyptian.

This murder aroused the British as nothing else had ever done, and created terror in the hearts and faces of the Egyptians, who had been getting more and more insolent for years. Now they were petrified, and their *volte-face* the only sudden thing about them.

Lord Allenby, who was our High Commissioner, drove down with an escort of the 16th Lancers, to deliver an ultimatum to the Egyptian Government, and I shall never forget the majesty and dignity of his drive. The streets were lined with stricken Egyptians, half dead with fear, and though they took a long time to recover, it was not long enough.

Just at this time a mutiny broke out in Khartoum, and it sounded as if there were going to be some fighting. An old friend of the Polish campaigns was commanding the British forces in Egypt, General Sir Richard Haking, and I went down to ask him whether he would employ me if fighting broke out. His greeting to me was, " My God ! You are a stormy petrel ! " I explained that I had only turned up by accident, and he was very nice and said he would use me if fighting broke out. The fact that it never did break out was due almost entirely to Colonel (now Lieutenant-General) Sir H. J. Huddleston's quick grasp of the situation ; his strong and courageous attitude suppressed the mutiny.

After the murder of Sir Lee Stack nearly all the tourists had cancelled their passages, the hotels were empty and the post-card vendors out of a job. This time I was staying at Mena House, a delightful hotel at the foot of the Pyramids. I often rode in the desert with Lord Allenby, and found my admiration for him growing with the days. I learned many interesting things about the Great War which I should never have known otherwise, and saw with a larger perspective.

Colonel Charlie Grant, who in the last war was G.O.C. Scottish Command, was chief of staff to General Haking, and always a most convivial companion.

The War Office, as a flattering inducement to me to remain in the Army, had offered me the command of the Sialkot Cavalry Brigade. The offer was only made to me verbally, and I refused it. Three weeks after this entirely conversational suggestion, with nothing put down in writing, I got a letter from my old bearer in India, whom I had not seen or heard of for over twenty years, saying that he had heard

I was coming to Sialkot, and asking me if I would take him on again. If only our postal service was half as good as their bush telegraphy! On the other hand, as there can never be any secrets in India, it is rather like living in an illuminated greenhouse.

The arrangements for my invalid stepmother completed and her return to England settled, I could turn my steps and my mind towards my new and unexplored home. Many of the improvements that I had planned had been carried out in my absence, and I was impatient to see them.

How far the Prypet Marshes stretch I do not know, for though I was surrounded by them, I never reached their limit during the many years I spent there. My house had belonged to a head forester, and was situated within a few miles of the Russian frontier, and although on that side my neighbours were highly undesirable, I was more than compensated on the other by my host and hostess, Prince and Princess Charles Radziwill.

Prostyn gave me a wonderful welcome, and I dropped into its life as easily as into a deep arm-chair, and should never have come out of it if Hitler had not precipitated me forcibly. It was a lonely spot, but I never felt the loneliness, for the countryside had so much to give, everything in fact that I had ever wanted, plenty of sport, lovely wild country and the sense of remoteness. The peace and quietude could be felt; the singing of a nightingale was a rude interruption. For the first time in my life I had found a place where I could get away from people, for much as I like them I do not like to feel encircled by them. The man who answered a greeting of " Good day " with the remark, " It isn't the day, it's the people you meet ! " should have come to Prostyn, where, if his theory held good, I should have been the best-tempered man alive.

In all the years that I was there I had only one unexpected but very welcome guest. I was outside my house when I suddenly heard my name called out, and looking round I saw a canoe, paddled by two women, with a man sitting in it. It turned out to be Rex Benson, who had been in Russia, and on his return had the enterprise to pass my watery way.

The house for my staff had been built, and I had made myself extremely comfortable, with an excellent Polish cook, and my old servant, Holmes, to look after me and run the rest of the establishment. When Holmes decided to go home to England he was replaced by my other soldier servant, James, who proved himself equally adaptable.

Matthews, my old groom since Brighton days, was given charge of all the riding horses at Mankiewicze. He took root, remained superlatively British, and always wore his bowler hat on Sundays. His only interest was horses; to Matthews a horse was the same in any language.

The country is absolutely flat, consisting of forests, meadows and marshes, but with a certain amount of arable land to give the peasant enough to live on—but no more. I found a new hobby, farming, and farmed enough land to supply my needs, except for the winter when the rivers are all frozen over, and the supplies were brought by sledges across the snow-covered country.

I decided that I would return to England every year for three months in the winter, chiefly to keep in touch with my old friends, but partly to get away from the intense cold of Poland. Then the duck have departed for a softer clime, and the rifle-shooting season starts, which holds little interest for me.

When I left the Army, Bob Ogilby was one of the very few people who realized what a wrench it was for me to go, and one day he sent me a book of Kipling's poems, with a slip of paper saying : " Read page x line z." That line read : " When the whole world's against you, the thousandth man will stand your friend." It was typical of Bob, who wastes no sympathy on you when you have no need of it, but stands like the Rock of Gibraltar when you do.

I went to Poland for three weeks, and I stayed twenty years, but to this day I could not tell you which season was the most fascinating. Each year I returned from England in time for the breaking up of the ice in the great frozen lakes and rivers. The sound of it was awe-inspiring with its booming thunder and cracking reverberations, like the destruction of Valhalla. Then suddenly spring seemed to shoot up from miles and miles of gentle wetness, the trees full of quiet green hope, and the yearly miracle of the awakening and arrival of the birds.

In the winter the journey from Mankiewicze to Prostyn

was covered in a sledge, straight across country which was now frozen, and the distance shortened to some thirty miles.

My first journey by night in a sledge was unforgettable. The country all white with snow with the trees standing like ghostly sentinels, the sledge drawn by horses with their bells jingling. Suddenly the road was lit by outriders on horseback carrying flaming torches, and turning the whole countryside into a shimmering fairyland.

The inhabitants of the Prypet Marshes are White Russians and a mixture of Russian and Polish, but if a peasant is asked if he is a Pole or a Russian, he answers : " Neither ; I come from here." Only a very small percentage of the peasantry had any form of education, though the percentage had been rising rapidly until interrupted by Hitler. In my early days at Prostyn most of the peasants were illiterate, had never seen a train and had no desire to move away from their respective bit of earth. Although knowing them to be primitive, I still had rather a shock when I saw a man performing as a chiropodist with an axe.

Primitive habits are not always only peculiar to peasants! One *soi-disant*, very *soigné* Pole was sharing a room with a man I knew. Upon opening an eye in the morning, my friend was electrified with horror to see this elegant gentleman using his—my friend's—toothbrush. He rose slowly from his bed, sauntered to the wash-stand, grasped the offending toothbrush and proceeded to scrub his toenails with it.

The natives of the marshes are most skilled watermen. To see them manning a canoe made of a single log, or finding the course of the river in a totally flooded forest, was really impressive. Their balance was equally amazing, and they ran along fallen tree-trunks coated in ice, whilst the rest of us were floundering and probably submerged in thick black mud. All their energies were devoted to remaining on top of the water, and their Blondin acts have been inspired by their dislike of getting into it. One day I dropped my pocket-knife into eight feet of water, and my boatman said he would get it for me. He retrieved it with his toes, and said he had not been in the water for several years.

My two keepers were German, and though they were very good at their work they suffered from rather cowardly dispositions. There were bandits in the forest, and rumoured to be in our neighbourhood, and my two keepers were frightened to death. I told them to come and sleep in my house, but they preferred to stay in their own cottages. Then they asked what I would do if the bandits made them come to my house, under the pretext of getting the door open. When I answered, " Shoot through the door," they hastily concluded that I was the more dangerous of the two and promptly came and slept in the house.

When the bandits were about I had the doors and shutters carefully closed, with only one window left open, the one opposite my bed. It was covered in wire mosquito netting, which I felt would keep out any bomb they might throw, while a man showing himself at the window would give me a nice easy shot with my revolver, which I kept under my pillow.

However, the bandits waited until I had gone away before they paid Prostyn a visit, and they consumed so much of my liquor that they left themselves incapable of looting anything else, and only took a most beloved old shooting-jacket.

General Sikorski was Prime Minister at that time, and I complained to him, saying it was no encouragement for a foreigner to come and live in his country if he was going to be set upon by savages. He told me not to worry, and that the matter would be dealt with. It was, and by the time I got back to Prostyn the police had killed five bandits, and my old jacket had been recovered, though unfit to wear. I was never bothered again by bandits.

I think I shot every day of those fifteen years that I spent in the marshes, and the pleasure never palled. I became absorbed by my healthy, easy life, so near to Nature and so far from the uneasy restlessness of those years between the wars. I became very out of touch with world affairs, and, I'm afraid, very uninterested. My greatest discovery at Prostyn was reading, a pastime for which up till then I had had no time and less inclination. Now that I had stabilized my one eye into steady action, I found that as long as I took care to sit in a good light I could pick up my education where I had dropped it at Balliol.

I read anything and everything, but still prefer adventure to any other subject, and rate Burnham's book *Scouting on*

Two Continents at the top of my list, in spite of its inadequate title. I found that I liked poetry, as long as it had a rhyme and a rhythm to it, like Rudyard Kipling's or Adam Lindsay Gordon's. I know nothing about music except to know that I like it, if it does not make me feel too sad. Polish music is too full of haunting despair.

I never listen to the wireless, and the theatre bores me unless it is a musical comedy or the circus. I hate good acting with its awful-seeming sincerity, and can make myself positively miserable thinking the whole wide world may be a hypocrite.

Twice when I went back to England the country was in the middle of a crisis, and both times, according to the rest of Europe, the country was rocked to her very foundations.

The first time was in the financial slump of 1931 after the pound had been devalued, and America had been enveloped by a wave of mass hysteria with suicides ten a penny, and I expected to find England plunged in gloom. Instead, on walking into the club, I found people sitting around quite calmly saying : " Oh, well . . . we can't go abroad this winter." There may have been panic in the city, but it was not apparent anywhere else ; the sangfroid of the Briton in a crisis gives him a lot of dignity.

On the second occasion I arrived on the day after the abdication of King Edward VIII. Europe had been bristling with stage whispers for months. In England I hardly heard the subject mentioned, and the attitude seemed to be : " It has happened." " It is over. . . . Long live the King."

No wonder grateful foreigners find refuge in England, with its sanity and its grumbles and its free opinions, and only one terrible drawback—its God-forsaken climate.

CHAPTER XI

SPORTING PARADISE

PROSTYN gave me a unique opportunity to study the fascinating complexities and peculiarites of bird life in general and wildfowl in particular. Until then I had been a typical example of the sportsman described, I think, by Wyndham

Lewis as : " A great lover of animals. He had shot them in every country." Certainly I had been too bent on destruction to have time to stop and wonder about their habits or home life, but I hope I paid my just retribution to these charming inhabitants of the Prypet Marshes by learning a little about them as well as trying to shoot them.

In Poland the miracle of the spring awakening synchronized with the migration, and every kind of bird appeared, always in the same order and timed practically to a day. Most of them were already in pairs ; mallard, teal, gadwall, pochard, geese, snipe, cranes, storks and pigeons, and the storks almost invariably returned to their last year's nest.

The number of duck varied considerably from year to year according to the amount of water in the river and lakes, and if the winter had been a hard one, heavy with snowfalls, when the ice and snow melted it caused unlimited spring waters, the duck would arrive in their thousands to the breeding grounds until the place was literally black with them. In a mild winter, luckily a rarity on those parts, there would be comparatively few duck and the waters seemed deserted.

The first shooting to be had in the spring was that of the drakes and capercailzie, both full of individual interest though not rated very high as sport.

Drakes were shot over call-ducks. The gun sets out before dawn in a small boat with a keeper, followed by another keeper in a boat with the call-ducks. On reaching the appointed ground, the boat is carefully concealed, hidden in the rushes, the call-duck anchored in front of the gun, and the whole manœuvre undertaken very quietly and carefully, as the mallard is a wary bird. The call-duck, although extremely intelligent, are very temperamental leading ladies, and if not in form remain absolutely and obstinately mute, but if in good voice start quacking immediately, and the drakes do not waste one second in putting in a hurriedly flattering appearance ; I have seen a loquacious duck with five or six drakes round her in a matter of seconds.

Call-ducks are the most amusing birds with characters as varied as human beings, and only one resemblance to each other—an utter lack of morals. They knew their masters with the unerring instinct of a dog. One day a keeper who had had his favourite call-duck stolen and had not seen her for weeks arrived at a friend's house and suddenly heard an invisible duck quacking loudly. It was his lost duck, who had recognized his voice, and got in a great state of excitement over the reunion.

When the call-duck refuses to quack, the gun becomes dependent on the cunning of his keeper, who imitates the call of the duck often as successfully as the lady herself. Call-ducks are invariably mallard, and when shooting other varieties it was better to rely on a good keeper to lure them ; I have shot garganey and ordinary teal, gadwall, shovellers and pochard to the quacks of my keeper.

Drakes often arrived on the water with such speed and from such unexpected directions that it was not possible to get a shot at them, and they would have to be frightened and shot at as they flew away.

Much of the attraction of shooting lies in the setting, and spring in Poland was brilliant with charm. Plants and bushes in their new green dresses, and acres of iris and giant buttercup bursting out of the water in a riot of fresh colour.

Capercailzie, our other form of spring shooting, is an acquired taste, and it took me several years before I would try it. It sounds a very ungentlemanly sport to shoot at a sitting male when he is calling to his girl friend, and it was not until I had tried and failed dismally to get anywhere near my capercailzie that my appetite was whetted to try again.

The chief delight of this shooting lay in spending the night in the forest, warmed by a huge log fire, rising long before dawn and hearing the creatures of the forest come to life. The cranes are the earliest risers with their shrill callings, followed by the snipe drumming and the woodcock rodeing and making such a quaint sound like a little snore followed by a short whistle. Gradually came the awakening of the later sleepers until they were all joined in a brilliant cacophony to herald the birth of a new day. At these moments I was full of regrets for all the dawns that I had wasted in my bed, when outside there was a whole animal world alive with urgency, busy with the family cares and daily task of survival.

The walk over the marshes was a moment I dreaded, with a perilous path of split tree trunks laid for us to walk over and usually covered in a coating of thin ice. I soon learned to shoe myself like the native, with my feet bound by a single strip, of linen, placed inside a sandal made of the bark of a tree, but, alas ! I could never attain the balance of the natives, and envied them the ease with which they ran across the logs as surefooted as on a road, and carrying heavy loads on their shoulders.

The capercailzie can only be detected by sound, and it is possible to hear him calling a quarter of a mile away. When he is calling he is conveniently stone deaf, and it is the only possible moment to move, as in between times his senses are so alert that, given the slightest warning, he is up and away and the stalk is over. If his calling is intermittent it makes the stalk a very long one, for during his call it is only possible to take at most three steps, but often only two, and he has an uncomfortable habit of breaking off his love-song with an upsetting suddenness and leaving the gun in the middle of a stride, balancing in a most uncomfortable position and not daring to move.

A successful stalk may allow the gun to reach a point only twenty yards away from his prey, but even if the caper is quite near it is still extremely hard to spot him in that queer light of an early dawn ; I have been under his very tree without being able to see him. Then at last comes the shot, at short range, and with a shot-gun, and full of blind assurance that it will be impossible to miss—until there comes the awful humiliating knowledge that one has missed. Our finest shots missed regularly enough to give this game its great attraction. Shooting woodcock in the evening when they were rode-ing was a form of spring shooting very popular on the Continent. Though I was assured it had no harmful effect I found that after several years the number of woodcock were diminishing considerably, and I felt it a form of sport that should be stopped.

Geese and jack-snipe were casual wayfarers, and passed through only in the spring and autumn, on their way to and from their breeding grounds in the Arctic Circle.

The hazel-grouse, no explorer and quite lacking in the pioneering spirit, stayed with us in the forest with the black-game and the capercailzie. The hazel-grouse gave us an interesting hunt ; he was called by a keeper whistling through a small chicken bone, which made one wonder who had first invented such a strange device.

When the ducks were nesting they were discreetly invisible, but after the ducklings were hatched they became very agitated when they spied our boats coming along, and would be seen bustling their families into cover of the reeds. Then the duck would try and distract our attention by flapping along in front of our boat, as if wounded, until she felt her young were out of danger, when she would fly back to them.

May brought a lull in the shooting, but a plague of mosquitoes, which the native did his best to defeat by burning smoke-fires outside his front door, and also outside the stables and cowsheds, as the animals were devoured and often the cows had their udders so badly bitten that they could not be milked. Mosquitoes disappeared when the hay was cut, to be replaced by a worse enemy—horse-flies. Even my wonderful marshland had a few drawbacks.

Pigeon shooting lasted over June, though at first it was frowned on by the peasant, who had some religious prejudice or superstition against the shooting of a pigeon. One day I opened the crop and showed it to a peasant, and he was so overcome at the amount of his grain that had been consumed by that particular pigeon that his prejudices melted on the spot.

July 15th saw the formal date of opening of the duck and snipe shooting, and in my opinion it was at least a fortnight too early, for the duck were still flappers, and had such soft feathers that one pellet would bring them down. All very flattering to our shooting prowess, but it suffered a cruel reverse two or three weeks later, when the birds had hard feathers and were strong on the wing.

By contrast the early snipe shooting was excellent, and it was the only period in which a big bag was procurable, as after a short stay with us of only a few weeks the snipe started moving off. When they first arrived with us, we had the unusual experience of seeing them perching on the bare branches of the trees, and hearing their drumming, that sound so reminiscent of a goat, and that comes strangely from such a small bird.

The solitary snipe—a bird little known in England—was another of our regular visitors : he is a much bigger edition of the ordinary snipe, and has quite different habits and flight. These snipe frequent the dry ground situated near to the marshes, and are an easy bird to shoot, as they get pig fat and fly very slowly and straight. They sit very close and gave us a grand opportunity for training our setters and pointers.

The Poles are very keen on horses, and are naturally fine horsemen, and as there is no hunting in Poland, at Mankiewicze we had a very amusing substitute, which was coursing on horseback. The grooms lead the greyhounds on horseback, and the hares are very strong, weighing anything up to twelve pounds, with occasionally a fox or a roebuck to give us a really good run for our money.

There was good coarse fishing, but I was no expert, and my record pike was an eight-pounder, though I have netted a thirty-five pounder. The natives trolled for pike with their lines held in their teeth while they were paddling their canoes, and they had another successful method when they fished in the reeds, with their canoes gliding slowly, slowly until they moved a pike. With their vigilant and expert eye they would mark the spot where the pike had come to a stop, paddle quietly up to it, drop a bell-shaped basket right on top of it, put their hand through a hole at the top of the basket, and pull the fish out. We used to spear fish at night in a boat with a fire carried in some contrivance attached to the bows. We paddled gently along, holding a three-pronged spear ready to drive into any confiding fish. Quite easy if the fish remained politely stationary ; not quite so easy if it moved off in a hurry.

One summer I had a very friendly little visitor in the shape of a turtle or tortoise. I was standing by a fence in the garden when I spied her coming towards me. She arrived within six feet of me and, quite regardless of an interested spectator, proceeded to dig a hole eight or nine inches deep with her hind feet. Then she laid an egg, dropping it carefully into the hole, and covered it by scraping sand over the top of it. She continued with this routine until she had laid either eleven or thirteen eggs altogether, when she covered them tenderly and ambled away.

I took a twig to mark the spot, and in September about three or four months later I dug up the eggs and found them just on the point of cracking. I placed them in a box of sand, and while I was doing it some of the little animals burst out of their shells. They were beautiful as jewels, all perfectly formed, and only about the size of a shilling. To my sorrow they all died, and I found out, too late, that I should have left them alone to feed on the white of the egg; then, in the spring, they would have dug themselves out and gone straight to the river.

Magpies in their hundreds were one of the biggest pests at Prostyn, but I had never bothered to shoot them until I saw one pecking the eyes out of a chick, when I started to wage serious war. I put down eggs filled with phosphorus, and within a few weeks there was not a single magpie left.

My keepers could never make out why they never found a dead magpie, but I think that—like all other sick wild animals—they went right away into the depth of the forest to die in solitude. The same instinct must guide them all. Perhaps they think, like Peter Pan, that " To die must be an awfully Big Adventure " and want to sample the thrill of it by themselves, or else they may regard death as a weakness which must be concealed from curious eyes. Who knows? But there must be some such explanation for the elephant cemeteries in Africa, where their skeletons are found often in the most inaccessible depths of the bush. My poor magpies, though of humbler degree, were possibly actuated by the same natural instinct, though I hope the elephant will forgive my *lèse-majesté* in suggesting it.

By the summer the flood subsided, leaving large areas of water where the duck collected in vast numbers. These areas were known as " saads," were most strictly preserved, and no one was allowed to disturb them in any way whatsoever.

In the beginning of my time on the Prypet Marshes our shoots were carried out with a modest form of comfort only. We camped out in small sheds, known as " Budans," closed in on three sides, but with the fourth open and facing a big log fire.

Later on Prince Charles had the shooting lodges repaired, and then we lived in perfect comfort, administered to by an adequate staff, always with an excellent chef.

Though luxury is not a necessity, it is only a fool who makes himself uncomfortable, and with the intensity of the Polish climate the comforts were very pleasant.

The seasons range from tropical heat in the early summer to the cold of the Arctic regions in the late autumn, and I soon copied the example of the Poles, who were adepts at clothing themselves to match the climate. In the summer I wore canvas trousers and native sandals, and in the autumn I clad myself in furs, but always very light ones, in which it was possible and comfortable to shoot.

At the end of August our shooting started in real earnest and on a very big scale.

The evening preceding the shoot we settled our things for the night in the shooting lodge, and then crawled quietly up to the edge of the saad to see and hear the duck getting up for their evening flight to their feeding-grounds. The sound of a flight of duck has been compared to the noise of shells passing overhead, but to me there is no man-made contraption that can compare with that breath-taking and most stirring of all animal sounds. It creates a feeling of suspended excitement, which no familiarity can destroy, and if I could choose one form of shooting only I should not hesitate—it would be duck.

My feelings on this fascinating subject are best described in the following poem:

WILDFOWL

How oft against the sunset sky or moon
I watched that moving zig-zag of spread wings
In unforgotten autumns gone too soon,
In unforgotten springs !

Creatures of desolation ! For they fly
Above all lands bound by the curling foam.
In misty fens, wild moors, and trackless sky
These wild things have their home.

They know the tundra of Siberian coasts
And tropic marshes by the Indian seas.
They know the clouds and nights, and starry hosts
From Crux to Pleiades.

Dark flying rune against the Western glow,
It tells the sweep and loneliness of things.
Symbols of autumns vanished long ago,
Symbols of coming springs.

PAI TA-SHUN

As we watched the duck flighting, the keepers came up to make hides round the saads for us to shoot from—always very comfortable and roomy enough to hold the gun, his loader and his other invaluable ally, his dog ; all, of course, very carefully concealed.

We dined early and went to bed, as we had to be up by 1 a.m. or 2 a.m. to get into our hides well before dawn, when the duck appear as shadows in the semi-darkness gradually taking shape, presently to be seen in their hundreds, even thousands, overhead. The most vital point for the guns is to prevent some reckless enthusiast from shooting too soon, and in our early days, before we had bought our knowledge, the first shot would send all the duck off and spoil at least half an hour of the shoot before they came back again, then never in the same numbers. Later we arranged it that one old hand should fire the first shot at a judicious moment and only when it was light enough to see properly.

The first half hour produced far and away the heaviest shooting, and I remember once emptying my first bag of cartridges in that time and counting ninety-two duck killed.

The shooting would go on for three or four hours, and at the end of that time there appeared to be just as many duck as there had been in the beginning, with only longer intervals between their departures and return, though they became a good deal more wary. By stopping after three or four hours, we ensured a second shoot on the same saad, often as good as the first, but with fewer guns, and if I shot a third time I went alone.

In a good season a gun could be counted on getting 150 duck, but I have often shot 180 and once 213. Our greatest difficulty was the pick-up : as the saads were surrounded by thick thorny bushes eight to ten feet high, it had to be a very bold dog that would face them, and the often icy water. At first I only had one dog, a black Labrador of mine known to the natives as the Black Devil, a perfect performer, but too big and heavy for our small wobbly canoes. Later we changed to springer spaniels ; they proved ideal for duck shooting. Instead of losing quite fifty per cent. of the bag as we did at first, we ended by retrieving nearly all we shot.

There is a great art in counting one's birds accurately, and nothing is more annoying than the over-optimistic gun wasting the time of both the keeper and the dog looking for mythical birds !

The best shooting, to my mind, was after October 10th, when the mallard had got their full plumage, and the drakes could be picked out easily and took a great deal of shooting. The shooting continued till the first heavy frosts, when most of the saads were frozen over with sometimes a patch left still open. One day in the late autumn the keeper told me of a particular saad that was still open, and I shot about one hundred and eighty duck and only stopped because retrieving in icy water was so hard on the dogs. The duck kept returning and returning, having nowhere else to go.

At the beginning of my shooting career in the marshes, I used ordinary 12-bore guns and number 6 shot, but by the end of it I had a pair of 12-bore guns taking 2¾-inch cases and another taking 3-inch cases, and used number 2 shot at the end of the seasons when smaller shot could be heard hitting the duck, but with little result.

Though far from being an expert, I did shoot over 20,000 duck to my own gun, so I had experience if not skill.

The autumn shooting included also driven hazel-grouse that were very difficult to hit driven over narrow rides in the forest; young black game were also shot, entailing a lot of hard work walking them up over dogs, but the results were much appreciated by gourmets. In dry years an occasional partridge looked in to vary our diet, but in the first week of December bird life ceased in the marshes, and only the capercailzie, black-game and hazel-grouse stayed with us, retiring late into the warmth of the forest to spend the winter.

When Prince Charles had inherited the property in 1921 it was estimated to contain eight elk (moose), but by careful preservation and keeping the terrain which attracts them very quiet, elk came in from all other parts of the country, and by 1939 the Prince's estate had eight hundred head on it. The elk were shot in the autumn, and only in the rutting season. The heads were the finest in Europe and won most of the prizes at the big Sports Exhibition held in Berlin before the war. The exhibition was sponsored by Goering, who, if he had no other qualities, was an enthusiastic shot and hunter, complete in fancy dress.

With the snow came the wolves; the keepers located them

easily by their tracks in the snow and shoots were quickly organized. Having located them, the keepers would surround the area with a cord tied up with bits of coloured cloth. For some reason known only to wolves, these flagged ropes inspired in them such fear that they could be depended on to remain inside the enclosed area. The guns were ranged along one side of the enclosure, the ropes removed from that side, and the wolves were then driven out to the waiting guns. The peasants were overjoyed when they were shot; they were very destructive and did a lot of damage among cattle.

The wolf is a fine sight in his full winter coat, and a much sought-after trophy, as his skin makes lovely rugs. He is a cowardly animal, and unlikely to find the courage to attack anyone unless he is cornered. One day some children were looking after their cattle when a wolf closed in to attack. Five of the children tried to beat him off, and he bit four of them, all of whom died from rabies, which disease is one of the dread curses of Poland, and was the arch-enemy of our dogs.

The big event of the winter was the wild boar shoot which was organized down to the last technical detail on the scale of a large battle-front. Pig-sticking enthusiasts resent the shooting of boars and demand to know why they should not be ridden. Naturally in that country of marshy forest it is impossible to ride a pig or to drive them out.

At Mankiewicze seven hundred beaters were employed for the boar shoot, three hundred and fifty at each end of the forest with the line of rifles in the middle. The boar were driven past the guns from one end to the other, and once, at the only shoot which I attended, I saw one hundred and forty-seven boar killed. It was wholesale slaughter, and bullets were ricocheting in all directions. As a sport it did not appeal to me at all, but the wild boar is a terrible enemy to the crops, and his demise a necessity. The Poles were wonderful rifle shots and it was a fine sight to see them shooting boars galloping across a ride.

Occasionally in the boar drives a lynx or bear would be seen, but we were not allowed to shoot the bear as they were rare in these parts and it was hoped to lure them to the neighbourhood. The peasants were most anxious that they should be killed as they stole their honey, but we were not allowed to oblige. One day the keepers found a moose that had been killed by a bear and the keepers thought that the bear had jumped from a tree to bring the moose down.

People wondered what we did with all the game which we shot, but nothing was ever wasted as there were two hundred keepers and their families on Prince Charles Radziwill's property, with none of the average British keeper's aversion to eating game. One can well understand a certain nausea at the idea of eating the animal one has guarded and watched, but the Polish keepers were too hungry to be bothered with finer scruples and meat is a luxury almost unknown to them. Moose and duck are a big delicacy to vary their monotonous diet of kasa, a form of oatmeal, black bread and sour milk.

Perhaps, inadvertently, I have been stressing too much the size of the bag in those never-to-be-forgotten shooting days in Poland, for to all good sportsmen the size of the bag means little and it is the quality which counts. The quality of the day, the setting, the friends, or just the intelligent working of one's dog can make a day memorable that has heard few shots fired.

The best moments at Prostyn to me were those evening flights when I waited alone, not far from my house, and felt the quiescent stillness of the coming night full of a tired magic, bringing the bustle of day to a peaceful close.

The Bolsheviks came to Prostyn in 1939, and they took all I had, my guns, rifles, rods, clothes, furniture, but they could not take my memories. I have them still, and live them over and over again.

CHAPTER XII

THE STORM BREAKS

THE year 1938 and the uneasy "Peace in our time" of Munich had repercussions even at my retreat at Prostyn, and this time we knew that Poland must be the crux of any war to come. I had written home to Lord Gort, the C.I.G.S., to ask if in the event of war he would employ me. His answer was evasive, indefinite and altogether disheartening, and it was quite obvious that he was not at all keen to use me.

Suddenly, in July, 1939, I was summoned to the War Office, and was asked if I would take on my old job as head of the British Military Mission. I was delighted and knew that I had to thank my friend General Beaumont Nesbitt for my appointment. At that moment he was the Director of Military Intelligence, had been to Poland in Lord d'Abernon's mission, stayed with me at Prostyn, and knew that I had a fair knowledge of the country and was on good terms with the Poles, so that I must have a certain usefulness.

It was a great relief to me to know that I should be employed, and I ordered some uniform, collected it with great difficulty, and returned to Poland in a far more cheerful frame of mind than that in which I had left it.

At lunch-time on August 22nd I had shot sixty snipe, and was sitting smoking my pipe and hoping to get my century, when my hopes were interrupted by the arrival of a man with an urgent message to ring Warsaw. I hurried to the telephone at Mankiewicze, got put through to the number, and found it was the British Ambassador telling me to come at once.

As I had missed the only train Prince Radziwill kindly lent me his car, in which I left early next morning equipped with my uniform and the clothes I stood up in, and no time for a last look round.

I went straight to our Embassy and met the Ambassador, Sir Howard Kennard, for the first time. He had the reputation of being a difficult man, but whether he deserved that reputation I do not know, and had no opportunity of judging, but I recognized at once his efficiency and capabilities, and no one could have done more for the Poles. He was most ably assisted by his counsellor, Mr. Clifford Norton, now our Ambassador in Athens, whose wife never ceased her work for the Polish cause, and earned their gratitude and affection.

Sir Howard Kennard immediately put me in the picture ; I realized that war was not a question of weeks, but of days.

Hitler was determined on war. He was ready and waiting and nothing was going to stop him, but with his usual fiendish cleverness he had managed to put the blame upon his victim, and so successfully as to dupe our people in Berlin. Our government, so busy with the placating of Hitler, prevailed on the Poles to delay their mobilization, so that there could be no action that might be interpreted as a provocation.

The next day, August 24th, I went to see Marshal Smigly-Rydz, the Commander-in-Chief of the Polish Forces. Smigly-Rydz had been an army commander in 1924 and was a man for whom Pilsudski had a very great affection; he had nominated him as his successor. He must have nominated him out of gratitude for his loyalty and integrity, for I cannot think it was for his capabilities, which were never fitted for the responsibilities which were thrust on him. I use the word " thrust " particularly as, to give Smigly-Rydz his due, I feel sure he never sought them.

I found that Smigly-Rydz had no illusions as to the imminence of war, but I found myself in strong disagreement with his proposal to fight the Germans as soon as they had crossed the frontier into Poland. The country west of the Vistula was terrain admirably suited to tanks at any time, but now, after a long long spell of drought, even rivers were no longer obstacles, and I did not see how the Poles could possibly stand up to the Germans in country so favourable to the attacker. Smigly-Rydz was adamant, and held the view that if he retired at all he would be accused of cowardice, and that he must stand at all costs and whatever the consequences. I then tried to persuade him to send his fleet out of the Baltic, where they would be trapped, and again I was given the same answer. His attitude of putting heroics before reason seemed to me to be short-sighted in the extreme, but finally I overcame his objections about the fleet; they succeeded in extricating themselves from the Baltic and proved of great value afterwards.

Warsaw was a hubbub of political crisis, the streets packed with people full of the anxieties and quavering emotions which precede a war and turn the actual declaration into an anti-climax of unspeakable relief.

All night the troops passed through—artillery, cavalry, infantry—until the streets rang with the monotonous sound of their marching feet.

The Poles were brimful of confidence, which unfortunately I could not share; on the night of August 31st I dined with some friends who had to be, almost forcibly, persuaded into sending their children away from Warsaw.

On September 1st, 1939, Hitler attacked Poland, and struck with unerring certainty by destroying, within the first few hours, practically every Polish airfield. The Polish Air Force was effectively grounded, but in any case the German Air Force was far superior in both numbers and training, and the Poles could have done little even had their airfields been left intact.

The same day the Germans bombed Warsaw, and with the first deliberate devastating bombing of civilians I saw the very face of war change—bereft of romance, its glory shorn, no longer the soldier setting forth into battle, but the women and children buried under it.

The Poles put up a heroic resistance to the weight of the advancing German tanks and infantry, but having no equipment, no planes, few guns and tanks, it was not within human possibility to stop them and the Germans swept on. Strangely enough, the trains still kept running, and the Hun never succeeded in stopping the communications.

England could give no help at all, but made matters worse by inflicting on us the perfectly useless, and extremely irritating, leaflet raids which had no physical effect on the Germans and no moral effect on us. We were crying out for bombs, not bits of idealistic paper, and Britain's efforts in the realm of propaganda were several years too late.

The Poles were fighting for their lives, but notwithstanding the issue they could not rise above their love of political intrigue, and allowed the armies to suffer by these senseless fomentations. For some political reason they were not employing General Sikorski, and there was a lamentable delay in employing General Sosnkowski, one of their ablest men who was to prove the only general to defeat the Germans in battle near Lwow.

We left Warsaw on the fourth or fifth day of the campaign, evacuating the embassy staffs, the French Military Mission and ourselves. At first I had Colonel Colin Gubbins as my G.S.O.1 and Major Roly Sword as my G.S.O.2, and Colonel Shelley, who had been passport officer in Warsaw, but by now my mission had increased considerably, and I had a number of language officers who had been working in Poland

and neighbouring countries, bringing the total to about twenty. A very good officer, Captain Perkins, usually accompanied me. He had had an unusual life, serving in the Merchant Service, and on leaving it had taken up business interests in Galicia. Later in the war his knowledge of the country and the Polish language were of great value in the special branch of Intelligence where he worked.

We left Warsaw at night and went towards Brest-Litovsk, but found our progress hampered by refugees. It was my first sight of that slowly-moving mass of heart-rending humanity, pushing and pedalling their incongrous forms of transport, clutching their children and their pitiful bundles, and trudging no one knew where. Fortunately the Germans never bombed at night during that retreat or the casualties would have been appalling.

The next day we stopped at a small village and received our daily dose of bombing. Mrs. Shelley, who was accompanying her husband, was tragically killed.

We had a number of women secretaries and clerks with us from various offices, and for the first time I realized that women, far from being an embarrassment in war, were proving themselves a genuine asset. Nothing could stop them from working even under impossible conditions, and I cannot praise them too highly for all the help they gave, but I was not the first or last male in this war to underrate the toughness and tenacity of women.

The German Intelligence was of a very high order. I give a small instance : one day I arrived in a town and sent an officer to the mayor to ask him to supply us with billets, only to find that they had already been assigned to us by instructions received from the German radio.

When we arrived in Brest-Litovsk I went to see Smigly-Rydz, who asked me to try and get help from England. Of course there was nothing to be done, and we were gradually retreating to the Polish-Roumanian frontier. Just before we reached what was to be our last stopping-place Sosnkowski cheered us with the first and only victory, and for a day we lived with the illusion that we might keep a footing in Poland and carry on as the Belgians had done in the 1914–18 War. We visualized a small corner as a symbol of resistance, but our illusion was dispelled by the entry of Russia into the war.

For Poland the entry was as unexpected as it was disastrous; it left her helplessly sandwiched between two mighty enemies.

We had heard that the Russians had mobilized, but we had no idea that they would attack us, for when they had crossed the frontier they pretended to come as friends and fraternizing with our troops. We were too glad to believe anything in our desperate plight, and were not unduly concerned by their presence over the border.

The evening of the Russian entry I again went to see Smigly-Rydz to ask him what he intended doing. I told him that if he was going to stay and fight it out on Polish soil I would stay with him, keeping several of my officers, and would send the rest home via Roumania.

Smigly-Rydz seemed to be suffering from a wave of indecision, and though he thanked me for my offer, he said that the Russian intentions were not, as yet, clear, but when he knew them he could make a decision and let me know his plans.

He inspired me with so little confidence that I told him I would leave an officer at his headquarters to ensure that there would be no loss of time in learning his intentions. I left Prince Paul Sapieha to report to me.

In less than one hour Prince Paul came back with the startling news that the Marshal had decided to clear out of Poland, and was crossing at once into Roumania.

Smigly-Rydz will never be forgiven by the vast majority of Poles for his decision to desert his army, and although I knew that he was not the right man to be in command of the Polish forces, it had never occurred to me he would throw aside his responsibilities in a hysterical rush to save his own skin. His behaviour was in direct contradiction to everything that I knew about the Poles, and my feelings at that moment are hard to express.

Our mission being now useless, we packed up and set off by car for the frontier, fifteen miles away. It took us three hours to make our way through the hordes of refugees. On arriving we changed into any plain clothes that we could get, were allowed into Roumania and started our journey to Bucharest by car. The whole country seemed alive with German agents, all perfectly aware of our identity, and the

Roumanian police were very busy inviting us to park our cars in certain enclosures, from which we should not have emerged as free men.

We arrived in Bucharest on the second day after leaving Poland. I drove straight to see the British Minister, Rex Hoare, who was a friend of mine. Although no doubt he was personally pleased that I had escaped destruction, internationally he found me an embarrassment. Our relations with Roumania were in mid-air, the German influence was very strong, and the Roumanians would have earned some kudos by handing me over to the Germans, or at any rate arresting us.

Luckily, Rex Hoare's personal friendship with the Roumanian Prime Minister saved me, and though he would not allow me to fly off in a private plane belonging to Arthur Forbes (now Lord Granard), which happened to be in Buchrest at that moment, he did consent to my departure by train. Armed with a false passport, I got away, but I imagine that it was only in the nick of time, as the friendly Prime Minister was murdered the same morning.

My next stop was Paris. Our Military Attaché took me to lunch at the Ritz, where I saw several French friends. They were all equally bitter and disgruntled with Britain for having stuck to her word to declare war on Germany if Poland was invaded. The French, with their usual realism, failed to see why we consented to ally ourselves to the Poles when it was geographically impossible to help them. The French were labouring under the impression that if Britain had not declared war the Poles would not have fought. It was far from the truth, but the French psychologically had no understanding of the Polish mentality, or they would have known that the Poles would have fought for their country if the whole world had opposed them.

After a few hours in Paris, I flew on to London, feeling rather disturbed by the attitude of the French and wondering what I should find in England.

I went straight to the War Office to see General Ironside, who had succeeded Lord Gort as C.I.G.S.

I was met with the remark : " Well ! Your Poles haven't done much." I felt that the remark was premature, and replied : " Let us see what others will do, sir."

No one who had not been there could imagine what the Poles were up against. The Germans had prepared for this war for years, and it was the world's first experience of the power of mechanized force used on a gigantic scale. It was the armed might of Germany against the weight of human bodies, and if heroism could have saved the Poles their story would have been a different one. At that particular moment I did not think it was for us or any other allied nation to deny them praise.

I made several more visits to the War Office to tell them all I could of the campaign, and had an interview with Lord Halifax at the Foreign Office. The Prime Minister, Mr. Neville Chamberlain, invited me to dinner with Lord Hankey and Sir John Simon, and was most anxious to know the effect of the leaflet raids ! My reply did not please him very much.

In England, later on, I learned that when the Russians crossed the frontier into the north-east they went straight to Mankiewicze and Prostyn. My servant, James, and Matthews, my old groom, were still there. The Russians asked them where I was. James told them that I had gone off to the war, and the Russians replied that if James was not telling them the truth he must know what to expect. The Russians, and in fact a good many of the Poles, too, imagined that I lived at Prostyn for the sole purpose of spying. But no one has ever informed me what I was going to spy on in a desolate marsh inhabited solely by birds and beasts.

After searching and not finding me, they treated James and Matthews quite fairly, saw that they were fed and paid, and some months later sent them back to England.

My worldly goods were carefully packed and were said to have been sent to the museum at Minsk for safe custody, but as the Germans burned the museum early on in their war against Russia, that was the last I ever heard of them.

Though I do not think one should be tied to one's possessions, as they so easily become one's master, I had several pangs over the loss of my guns and old shooting clothes. I vaguely hope that some omnipotent commissar is not strutting around in my fur coat.

The Polish campaign, though bitter with the taste of defeat, had made me aware of several new developments in warfare. The first—perhaps a premonition—was that with the speed and mobility of mechanized war it would be very easy to be taken prisoner. The second was the newly-acquired power of the air, and the terrorizing effectiveness of bombing, though we were still far from being alive to its full capabilities. The third was a grasp of the full meaning of those strange words " The Fifth Column."

The Fifth Columnist as an enemy was most dangerous ; he could be felt but not seen, and as an individual he was loathsome as he turned against his own and loved money or power better than his honour. That he was a foul weapon to be seriously reckoned with we found to our cost in every country that was overrun. The Fifth Column was a canker which spread swiftly and ate deep into the heart of a country. By a miracle we were spared its activities in Britain.

CHAPTER XIII

THE UNHAPPY NORWEGIAN CAMPAIGN

JUST after I got back I heard that Tom Bridges was in a nursing home at Brighton. I went down to see him and found him desperately ill with chronic anæmia. He had always been so vividly and vigorously alive that it was pathetic to realize that his life was coming to an end. Soon after I had left him in France in 1917 he had lost a leg and had never held another active command. He had had a lion cub as a pet, and when he came round from the anæsthetic after having his leg amputated, the first thing he said was, " I hope they have given my leg to the lion." He had held many quasi-diplomatic posts, one as our representative on the Balfour Mission to the U.S.A., and his last as Governor-General of South Australia which must have given him full scope for his flair for people.

I retired to hospital for some treatment and found myself filled with diffidence and doubts. I was extremely anxious about being employed again, as I knew there were various people at the War Office who considered me out of date, and one charming man had been heard to say that he supposed Carton de Wiart was anxious to come back and collect some more medals. Also I was haunted by the old spectre of medical boards which invariably made me feel as if I were knocked together with tintacks and tied up with bits of string.

Whilst I was in hospital Tom Bridges sent a friend to see me to ask what I thought of the general situation. The friend told me that Tom's end was very near, but even though he must have been aware of it he did not allow it to dull his interest in the great issues which were at stake. I never saw him again, for he died two or three days later, and if " To live in the hearts of men is not to die," then Tom is still with us.

To my intense relief General Ironside appointed me to command the 61st Division, a second-line Midland Territorial Division which I took over from General R. J. Collins, who later was made Commandant of the Staff College. The A.D.M.S. said that I must be " vetted," but I assured him that I had been passed fit in Poland only a few weeks before and that it was a waste of his valuable time to examine me again !

My headquarters were at Oxford, and it amused me to think that when I left the place forty years before it had been to avoid being thrown out.

My command stretched from Birmingham to Portsmouth, Cheltenham to Reading, but I managed to cover the ground in a fortnight to impress on the troops what I expected from them.

That winter, which was afterwards known as " The Bore War," was dangerously static in Europe, but we were training hard and trying to equip ourselves, and were not fully conscious of the stagnation. France had lulled both herself and her Allies into a state of confident apathy with the Maginot Line, and personally I was in utter ignorance as to where it either began or ended, I visualized it stretching magnificently and impregnably from frontier to frontier and ending up somewhere in a sea, and it was rather a shock when I learned eventually that the Maginot Line simply ceased—and that a boy on a bicycle could scramble round the end of it ! With the rest of the world I put great faith in the French Army, and believed it to be of formidable strength and most modern equipment. We did not know then that it was suffering from a deadly disease known in

France as *le cafard*, which can destroy eventually the mainspring of an army—its Spirit. The women of France were also badly infected, for they had no work, no husbands, no sons or lovers. Their boredom was complete.

April, 1940, saw Norway appearing on the scene. The Germans were known to be bringing great pressure to bear on the Norwegians, and we did not know if it lay in the power of Norway to withstand the persistent naggings of Germany.

At that time the war was mainly a sea war with our Navy playing its traditionally valiant part. Captain (now Admiral Sir Philip) Vian, commander of the destroyer *Cossack*, had stirred the imagination by his brilliantly timed boarding of the *Altmark*. She was a German auxiliary cruiser driven aground in Norwegian territorial waters, and in the rat-infested holds Captain Vian found and released 299 British sailors who had been captured by the *Graf Spee* in the South Atlantic.

Shortly after the Germans made their first landing in Norway, we responded by a gallant failure at Narvik. In the middle of one night there was a telephone message for me to report to the War Office. It dawned on me the reason might be Norway, especially as I had never been there and knew nothing about it. Norway it was, and I was ordered to go there immediately to take command of the Central Norwegian Expeditionary Force. Unfortunately I was not to take my own division, the 61st, for the Force was to consist of a brigade and some odd troops sent from Northern Command, together with a French Force composed of Chasseurs Alpins under General Audet. These troops were to proceed to Namsos.

I was told that I could have time to collect a staff, but I felt it was of more importance for me to be on the spot when the troops arrived. My A.D.C., Neville Ford, was away for the week-end, so I took Captain Elliot, who was one of my brigade majors.

Having got my orders, I collected my kit and flew up to Scotland the next day, April 13th. We were to fly across to Norway the same night, but were delayed by a blizzard, and took off next morning in a Sunderland. We did not seem set for victory from the start, as poor Elliot was sick the whole way over, and on arriving at Namsos we were attacked by a German fighter. Captain Elliot was wounded and had to return to England in the same plane to spend several weeks in hospital.

While the German plane was attacking us we landed on the water and my pilot tried to lure me into the dinghy which we carried. I refused firmly, having no intention of allowing a Hun plane the pleasure of pursuing me in a wobbly and clumsy rubber dinghy when the Sunderland was still on top of the water. When the German had fired all his ammunition he flew off, and one of our Tribal Class destroyers, the *Somali*, sent a boat over to take me on board. On board I found Colonel Peter Fleming and Captain Martin Lindsay, and whoever may have been responsible for sending them, I thank him now, for there and then I appropriated them, and a better pair never existed. Colonel Peter Fleming from being adventurer and writer turned himself into general factotum number one and was the epitome of :

> Oh, I am a cook and a Captain bold,
> And the Mate of the *Nancy* brig
> And a Bo'sun tight, and a Midshipmite,
> And the crew of the Captain's gig !

Captain Martin Lindsay, explorer and traveller, picked up the bits where Peter Fleming left off, and between them they were my idea of the perfect staff officers, dispensing entirely with paper. Peter Fleming managed to find us good billets in Namsos, and a motor-car with a driver.

I had made only one request to the War Office with regard to this expedition. I had asked them to try and arrange that the landing at Namsos should not be made by untrained and untried troops. They had fulfilled my request and by the time I arrived the Marines had already made a preliminary landing and were holding a bridge-head south of the Namsen river.

The troops were being sent to another fjord about a hundred miles north of Namsos called Lillesjona, and the evening of my arrival the *Somali* took up up to meet them. We arrived next morning to find the troops on transports, but as the transports had to return to England we had to transfer all the men to destroyers at once, notwithstanding a great deal of interference by German planes. At Lillesjona I had a conference with Admiral Sir Geoffrey Layton on his flagship, after which I was taken on board the *Afridi*, commanded by Captain Philip Vian of *Cossack* fame, who showed me every consideration and kindness, although I must have been an inconvenient guest.

When we were returning to Namsos, I got a signal from the War Office saying that I was to be an Acting Lieutenant-General, but as I felt in my bones that the campaign was unlikely to be either long or successful, I did not bother to put up the badges of my new rank.

The Norwegian coastline was lovely to look at, with the majesty of its rough mountains covered in snow, but from a fighting angle the view had no attraction for me, as obviously in this type of country one would need very specialized troops.

We reached Namsos in the evening and started to disembark troops at once. It was soon evident that the officers had little experience in handling men, although they had a first-class commander in Brigadier G. P. Phillips.

In Norway at that time of the year there were only about three hours of darkness, and landing troops with the whole country under snow, and a vigilant and attentive enemy, was no easy matter.

The troops were only too anxious to do what they were told and to be quick about it, and it says much for them that not only did they succeed in landing, but they completely obliterated all traces of their landing. The Germans who flew over next morning suspected nothing.

My orders were to take Trondheim whenever a naval attack took place. The date was unnamed, but I moved my troops up to Verdal and Steinkjer (both near Trondheim), from where I would lose no time in synchronizing with the naval attack when it came.

The following night we had to land French troops—the Chasseurs Alpins under General Audet. Although far better trained than we were, and experienced at looking after themselves, they did not obliterate the traces of their landings. The next morning the Germans saw that troops had been put ashore, and the French made themselves still more noticeable by loosing off their machine guns at them, which succeeded in making matters much worse. The Germans responded by more and more bombs, and in a matter of hours Namsos was reduced to ashes. The casualties were not heavy, as by that time my troops were all forward, and the French bivouacked outside the town. I went up to the front with Peter Fleming soon after the bombing started, and by the time we returned there was little of Namsos left.

The French Chasseurs Alpins were a fine body of troops and would have been ideal for the job in hand, but ironically they lacked one or two essentials, which made them completely useless to us. I had wanted to move them forward, but General Audet regretted they had no means of transport, as their mules had not turned up. Then I suggested that his ski-troops might move forward, but it was found that they were lacking some essential strap for their skis, without which they were unable to move. Their other equipment was excellent ; each man carried some sixty pounds and managed his load with the utmost ease. They would have been invaluable to us if only I could have used them.

The British troops had been issued with fur coats, special boots and socks to compete with the cold, but if they wore all these things they were scarcely able to move at all, and looked like paralysed bears.

As far as planes, guns and cars went, I had no trouble at all, for we had none, though we commandeered what cars we could. Landing facilities were conspicuous by their absence, and, to make matters worse, we were being supplied by ships larger than the harbour could take. How the sailors got them in and out of these harbours remains a mystery never to be understood by a mere landsman.

The Hun bombers destroyed our small landing-stage. They had the time of their lives with no opposition whatsoever. Some of the ships carried A.A. guns and a few days before the evacuation I was sent some Bofors guns. The Bofors never actually shot down a Hun plane, but they managed to disconcert them and had a nuisance value, at the same time giving us a fillip at being able to shoot at them.

On one of our more hopeful days an aircraft carrier miraculously cleared the skies of German planes and stayed several hours, but as there were German submarines about it was not able to remain close to the land, and had to go out to sea again where some of the planes could not return to it.

My headquarters in Namsos was one of the few houses

to escape destruction, but after the bombardment I moved out to a small farm on the south side of the river Namsen, where we were not bothered much by the enemy, and it was easier for me to get to the front-line troops.

Two or three days after we had occupied Steinkjer and Verdal, about forty or fifty miles south of Namsos, the German Navy gained its one and only victory of the war, for their destroyers came up Trondheim Fjord and shelled my troops out of these two places. We had rifles, a few Bren guns and some two-inch smoke bombs, but none of them were either comforting or effective against a destroyer.

The troops at Verdal had a particularly bad time. The road ran through the town on the shore of the fjord in full view of the ships, and the troops had to take to the snow-covered hills, ploughing through unknown country in eighteen inches of snow, only to be attacked by German ski-troops. There is no doubt that not many of them would have survived had it not been for the handling of the situation by Brigadier Phillips.

We retired to positions north of Steinkjer and out of reach of the German naval guns, where we were able to hold on. Steinkjer was being heavily bombed and shelled, and it was not surprising that the population in these small towns lived in deadly terror of our arrival. Our intentions were excellent, but our ideas of ultimate deliverance invariably brought the whole concentrated weight of bombing on top of the heads of the population. At the time I felt irritated by their lack of interest in us, but afterwards I realized that unused as they were to the horror of war they were stunned by the invasion, and had not had time to come round.

Still I waited for news of our naval attack which was to be my signal to take Trondheim, but still it did not come. Hourly it became more and more obvious to me that with my lack of equipment I was quite incapable of advancing on Trondheim, and could see very little point in remaining in that part of Norway sitting out like rabbits in the snow. I wired the War Office to tell them my conclusions, only to get back the reply that for political reasons they would be glad if I would maintain my positions. I agreed, but said that it was about all I could do. They were so relieved that they actually wired me their thanks.

Now that my chances of taking Trondheim had gone, I sent Peter Fleming to the War Office to find out their future plans. He came back after a couple of days and told me that plans and ideas about Norway were somewhat confused, and adding : " You can really do what you like, for they don't know what they want done."

About this time a complete staff turned up, but I was not very pleased to see them. They took up a lot of unavailable space, there was not much for them to do, and Peter Fleming and Martin Lindsay had more than fulfilled my requirements. We had already been given one most useful addition—Major R. Delacombe—and I felt that soon we would be all staff and no war.

During these last few days I was offered more men. Lack of accommodation and the fact that my only line of communication was a single road and a small railway line functioning spasmodically forced me to refuse them. They were the type of troops that I should have been delighted to have under me, for they were Poles and the French Foreign Legion, but if I had accepted them it would have made evacuation still more difficult.

Several staff officers were sent over in the *rôle* of liaison officers, but I don't think they cared much about the job, for they seemed very intent on departing as soon as they could. One of them was particularly amusing : he was so anxious that his plane should not go off without him that he thought he would like to go and sit quite near it in a sloop which was in the fjord. A Hun promptly dropped a bomb on the sloop and sank it, but the gallant officer was not drowned and made a safe return to England, where his report must have been illuminating.

My farmhouse headquarters provided us with some amusement and excitement from the air. My new staff had not seen these air antics played by the Hun, and were startled one day when a German plane came down the road, flying very low and machine-gunning us. It is a most unnerving and unpleasant sensation to be peppered at from a plane bearing straight down on one, and takes a lot of getting used to.

One addition to my staff had given me the greatest pleasure, an officer who had been my A.A. and Q.M.G. in the 61st Division, Colonel C. L. Duke. With his unfailing energy and knowledge he managed to put a lot of order into chaos, and if I were asked who was the best officer I had ever had under me, I should answer Bulger Duke. After Norway I helped him to get command of an infantry brigade; he was captured at Singapore and all his energies wasted for five years in a Jap prison.

Just as we had settled to an uneventful routine with my troops in their new positions, wires started to flash to and from the War Office. First to evacuate, then to hold on, then to evacuate, then suddenly it was suggested that I should retire on Moesjen, about a hundred miles to the north of Namsos. I knew the road to be covered in deep snow and impassable for infantry, and I could see no point in the move and wired the War Office to that effect. Meanwhile I sent Peter Fleming and Martin Lindsay to reconnoitre the route in a car, and they took twelve hours to cover forty miles.

I believe the War Office considered me very unenterprising for opposing their suggestion, but I felt at that moment the move only looked feasible on a map.

More orders came to evacuate, and this time I started to set about it. General Audet came to see me and begged me not to leave his troops until the last when the hour came to embark. He seemed much moved, and on my assuring him that not a single British soldier would be embarked until every Frenchman was on board ship, I had a narrow escape from being embraced and was told that I was *un vrai gentleman*.

Gradually we retired towards Namsos, where we were to embark. The evacuation was to take place on two consecutive nights. I intended sending the French troops off the first night, and they had all gone down at dusk to be ready to embark. We waited—no ships turned up. There was no word from the Navy, and I must admit to feeling anxious. Just before dawn I had to move the troops up into their positions again, leaving them, depressed and disappointed, to await another night.

I was getting more and more anxious as Mr. Neville Chamberlain had told the House of Commons that General Paget's force had been evacuated from Andalsnes, which left me the only unenvied pebble on the beach. Alone against the might of Germany.

In the course of that last endless day I got a message from

the Navy to say that they would evacuate the whole of my force that night. I thought it was impossible, but learned a a few hours later that the Navy do not know the word.

Apparently there was a dense sea mist quite unsuspected by us on shore, and this had prevented their coming in the night before, but Lord Mountbatten managed to feel his way into the harbour, and the other ships followed him in. It was a tremendous undertaking to embark that whole force in a night of three short hours, but the Navy did it and earned my undying gratitude.

As day was breaking the Germans spotted us leaving the fjord and bombed us heavily. We lost the *Afridi* and a French destroyer and I lost my chance of being sunk. Having known the *Afridi* so well I asked to go on board, but had been told she was not coming in that night. When I found that she had come in after all I asked again to go in her, only to be told that my kit had been put on the *York* and it would be best for me to go in her instead. I did, and missed a very great experience. Unfortunately the wounded from the French destroyer had been put on board the *Afridi* and nearly all of them were drowned.

On my sixtieth birthday, May 5th, we arrived back at Scapa Flow exactly eighteen days after we had set forth. Captain Portal, who commanded the *York*, thought it was a most fitting occasion for a bottle of champagne. He must have known that to me the taste is extra good after a surgical operation or a major disaster.

Though Norway was the dullest campaign in which I had taken part, it had several redeeming points. It had given me my first opportunity of seeing the Navy at work, and working with them my admiration for them had grown with the days. We caused them endless trouble, and forced them to do extra and unusual jobs, but instead of showing any signs of resentment they gave us all the freedom of their ships.

The War Office had done its level best to help us, but they had not the power, the equipment or the facilities to make that help effective. Politically, Norway was worth a gamble, and I am sure the gesture was important, but I never feel that the whys and wherefores are a soldier's business. To me war and politics seem bad mixers, like port and champagne.

But if it wasn't for the politicians we wouldn't have wars, and I for one should have been done out of what is for me a very agreeable life.

Later the Norwegians sprang into life with their now famous resistance movement, and were content to suffer tortures rather than yield to the easy way out; they earned the respect and admiration of the world.

Although it meant two retreats within nine months I was glad that I had been sent, and notwithstanding the debacle I never doubted the ultimate issue.

CHAPTER XIV

ITALIAN PRISONER

A FEW hours after I had arrived in London, Admiral Sir Roger Keyes came to see me. He was under the impression that I was feeling let down by the Navy, owing to the intended attack on Trondheim not having taken place. I told him that, naturally, I had been very disappointed, as the non-appearance of the Navy had knocked out all idea of attacking the town, but I assured him that I had never for a minute blamed the Navy. I knew that the blame lay in the circumstances, and every man in my force knew it, too, and I hoped Keyes left convinced of my sincerity.

The 61st Division, still stationed at Oxford, had been given to General Schreiber, and I had some difficulty to get it back. I succeeded, and soon after Ireland became a key-point in invasion rumours, attention was switched to the west and my division was sent to Northern Ireland.

I can never believe the Germans had any intention of invading Ireland, but I am very grateful for any reason which sent us there, for it was an ideal training ground for troops and the division improved enormously from the moment of our arrival.

I had been to Northern Ireland several times to stay with Bob Ogilby, who owned the delightful property of Pellipar in Co. Derry, but we had been busy shooting and I had never ventured much farther than the neighbouring estates.

I had imagined the Northern Irish to be very akin to the

Scots, suspicious of Sassenachs and rather slow starters. Whether war was responsible for the dropping of all barriers or whether it was the charm of that greatest of our ambassadors, the British Tommy, I do not know, but Ulster received us to her bosom.

The division was scattered between Co. Antrim, Co. Derry and Co. Tyrone, with my headquarters at Ballymena.

Neville Ford was still with me as my A.D.C., but he was hankering to get back to troops, and I felt I must let him go. I replaced him with one of my best friends, Arthur Fitzgerald, an Irishman from the south. He had broken his back racing some years before and had difficulty in getting passed by a medical board. He had scraped through somehow, and joined me at my headquarters. His help and companionship meant much to me. His wife very kindly ran our domestic establishment and guided the efforts of our excellent Cypriot cook, Nicholas, and we fed really well.

The faithful James had turned up at my headquarters at Oxford, having been returned by the Russians just in time for the Norway adventure. I had him re-enlisted in the course of a few hours, so he may have thought he had arrived at an unfortunate moment but he never said so and was now looking after me with his usual nonchalance as if he had never heard of the word retreat.

I had a very nice and efficient chauffeur called Hailes, and with my scattered division I soon got to know and love the country and enjoyed the long drives. Wherever we found ourselves we were housed most comfortably in charming houses with hospitable people, whom I now count among my good friends. Lord and Lady Antrim, Sir Hugh and Lady O'Neill, Mr. and Mrs. Carruth and all their charming family, and Mrs. Sinclair of Holy Hill, who, an American herself, must have surpassed every American idea of hospitality.

The inhabitants of Ballymena were the kindest I have ever known ; they plied us with everything, but best of all with their goodwill, and I never pass through without seeing Jane McCurry, the fishmongress of the town, who always gives me a cup of tea.

When we arrived in Northern Ireland the General Officer Commanding was Major-General Sir Hubert Huddleston, but he was sent suddenly as Governor-General to the Sudan which was the country which he knew and loved so well, and where he had already made a great name for himself.

He was succeeded in Northern Ireland by Lieutenant-General Sir Henry Pownall, who had been Lord Gort's Chief of Staff at Dunkirk. I have a great personal liking for Pownall, and I know he will not resent it if I say that his advent in Northern Ireland brought a great black cloud to hover over my head, filling me with depression and foreboding. The cloud burst and I received a communication from the Military Secretary stating baldly that I was too old to command a division, and should have to go. I answered that I would not go unless I was turned out. I fought the decision on the ruling that I was the only senior officer who had been through the two campaigns of Poland and Norway, and though it was true they were both disasters, it was hardly my personal fault. I felt I was one of the few soldiers to have any idea of what we were up against.

The War Office turned to Pownall and said that I should have to go unless he specially recommended I should be kept on. Pownall was not prepared to recommend me, as I was in exactly the same position regarding age as several other divisional commanders, only they seemed to be less truculent.

The decision was a bad blow to me, for I felt that the division had improved enormously and that it was in some small part due to me. Also I could not bear the idea of being out of the war, and wondered what on earth I should do with myself.

My despair was interrupted, for on April 5th, 1941, I received another urgent message to report immediately to the War Office. This time the offer was a real prize, for it was to go to Yugoslavia and form the British Military Mission.

Although I had never been there, the idea of Yugoslavia had always appealed to me. We had not been allowed into the country before as the Yugoslavs had not wanted to annoy the Germans prematurely, but now they felt the hour had struck and the prospect was alluring, as I understood them to be the toughest of fighters and utterly unscrupulous.

The War Office intended that I should fly from Plymouth in a Sunderland, taking Arthur Fitzgerald as my A.D.C. and the indispensable James. The Sunderland failed to materialize, and I was sent to Newmarket instead to fly in a Wellington which had no room for Fitzgerald and James, and it was decided that they were to follow in a cruiser.

The Wellington was an ordinary bomber, and as I was climbing into it the Air Officer Commanding the area, Sir John Baldwin, told me that he had sent ninety-four Wellingtons to the Middle East and only one had failed to arrive. I crossed my fingers and fervently hoped that mine would not be the second.

Our first stop was Malta, where we arrived in the morning and spent the rest of the day. I lunched with General Scobell in command of the troops, and he took me around the island, which was already scarred from end to end. That evening I dined with the Governor, General Dobbie, and took off late that night to fly to Cairo and get my final orders from General Wavell. When I was waiting at the aerodrome to board my plane there was an R.A.F. mechanic standing by it who volunteered the information that he himself had looked over the engines that afternoon and found them in very fine condition.

I have a useful and unfailing capacity for sleep in almost any circumstances; I fell asleep immediately, but kept my earphones on. Two or three hours later my slumbers were disturbed by the repeated word " S O S . . . S O S . . . " and it eventually penetrated my consciousness that the signal was ours. At that instant the pilot sent me a message saying that one engine had failed, but he was hoping to make land and I must prepare for a parachute jump. I did not mind the prospect of the jump, but I hated the look of the small hole through which I was expected to hurl my elongated body attached to the parachute. As I was complying with the order the pilot sent another message that the other engine was failing and he must crash-land on the water. As we were dropping I heard the echo of that R.A.F. mechanic's voice saying : " The engines are in fine condition," and I wondered if he had his tongue in his cheek as he said it.

We made a clever landing on the water, though most of us suffered some damage and I personally got a blow on the head and lost consciousness. The first thing I can remember was being pushed through an opening in the top of the plane feeling myself soused by a wave and instantly restored to consciousness. Afterwards I never had the vestige of a headache, and imagine a few hours in a cold sea must be the perfect cure for concussion.

When we crashed we found ourselves about a mile to a mile and a half from the shore, but as there was a strong cold northerly wind blowing us rapidly inshore, when the plane did finally break in two we could not have been more than half a mile away from land. We made the annoying discovery that our rubber dinghy had been punctured and was useless to us : if only it had been seaworthy we might have been picked up. We had all managed to remain on the wings, with the seas breaking over us, but when the plane finally broke we had no alternative but to swim ashore and take pot luck of what we found there. Several of the crew were damaged, one with a broken arm, another with a broken leg, beside many cuts and bruises, and we had to help them as best we could.

We managed to make the shore to be greeted by native policemen in Italian service, one of whom pointed a rifle at me. I told him in forcible Arabic to put it down, which he did ! Then I asked him the whereabouts of the British forces, and when he answered they had left yesterday we chewed the bitter knowledge that if we could have flown on for another few minutes we should have landed among our own people.

Our appearance cannot have been very impressive, for I was barefoot, having removed my boots for the swim, and I had lost my cap as well, and the others were in much the same state. The only thing I had managed to salve from the wreck was my bamboo walking-stick, which I had found floating about inside the plane. It turned out an invaluable friend as I secreted some bank-notes inside it and saw that we were rarely parted again.

An Italian priest came up and took us to a small café, where we were given coffee and something to eat before being taken on to the hospital for attention. On the way I asked the police if there was any chance of finding some transport to take us to our own lines, but they pretended there was nothing available, obviously determined not to let us out of their clutches. The Italians had not arrived yet to occupy the town, but when they should arrive the police wanted to impress their Italian masters with their courage and ingenuity in capturing us.

The native doctor who was in charge of the hospital mended us to the best of his ability, and when I was alone with him he treated me to a brilliant verbal description on the illegitimacy of all Italians . . . later no doubt he was equally graphic over ours.

As we were being attended to we saw a British plane over our heads, obviously in search of us, and we cursed that punctured rubber dinghy; our hearts sank low as the drone of the plane faded into the distance.

My pilot told me that he felt certain that our plane had been sabotaged, as it was unlikely that the Wellington would fail on one engine, let alone on two, such a short way out from Malta. My mind switched back to my crossed fingers when I felt Sir John Baldwin to be tempting Providence, and I thought several more unpleasant thoughts of that R.A.F. mechanic, and wondered if he knew how far we would get.

Two hours later two Italian staff officers appeared, questioned me and took me off. They left my crew to be picked up later, and although they were taken to Italy, I am sorry to say that I never saw them again. I believe the pilot was shot by either the Germans or Italians. During the whole of our unpleasant experience the crew had never allowed their spirits to sag, and if the Italian staff officers had not put in their untimely appearance we had every intention of walking out of the hands of the police when night fell.

By this time I had acquired a pair of sandshoes and was feeling correspondingly elegant. The staff officers took me to Bardia, where I was given an excellent lunch by the Mayor. The mixture of concussion and a good lunch must have dimmed my sensibilities, for I was still far from realizing what had happened to me.

We were sent to Benghazi, where I was put into a small hotel bedroom for the night, heavily guarded by a zealous sentry who, though he did not actually sit in my room, spent his time putting his head round the door to make sure I had not disintegrated into space.

It was there and then, in that small bedroom, that I felt the walls close around me, shutting me in alone with the inescapable fact that I was a prisoner. Often in my life I had thought that I might be killed, and though death has no attraction to me, I regard it more or less phlegmatically.

People who enjoy life seldom have much fear of death, and having taken the precaution to squeeze the lemon do not grudge throwing the rind away. But never, even in the innermost recesses of my mind, had I contemplated being taken a prisoner. I regarded it as the calamity that befell other people, but never myself. In the ordinary sum of daily events I seemed to have a fairly equable philosophy, but it could not rise to this, and I faced despair.

To make matters worse the Italians were hatefully full of themselves, for they had had a bumper week with a galaxy of generals in the bag, and they rolled out the names to me, General O'Connor, General Neame, General Gambier-Parry and several brigadiers as make-weight. Their recitation succeeded in depressing me still further, for though I never think of the Italians as great warriors they did seem to be having all the luck.

My second night was spent at Circe in a hospital, and on the third day of my captivity I arrived at Tripoli. At Intelligence Headquarters I was first handed a whisky and soda—I suppose the traditional entry to an Englishman's heart—but as I detest whisky it availed them nothing and beyond my name and rank they were not very much wiser. I met Captain Camino, who had lived in England many years and afterwards proved himself most helpful to many British prisoners of war. Later Captain Camino took me on to the cavalry barracks, where I was treated as an honoured guest, and I wish that I could meet some of those officers again and thank them for their courtesy and kindness to me.

Brigadier Todhunter was brought to the same barracks, and, as it turned out, he and I were to share our captivity for another two and a half years.

We were transferred on board the ship which was to take us to Italy, but we were the first to arrive and had to wait three or four days in the harbour until we filled up with prisoners of war. A visiting Italian general kindly produced an English officer's cap for me to wear, swathed it in a red band and restored me my dignity!

I was recovering from the shock of finding myself a prisoner, and was beset by one idea only—how to escape. Our bombers were bombing us nightly, but so far unsuccessfully, and I longed for them to hit our ship to give me a chance of getting away in the confusion. The only hit made in the four days we were sitting in the harbour was on a small vessel at least a quarter of a mile away from us.

I was made very comfortable on board, with a cabin to myself, excellent food, and all the Italian officers extremely polite. An Italian staff officer had been put in charge of Todhunter and myself, and although in Tripoli we had found him rather pompous, later he thawed completely and we both became very attached to him and knew him as Tutti-Frutti.

The ship filled up and we sailed for Naples, hoping to be attacked by one of our submarines, but we never saw a sign of one, and reached Naples far too safely for our liking, wondering if Britannia ruled the other seas, as she did not appear very possessive in the Mediterranean.

At Naples Tutti-Frutti hustled us straight to a train, where we learned for the first time that our destination was Sulmona in the Abruzzi.

We were met at the station by the Commandant of our prison, Colonel Damiani, who seemed a nice man. He was in the Grenadiers, a crack Italian regiment. He took us to the Villa Medici, where we were to spend the next four months. It was a charming-looking villa surrounded by a pleasant unostentatious garden, with a lovely range of mountains to the east and very high hills in all the other directions. I was given a room to myself, but noticed with regret that we seemed to be heavily guarded.

The latest arrival in a prison camp has about one hour of a popularity that he never attains again during the rest of his captivity. He is news personified and as exciting as a Red Cross parcel. For my one hour the prisoners crowded round me, introducing themselves and asking questions, but out of nearly a dozen faces I saw no one familiar to me except by name and reputation.

Father of the camp by seniority was Lieutenant-General Sir Philip Neame, who had been captured the week previously with General O'Connor and Brigadier Combe, constituting a small triumph for the Hun and a serious loss to ourselves.

Neame had been commander of Cyrenaica and O'Connor was commanding British troops in Egypt, and together with Combe they were driving in Neame's car in the desert, took a wrong turning and ran slap into a body of Germans, who handed them over to the Italians.

Air Marshal Boyd was the oldest inhabitant of the villa, having made a forced landing in Sicily in 1940, and burned his plane. He had been taken prisoner with his personal assistant Flight-Lieutenant Leeming.

General Gambier-Parry was also incarcerated with us, having been captured at Mechile when the Armoured Division were surrounded by the Germans. Taken with him were Todhunter and Colonel Younghusband.

The first buzz of excitement over, O'Connor came up to me and said that we had a mutual friend, Anthony Muirhead, who had been an M.P. but had died. O'Connor knew that he had stayed with me in Poland. Straight away O'Connor and I paired off, and through adversity I found a very good friend.

Although heavily guarded, Sulmona offered us certain privileges which we did not appreciate fully until we had lost them. The country around was very beautiful, and we were allowed out for long walks and even picnics lasting the whole day with only one officer as escort. We were permitted to go shopping in the town, which was lucky from my point of view, for I possessed nothing at all except my bamboo stick and I had to replenish my wardrobe from the beginning. The quality of all my purchases was excellent, most of my clothes coming from the Unione Militare, the Italian equivalent of our N.A.A.F.I. One of the most treasured possessions is a little tin shaving mug embossed with a nursery rhyme in Italian which has travelled with me ever since Sulmona to do its shaving duty. It sometimes gets a rise in the social scale and goes for picnics. Money was arranged through government channels ; we were allowed a certain amount of our pay which helped towards buying food extras ; wine, cheese, fruit, etc. These were the days before Italy ran short of food herself and several months before the regular stream of Red Cross parcels.

The Commandant, Colonel Damiani, had an English wife, and continued to be most fair, just and pleasant to us. We had two guards to look after us. One of them, Lieutenant Ricciardi, was a most outstanding young man. He was tall and dark, with a quiet distinction, but with a disquieting shrewdness far beyond his years, and he knew our form exactly from A to Z. He was known to us all as "Gussie," and although he was extremely correct in his behaviour, we felt his underlying sympathy.

In the beginning our guards used to come and dine with us occasionally, but this was soon stopped, as it was feared we might be getting too friendly.

Dick O'Connor and I discussed escape plans from morning till night, but Sulmona was a most difficult place to get away from; it was far from any frontier, and the coast of the Adriatic was heavily guarded. There was another camp three or four miles off, and escape attempts had been made by several officers, but they had always been recaptured. We could have got out of our grounds without much difficulty, but only by abusing certain privileges given us by Gussie, and we could not bring ourselves to let him down to such an extent.

We were allowed to write as many letters as we liked on our own notepaper, but very little mail filtered through to us and practically no parcels.

Most of the prisoners embarked on some hobby or other, and the display of talent was remarkable. General Neame, well known as a big-game hunter, discovered a latent talent for embroidery and also started on the book he has since published, called *Playing with Strife*. O'Connor applied himself assiduously to learning Italian, a feat which was to be remarkably useful to us in the future, though no one could induce me to learn it. I can still see the look of hurt disappointment on the face of one of our jailers when he asked if we would care to take the golden opportunity of learning Italian, and I answered : " I don't want to learn your bloody language ! " If the truth were known I had absolutely no wish to learn anything. I had become a recent disciple to the cult of sun-bathing, and if you indulge long enough you attain a kind of Nirvana, the suspension of all thought and action, highly to be recommended for a life in prison. My only intensive study was the life and love story of the most charming little lizards who inhabited our terraces and, like me, had an urge towards the sun.

General Gambier-Parry was amused with the lizards, too, but he was also a most gifted man, made delightful sketches, was a first-class " forger " and a knowledgeable musician. But the lizards were more than enough for me. We slaughtered flies for them, placing them temptingly on the wall quite near us. Later, when lizards had got used to the sight of us, we balanced the flies on our hands and one lizard became tame enough to feed off us, although he would not allow any patting familiarites. I loved their aloof dignity and ungreedy natures, and found them fascinating, which perhaps shows what we were reduced to for our amusement.

Combe, Younghusband and Todhunter were enthusiastic gardeners and launched out into the poultry and rabbit world. Todhunter had to be removed from the rabbits, as he seemed to be the only person in the world who dissuaded them from breeding. He was transferred to the more erudite occupation of collecting the news from Italian newspapers and making a résumé of them in English, which he managed brilliantly, leaving the rabbits to think out things for themselves. Combe, by way of contrast, induced tired old hens to lay without any food whatsoever. He showered on them affection, which is the one thing very rarely offered to a hen, and was rewarded with prolific results.

I think that my birthday was the inaugurator of all birthday feasts, falling as it did about three weeks after our arrival. From then onwards they were solemnized with the inevitable rabbit, wine, cake and any morsel of excitement devised by Sergeant Bain, who ran our house-keeping, and Sergeant Baxter, who cooked for us.

The batmen were an excellent lot, and if we had been asked to pick them personally we could not have picked better men. My own batman, Prewett, had been in the Royal Gloucestershire Hussars, and I felt that there was a bond between us, and I hope he felt it, too.

My chief pleasure at Sulmona was the walks, as I think I am one of the few men who enjoy walking for its own sake, without trying to get anywhere or trying to kill something *en route*. With my mania for exercise, I do not understand any pace under four miles an hour. Some of my fellow prisoners grumbled at me and said I took all the pleasure away from a walk by walking so fast. I admit to being a very unattractive walking companion, for hurtling through the air makes me oblivious of all conversation as well as the view.

Sometimes we went for a picnic to a reservoir half-way up the mountainside, where some of the more intrepid of us bathed. I was content to watch as I dislike icy water, and think swimming the most boring of entertainments, and I enter the water under protest. At Sulmona, in the garden, we had a small goldfish pond which occasionally attained the right temperature for me after the sun had boiled it hard, but the reservoir was no temptation.

On one of the walks I was leading the way down the mountainside and got separated from the rest and only re-appeared in their midst long after they had arrived at the bottom. I found Gussie white about the gills and seething with controlled annoyance, thinking that, for all he knew, I might have been escaping. I got severely reproached.

From our villa we could see a hotel high up in the mountain and perched like an eagle's nest. It was known as Ter-minillio. Later it became famous for the sensational rescue by air of Mussolini by the Germans, after he had been imprisoned by his own people.

Summer wore on and fireflies in their thousands lightened our darkness, and into the middle of our almost human existence came the word that we were to be moved. It was rumoured to be a much more suitable jail somewhere near Florence. Our guards waxed enthusiastic over the description of it. They made it sound as though it combined the charm of the Garden of Eden with all the amenities of a modern country club. Our hearts rose in anticipation. . . .

CHAPTER XV

PRISON LIFE AT VINCIGLIATI

It was October when we left the Villa Medici. We all set off, escorted by Gussie, to be met at Sulmona station by two more prisoners who were to come with us. They were Lord Ranfurly and Lieutenant Smith, R.N.V.R., and they had been sitting in the neighbouring prison, although Ranfurly had been Neame's A.D.C. and was taken at the same time.

I had not met Ranfurly before, but he came up to me and told me that the first piece of information he had gleaned from the Italians was that I had dropped into their hands. As the last he had heard of me was that I was commanding a division in his native country, Northern Ireland, he did not believe them and was very surprised to hear I was in Sulmona.

We arrived at Florence and Todhunter and I were very touched to find our first escort, Tutti-Frutti, at the station to meet us ; he risked a severe reprimand for being there. Then we were put into cars for this delectable drive to our new paradise. We were all very busy scanning the countryside and wondering whether or not it was going to be good "escaping" country. We had been told that Vincigliati was at Fiesole ; the Italians breathed the name with such enchantment that I could well picture all the charms of *Decameron Nights* and was only wondering what we should do by day.

Whether the Castello di Vincigliati is rococo or baroque I do not know, but I do know that Queen Victoria lunched there and Queen Elizabeth did not sleep there, and I know better still that I thought it was the most horrible-looking place I had ever seen. It was a fortress, nothing more or less, perched on the side of a wretched hill, surrounded by ramparts and high walls, bristling with sentries all armed to the teeth. Our hearts, which had risen so high at the idea of leaving Sulmona, sank within us ; we were a silent, despondent bunch as we entered this vault of a prison.

We were in a small way consoled by the aspect of our new Commandant, the Duke of Montalto, who had been educated at Cheltenham, spoke perfect English and seemed to understand the British outlook and mentality. He had another guard with him, Lieutenant Visocchi, who spoke fluent English with a broad Scottish accent, having finished his studies in Edinburgh.

To our relief we were assigned a room each. I was ushered into a vast semi-basement apartment. Giving one look at it, I thought of the cold winter that was almost upon us, and asked for something simpler and smaller. Gambier-Parry took the large Spartan room, and I retired up to the first floor to a tiny room where I could raise a glorious fug with one electric fire in a very short time.

The *castello* was a deceptive sort of structure, for from the outside it looked enormous with its ramparts and walled-in gardens, but the house itself was quite a moderate size, built in an inner circle on four floors.

We learned that Vincigliati had belonged to an Englishman, a man called Temple Leader, who had been a Liberal Member of Parliament. We considered he had restored the *castello* in the most thoughtless fashion, giving all his attention to what went on above ground, and regardless of the many underground passages that he had sealed up. He made things very difficult for us.

Our lives became very different from what they had been in Sulmona. We were fully conscious every moment that we were prisoners ; we found that we had no priviliges, no picnics, no shopping, in fact nothing at all except what we ourselves could provide in the way of amusement.

Montalto was not to blame for this overwhelming severity, for he was undoubtedly sympathetic to us and eventually got removed for his sympathies, but he had a lordly overseer, one Colonel Bacci, who was commanding officer of the two or three neighbouring camps, and he certainly wasted neither love nor sympathy upon us.

Life having become disagreeably rigid with enforced discipline, we instinctively organized ourselves into a more or less civilized community, keeping up certain standards which were important to us, like changing for dinner, having baths twice a week, saying " Good morning " and keeping off politics and religion.

There were several additions to our prison; we were joined by Brigadiers Hargest, Stirling, Miles, Armstrong, Vaughan and Fanshawe. Hargest and Miles were New Zealanders, Stirling an ex-13th Hussar, Armstrong a South African, Vaughan in the Indian Cavalry and captured with Gambier-Parry, and Fanshawe in the Bays.

There was no sun to distract our thoughts, and only formal afternoon walks under heavy guard for air and exercise. Most of us were busy memorizing the country when we were out walking. It was a strain for me—I was born with no sense of direction and had only the sun and the moon on my side. We were abruptly switched from one walk to another when it was thought that we were getting to know it too well, but in spite of this, the knowledge we got from our walks was considerable, and turned out most useful. We were allowed to walk in any attire we liked, so I was always encased in innumerable sweaters which at a speed of four or four and a half miles per hour served the purpose, for me, of a Turkish bath.

The hobby mania became notably more persistent. Hargest and Miles joined Combe and Younghusband with the garden and coerced an amazing variety of vegetables and salad out of the unfriendly earth inside the castello walls. I let all my sadistic instincts loose upon the snails in their garden, became catcher-in-chief and saved the salad from worse than death.

Stirling had the most desirable effect on the rabbits and through his efforts they may now be Italy's enemy number one. But he ensured the success of our birthday feasts.

Vaughan took over the housekeeping with the help of Ranfurly, and with the arrival of Red Cross parcels it became a serious and difficult business; they were under strict supervision by the Italians, had to put all the food into store after careful examination of every tin or packet, and then to dole it out to our hungry satisfaction and try to provide us with some little surprising extra every day. We could no longer buy *ad lib.*, though there was an Italian sergeant detailed to do our shopping who found us wine and fruit and sometimes cheese, but by this time Italy was beginning to feel the pinch.

Boyd was an expert carpenter; in spite of the lack of material he made some charming things—boxes and tobacco jars—and took on Leeming and Dan Ranfurly as pupils. They became quite adepts; it kept them amused for hours.

Gambier-Parry had, to me, a most envied gift—sketching. He found inspiration in our hateful surroundings and did some delightful sketches of Vincigliati, in between his study of forgery, which could no doubt earn him a steady income in the underworld. He was also a musician of appreciation and organized weekly high-brow concerts to the pleasure of everyone except myself, as classical music is beyond me. Dan Ranfurly descended to my level and supplied us with all the old tunes which I know and love, and can hum.

In the evenings, after dinner, we played cards, starting off with poker, which I soon gave up as I invariably lost, being the worst card-holder alive as well as the worst player. Dan Ranfurly, who was our most expert gambler, did me the good turn of teaching me how to play backgammon, which proved a more sympathetic medium for my character. Eventually some gruelling coaching on Dan's part brought me to the pitch of playing with the best performers. Chief backgammon expert was Neame, but it made me perfectly furious to play with him, as he always seemed to have the luck of the devil. I never realized how funny my fury was until Dan produced a revue, with one scene depicting Neame and myself baring our teeth over our post-dinner game, myself using the most foul language, and ending with the pent-up phrase : " You have all the —— luck of a fat priest! "

Considering that we saw each other day in, day out, and at every meal for two and a half years, it was extraordinary what quiet harmony reigned among us. Beyond an occasional over-stretching of taut nerves when there was an escape plan on hand, I cannot remember any rows ; having the luxury of our own rooms, we could beat a strategic retreat whenever we got sick of the sight of each other. I cannot say that I think prison has an enlarging or ameliorating effect on a man's character, and I doubt if any of us were improved by the experience. Personally I made no searching discoveries of my soul, and still less of anyone else's, for living in such close proximity with one's fellow beings makes one positively shy of intimacy. It is shattering to be faced with it every day. Dick O'Connor and I were very close and were the antithesis of each other in many ways, which explains why we got on so well. I think all my friends are at opposite poles to myself, as I am sure that I could never stand anyone with my own defects.

Although Vincigliati itself was a bitter disappointment to us with its impregnable and unrelenting appearance, the actual move acted as a tremendous impetus and spur to our escape plans. From the moment we arrived in Vincigliati we never thought of anything else at all.

The ideas and the working out of the plans gave us a zest and a vital interest that nothing else could have done. Personally, without this one thought, I imagine I should either have become disgruntled, irascible and peppery, or else have reached the state of apathy I slide into in hospital when, after a long illness, I start to dread the mere idea of recovering and am perfectly content to stay in bed, preferably for ever.

In prison time passed in the same manner as in hospital, the hours very slowly but the weeks very quickly, and one needed a fixed idea or an effort of will not to get demoralized.

Dick O'Connor was as keen on escape as I was, and he and I talked plans, thought plans and dreamed plans until we must have shown contours all over us. It acted as a stimulant not only to our minds but to our bodies, for we knew it was essential to keep at the peak of physical fitness if we were to be able to seize an opportunity when it appeared.

I did a few reluctant exercises, with my ears well back, but kept most of my energies for my running walks. Dick took his training far more seriously and went in for extensive breathing exercises, showing such control that he must have been more than half way to becoming a Yogi.

The first plan we conceived was an escape by night.

The Italians, not content with the already Machiavellian planning of Mr. Temple Leader, had built yet another eight-foot wall to confine us into a still smaller space where we could be watched easily by the guards without any danger of their fraternizing with us. We proposed to climb this wall and tiptoe past the guard-room to the foot of the stairway, which led on to the highest part of the rampart over on the far side of the grounds where there was no sentry. The *castello* was locked at night, and we planned to drop over the ramparts into the moat about twenty feet below.

To get ourselves into training we made a practice course inside the main building which had a small courtyard, and every morning at the crack of dawn we got up and tried negotiating the sort of obstacles which we should meet on our way out. Luckily the Italians had no love for the early morning and it was our one uninterrupted chance of being free of them.

There were four of us in on this plan—Boyd, O'Connor, Combe and myself, and we were encouraged and helped by all the others whose turn would come later. We went up to the first floor, and came down on a rope as we would have to do over the final rampart. Having only one hand I could not manage it unaided, and Sergeant Baxter used to let me down, exactly as he proposed to do for the actual escape. Baxter was the most unselfish and gallant man, always ready to help as long as there was some danger to himself involved, and as enthusiastic over our escape as he would have been for his own. He was an ardent weight-lifting devotee, performed every gymnastic, and let down my eleven stone and over-six-foot body as if I had been a baby in a blanket.

One morning during rehearsal, O'Connor had a bad fall with the first trial of carrying a rucksack. It upset his balance by forcing his weight backwards, for which he had not allowed. We were worried whether his accident would arouse the suspicions of our guards who were all of them extremely astute and hotted up to strict surveillance of us by the new Commandant, Captain Tranquille, who had replaced the too friendly Montalto. Captain Tranquille had the reputation of being very anti-British and was heartily disliked by all the prisoners except O'Connor and myself. He had a saturnine appearance and very little *joie de vivre*, but Dick and I found him just, though very strict, always most polite, and we felt that he liked us in spite of our nationality.

Our first escape plan was so involved and intricate that we had committed the grave error of putting it down on paper complete with a map drawn by Miles. The mistake proved fatal and was never repeated, and from that moment on, all plans were carried in our heads and our memories were not allowed to fail us.

The one essential to our plan was a wet and windy night when the *castello* would be creaking with ghostly noises and we should stand a better chance of getting past the guard-room unheard. Needless to say the weather grew finer day by day, until we craved a cloud and ran in and out like anxious hens searching for a drop of water.

Whether our anxiety was contagious or whether our wide-awake guards spotted something suspicious, I do not know, but one fine day we were sitting after lunch when suddenly there was a clatter in the courtyard, and the unmistakable stamp of soldiers and at that moment into the room burst Captain Tranquille, who ordered all the officers to herd into one room and the servants to get back to their own quarters. It was a search, and our first one, although I believe searches ought to have been made periodically for precautionary reasons.

The orders were that each officer was to be taken out separately to witness the searching of his respective room, after which he was to go straight out into the garden without any opportunity of communicating with the rest of the prisoners.

Neame was the first to be taken out. His room was searched, and when nothing was found he was set free. Somehow he eluded the watchers, shot up the stairs to O'Connor's room where he knew the plans to be hidden, retrieved all the incriminating documents, crawled out along the narrow channel between the top rooms and the battlements and, finding a conveniently loose tile, shoved the papers under it. He came down again looking amazingly unconcerned, but was unable to impart the wonderful news to any of us.

In turn we were taken up to our rooms and searched, but naturally owing to Neame's brilliant exploit nothing was discovered, and the *tempo* of the hunt was slowing down, with the searchers visibly bored with no results.

The Commandant strolled on to the battlements to sniff the air, he gazed round at the beauties of the countryside, looked up, saw the raised tile above his head, put up his hand . . . and produced the plan. All was over for us, but I think no one was more astonished by his discovery than the commandant. For the searchers of course it was the breath of life, and they practically whooped with delight, visualizing some rapid promotion and a row of medals.

Next day General Chiappe, the corps commander, came and gave us all a lecture on the dangers of escape. He was a very nice man ; his lecture consisted mostly of regret that we had been found out, and the inference was that in like circumstances he would have done as we had.

This time we were not punished in any way, but more stringent restrictions were placed on us, and the *castello* walls festooned in brilliant floodlighting until we must have looked like the Paris Exhibition on a gala night. No longer were we allowed our *dégagé* attire for the walks ; we were ordered to wear our complete uniform and were escorted by still more guards, until the whole proceeding annoyed me so much that I refused to go out again.

My refusal was probably a great relief to the guards, not

only because they would not have to walk so fast, but because they may have thought indolence a sign that my spirit was cracking and that I would resign myself to spinning spaghetti on a fork and sleeping in the sun. As a matter of fact, my sulks produced a far better way of getting and keeping fit; it took half the time and had twice the effect. The guards slept in a different part outside the *castello*, and were not early risers so, as we had the whole house to ourselves in the early morning, I used to climb the one hundred and twenty steps of the *castello* twenty times without a pause carrying a rucksack with roughly twenty pounds in it, and dressed in several woollen sweaters and mufflers. Many of the others did the same, and especially Dick, who not content with twenty times, risked heart disease and was still alive after seventy-five climbs! These efforts, I still believe, were quite unsuspected by our guards, though they must have wondered sometimes how I continued to survive my seemingly lethargic existence.

Our next attempt at escape was to be made by day, and as a contrast from our last complicated failure, it was to be a very simple plot.

The rest of the prisoners were to try to draw the sentries away from a particular spot where O'Connor and I were to get over the ramparts, drop down and make for the hills. If we were successful Combe and Boyd were to follow an hour or two later.

That the ropes had been confiscated in the big search constituted a great loss, and we had to make some out of our sheets. O'Connor and his servant, Collins, made a very neat job of them by rolling them round tightly and binding them up with twine. Then as they were conspicuously white, it was thought advisable to stain them brown with wet earth, and they were then hung up to dry in O'Connor's bathroom next to his bedroom.

The jailers made a nightly tour of our rooms to see that we were tucked up safely and not meandering around with felonious intent, but up till that one particular night they had kept strictly to the same ritual and order of search. Of course, that night they chose to pioneer, advanced through O'Connor's bathroom and nearly hung themselves on the improvised rope strung across the room to dry. At once there was another clamour of excitement, and we were all roused and searched; but this time nothing was unearthed, and the authorities were unaware of who had meant to escape.

No punishment was administered, and we subsided to regain our breath and allow the jailers time to lull themselves into a feeling of security.

The Red Cross parcels and mail were coming through with wonderful regularity, and if there is anyone in the world who decries the Red Cross, he or she can never have been a prisoner. Words are inadequate to describe how much they meant to us, and not just for the food they brought, but for the fact that it meant we were not forgotten by those at home. We devoured the letters as eagerly as we devoured the food, and I think a cheerful letter did more for us than a vitamin tablet. Ever since prison days I have had a very different attitude to the post, and have voluntarily kept up a voluminous correspondence which would have struck horror in my heart in the active years before my capture. As the days went by the parcels became more and more wonderful. The contents kept us fighting fit with the aid of the *castello* steps, Vaughan and Ranfurly's fair distribution, and Baxter's cooking. Out of each parcel we kept our own sweets and some of our tobacco, and every day after lunch O'Connor and I sneaked upstairs to my room and had a childish stuff of sweets, and revelled in it. I love sugar, and pretend that it keeps me warm, and I have to be disagreeably firm with myself not to indulge too freely at the expense of my figure. Soon Dick and I renounced our stuffing, for we knew we must save all our supplies against the day of escape, and instead of eating we started collecting and concealing in unsuspected corners of our rooms.

The Red Cross sent representatives to see us three or four times during our two and a half years of imprisonment, and once the Papal Nuncio came in the guise of Father Christmas loaded with cigars, wine and a gold watch to raffle. It was won by Gambier-Parry. Otherwise we had no visitors, and were quite out of touch with the outside world, although news filtered through from the guards, and a more biased version from the Italian newspapers from which Todhunter still made his excellent résumé, diluting the news to its proper proportions.

Through the good offices of a mutual friend, I received great kindness from the Marchesa Origo, who, in the early days, sent me presents of tea for which we were most grateful. Once the Marchesa sent me a letter which I was not allowed to touch. It was held up for me to read at a distance of about three feet, a most mysterious proceeding, the reason for which I never fathomed.

We had applied for a doctor to swell our community, and had been allotted not only a very good doctor but a most helpful man. Another Vaughan by name; at heart he was a real insurgent and showed the right spirit by having a go at the Italians whenever he could.

Stirling had been sent to Rome from Vincigliati to be court-martialled by a Fascist court, not because he had over-run Italy with his rabbits but because months earlier he had written on a postcard that Italians were bastards. Stirling's powers of rhetoric were colossal; he practically persuaded the court that not only was it a term of endearment in English, but a compliment as well. He was sentenced to two years' imprisonment, but returned to Vincigliati and heard no more about it. Either the Fascist court judged honour to be satisfied, or that, indubitably, he was right!

Censorship of our letters was of the simplest; it consisted of erasing every word that the censor did not happen to understand. As my own handwriting is quite undecipherable even to myself, it meant that several friends of mine received letters or cards from me with only the name and address intact.

Books were a godsend, and we accumulated nearly a thousand volumes in our library, but the authorities wrenched a great deal of the aesthetic pleasure away from the books by tearing off their bindings before allowing us to handle them, thinking the covers might be concealing contraband. The books looked sad in their mutilation, devoid of individuality, and it almost hurt to read such bald bare words.

One day the order came through that our so-called jewellery was to be confiscated, as some kind of reprisal. I believe the Italian officers in prison in India had been selling their jewellery for money and the authorities decided to take their things away. Our jewellery merely consisted of watches, a few signet rings, and in my case a key-chain with all my lucky mascots hung on it. I felt very sad and rather apprehensive as if I was giving away my luck.

In prison life is made up of very little things, small pleasures and small hurts. It is like living in miniature—puppets in a puppet show—and one could not help a slight resentment when the jailers reduced us to still smaller size.

To the regret of O'Connor and myself Captain Tranquille had been succeeded by another commandant, but before leaving Tranquille came to say good-bye, and to tell us that he wanted to go and fight. I believe he went and fought against the Russians and was killed. His successor was suspiciously ingratiating and rather nauseated us with his attitude, which was utterly unlike the correct sympathy of the preceding commandants.

The next escape on the books was to be a gallant solo by O'Connor, who was nothing if he was not a trier.

Our studies of the life and habits of our guards and sentries would have put all Maeterlinck's observations of the bee into the shade. There was no movement, meal or machination of which we were not aware. At 2 p.m. the sentries changed on the ramparts, and there were just two or three seconds when, with a pinch of luck, it might be possible to leap over the battlements and get away unnoticed. O'Connor was determined to try. After lunch we were all posted to different portions of the grounds to watch, and give the signal all clear. O'Connor appeared, clad in a light raincoat covering a large pack on his back, and at the given signal Hargest and Miles legged him up the wall.

There was a desperate two seconds' delay when the wooden block he was carrying for attaching his rope caught in his belt, but he managed to free it and was over the parapet in a flash with a remarkable display of agility. We heaved sighs of relief feeling that at least he had got away, when, to our dismay, we saw a sentry running along the battlements towards the spot where Dick had disappeared, and we knew that he must have spotted something. Those two seconds' delay were responsible, for apparently the sentry had seen the flick of a vanishing hand as Dick was disappearing. He covered Dick with his rifle but did not shoot, calling for the carabinieri to come up and arrest Dick. Up stormed the ingratiating Commandant, at last shown in his true colours, screaming hysterically, first at the sentry for not shooting O'Connor, and then at the rest of us for being accomplices, and in general behaving like the swine that he was.

O'Connor was sent to his room, and we were all sitting rather depressed when Gussie put his head round the door and said: "The General is quite all right," which was typical of his nice character and took some of the sting out of the situation. All the same, nice as Gussie was, his powers of observation were uncomfortably acute, for when discussing Dick's attempt he said he had noticed that morning that the general had not shaved and wondered what it meant. As Dick is very fair and has practically no beard at all, it shows how little eluded Gussie's eagle eye.

The next day General Chiappe appeared again, and Dick was sentenced to one month's solitary confinement in another fortress, and the rest of us admonished and told that we could never escape from the *castello* alive.

As a nice distinction between a cad and a gentleman, General Chiappe rewarded the sentry for not shooting O'Connor and severely reprimanded the Commandant for his hysterical outburst.

We were subjected to more floodlighting and a further surfeit of barbed wire, and the whole regime was tightened up by sending away all our friendly guards, both Gussie and Visocchi, and replacing them by jailers in every meaning of the word.

The unpleasant Commandant was replaced by a most charming man, Major Guillaume, of whom I think most kindly to this day. Sorry as we were to lose Gussie in one way, we were rather relieved in another, for we should never have succeeded in getting out when we did as he would undoubtedly have spotted any plans in progress.

Gussie was replaced for the worse by a man we knew as Yellow-Belly, though I believe his name was Janicelli, and some other guard not kindly disposed to us. Altogether we were deploying about two hundred men away from the more active theatre of war. What with the accumulation of guards, floodlighting, sentries and barbed wire, the ramparts took on a forbidding aspect, and as it no longer seemed possible to go over the top of them, there was only one thing left to us, to go underneath. Immediately we deflected our attention from the great outdoors to the possibilities within.

CHAPTER XVI

PLANS FOR ESCAPE

THE *castello* with its crazy planning ought to have been a labyrinth of secret passages, leading straight to the top of the highest mountain or into a lovely lady's boudoir in a neighbouring villa, or at any rate somewhere outside its own radius. But no—all the passages led stupidly into another one, like a dog chasing its tail. We spent days on false trails and fruitless tappings before we came to the conclusion that as there was no tunnel suitable we must make one, starting from inside the *castello* and emerging the other side of the rampart walls, choosing the nearest point compatible with safety.

By a process of elimination we whittled the possibilities down to a starting-place somewhere behind our dining-room, which was only thirty or forty feet from the ramparts and separated from them by a disused chapel, which had been blocked up by the Italians.

The chapel formed the outside of the *castello* at the north-west corner directly under the high tower, and one side of it was against our dining-room, only separated by a small landing and a lift well. The lift well was used solely for bringing up our food from the kitchen below inhabited by our servants; Neame discovered that by lowering the lift we could stand on it and use it as a platform from which to bore through the wall into the chapel.

Our worst enemy was going to be noise, so we decided to limit our boring efforts to the early hours of the morning before our guards were about, and soon after lunch during their siesta hours.

The tools were pathetically elementary; all that could be found were some broken kitchen knives and a small crowbar and these weapons could never have chiselled their way through rock and stone but for the inflexible will and fixed determination of the men who wielded them.

After a few days of chipping and scraping we made an entry to the chapel and found it an eminently suitable starting-point with high windows that could not be looked into from the outside, and plenty of cubic space for the spoil.

Between the chapel and the sealed door into the court-yard was a porch about three steps lower than the floor of the chapel, and we decided this was the best spot to start operations, dig down for about ten feet and then drive a gallery straight under the ramparts emerging on the outside.

The escape party this time was to be Boyd and Combe, Hargest and Miles, and O'Connor (when he returned from his solitary confinement) and myself, and our thanks and gratitude are due to all our brother officers and men who helped us unstintingly and unswervingly for unselfish ends.

Neame with his sapper's knowledge gave us the lay-out for our labours, and with such a degree of accuracy that at the end we were hardly a centimetre out. Boyd and Ranfurly made the cover for our hole from the lift shaft to the chapel, and Ranfurly plastered it over and it was never detected.

We worked in shifts of two chiselling in the tunnel, with four watchers standing at various vantage points ready to give warning. From Vaughan's bedroom we found we could watch the gateways and see anyone approaching either the main or the servants' entries, and from his bathroom we had a complete and commanding view over the sentries, and when we pulled down the lattice blinds we could see without being seen.

Sergeant Bain made two essential contributions to our success; being a qualified electrician he fixed up a system of warning bells between Vaughan's room and the tunnel and also an electric light for the workers to work by.

As I was unfortunately unable to help with the digging I was given command of the watchers and the warning system. Whenever a sentry came within earshot of the tunnel, the bell was pressed and all work had to be stopped instantly, as it was if an Italian was seen to enter the *castello* gateway.

When we first started it seemed to us, the watchers, as if the noises issuing from the tunnel were positively alarming, and must reverberate to the ears of every sentry unless by a merciful Providence they happened to be stone deaf. Knocking was the most dangerous. Apart from the noise it seemed to shake the whole *castello* as well, and we were thankful when the silent knife could be used instead.

Occasionally I treated the diggers to a false alarm to keep them mobile and to see how quickly they could get out of the tunnel and into their rooms if the necessity arose. Not a very popular form of diversion !

It is extraordinary to think that for seven long months, and for at least four hours a day, the tunnel was our breath, our life and almost our food, and that we chiselled and bored and knifed and dug practically under the feet of the sentries and that they never suspected anything. Often whilst watching I would see a sentry pause and seem to listen, and I would think : " Oh God, he's heard something ! Now he'll find them, he can't help it." I found myself cursing the diggers with ungrateful curses for the noise the poor devils made, and I would ring the bell and wait . . . and then the sentry would turn on his heel and walk back again to his box and I knew that I had been a fool and panicked for nothing, and that the sentry had only heard some inoffensive sound which had not even caused him to be inquisitive. All the spoil was put into the chapel and eventually reached a height of ten feet.

Soon after our start Dick O'Connor came back and though silent and uncomplaining about his treatment, I learned afterwards that he had had a most insanitary time, but all that he would vouchsafe was that his Italian had improved considerably, and later I reaped the benefit of his learning. His solitary confinement had not dampened his enthusiasm for escaping ; in fact he seemed keener than ever and was most enthusiastic over our latest exploit. Being the king of administrators he took over command of all operations and perfected them to the last detail.

Neame gave us a weekly inspection to measure our progress, which varied from feet in some weeks, to an inch in others, according to what the diggers were up against, and the zeal of our sentries.

During digging hours all the other inhabitants of the *castello* acted as decoys, and assiduously made rival noises to compete with us, chopping wood, carpentering and even encouraging Combe's hens to be in league with us.

Gambier-Parry was putting in hours of concentrated endeavour, forging our papers. By the time he had finished they were perfect down to the final detail. Being also our musical director he was sent catalogues of Italian records all embellished with the portraits of the leading singers and musicians with the most speaking likeness to ourselves, and he used them for our identity photographs. My double looked the most awful thug to me but the rest found it a remarkable likeness, and I lost another illusion. Gambier-Parry had managed to purloin an Italian identity card and to copy it six times with all the necessary stamps, signatures and descriptions and on the correct paper. It was a work of art as well as devotion but proved a bad strain on his eyes. Being an artist, he had been allowed all the pens and indelible inks and materials necessary to the perfection of the papers, and his copies could not be told from the original.

We were laying in our stores against the great day, but taking infinite pains to conceal them from curious eyes, and we were in general trying to behave in as innocent and unprovocative a manner as possible, so as to encourage our guards to relax their strict vigil.

In the middle of our diggings, the Crown Princess of Italy, a daughter of King Albert of the Belgians, brought Castellani, the world-renowned doctor to Florence, to see me with a view to having me repatriated. I had been examined two or three times before for the same reason, although I personally was against it, because it would have meant I could take no further part in the war. The Crown Princess knew my Belgian relations and had tried to do many kind things for me, but they had all proved most difficult with the Fascists in power.

Castellani owed much to England, where, besides earning fame and gathering a knighthood, he had also gleaned a great deal of money, but from the time of the Abyssinian campaign his allegiance had swerved and he had become completely anti-British. When he came to examine me it was almost amusing to see how nervous he was of being thought in any way pro-British; he insisted on the Camp Commandant remaining in the room with us during the whole of the examination. I believe he did eventually recommend me for repatriation, but by the time word came through the bird had flown.

The tunnel was nearing completion, spring had arrived and our enthusiasm was running high. It was extraordinary that the interest and keenness had never waned for one minute, even when the difficulties seemed insurmountable and progress reduced to almost nothing. I can only put it down to the fact that, whether working or watching, each man was necessary to the others, and the idea of being essential kept us strung up without the danger of cracking. Our physical fitness due to the daily routine climbs, must have gone a long way towards keeping us unnervy, and the co-operation we received from all the others was the height and depth of every man's unselfishness.

The plan of escape was formulating. We decided that our best chance of getting clean away lay in going early after dinner when it was dark, so that we should have the benefit of the whole night before us to put as many miles as possible between ourselves, Vincigliati and the daylight. Our chief worry was the nightly round and inspection of our rooms by the Italian officers at 1.30 a.m., as we knew if we could avoid discovery then, we had until 11 a.m. the next morning before another inspection took place. We decided to try and deceive the guards with dummies in our beds, made possible because we had just started sleeping in mosquito nets, so the guards could not peer too closely at us ! Our batmen took over the job of making the dummies, and after seeing mine I can well understand the saying that no man is a hero to his valet ! At our trial inspection I was horrified at the object which met my eyes but as the rest of them said it was a striking likeness I kept a hurt silence and tried to forget.

Once out of the tunnel the party was to split up in pairs and find their ways to the frontier by different routes. Dick O'Connor gave me the greatest proof of his friendship by very generously saying that he would come with me, for ours was the more difficult plan. Being minus one eye and one hand I felt my appearance too noticeable to risk a train, and that our only chance lay in evaporating into the mountains, and trying to gain the Swiss frontier on foot. The others were going to Florence to take the train to Milan, and from there wend their devious ways into Switzerland.

We had all been collecting garments befitting our chosen spheres of life. Dick and I were to be peasants, and to account for any peculiarities in our Italian accents we had come from the Tyrol. I had an ancient pair of corduroys lent me by Gambier-Parry, a nondescript shirt and pull-over of my own, and a rag tied round my neck as a scarf, and Dick wore much the same. Luckily I had bought a pair of mountain boots in Sulmona, and they were the softest leather and the best boots I have ever had. As I had not been out of the grounds for months, just before the time for our escape I thought it wise to indulge gingerly in one or two walks, so as to get the feel of my boots again, and give my feet warning of how much might depend on them.

The tunnel finished, all we needed was a wet and preferably windy night to keep the sentries in their boxes and drown the noise, but rain is not easily come by in Italy in the spring, and we imagined we would have to learn a further lesson in patience. Neame was to be arbiter of the weather and his word final.

At last about March 24th, 1943, the right evening seemed to have arrived and we were preparing to go, when the weather suddenly changed and Neame called the night off. His decision engendered some strong feeling, and one of the escapers was sure we should never have a more suitable night. He was proved wrong, for the very next night presented itself as perfect for escape purposes. Neame gave the word and after dinner we all trooped upstairs to change, fetch our packs and assemble in the dining-room. Just as we were all in our escaping clothes there was a warning signal on our buzzer; an Italian officer coming into the *castello*. But after a few minutes of tense waiting it proved to be a false alarm, and down we streamed for our exit from *Campo Concentramento No.* 12.

Neame and Ranfurly preceded us, Neame to see that all was well with the tunnel and Ranfurly armed with a long knife to cut away the last piece of earth dividing us from the great outdoors.

O'Connor and I were the last to go, and as I crawled along that tunnel I had no nostalgic feelings; I was praying that I might manage all the obstacles in front of me without holding the others back. They had all been so good in letting me in on all the escape plans, and never made me feel that I was an embarrassment or not pulling my weight, and I did not want them to regret having taken me with them. Besides my twenty-five pound pack, I had a burberry over my arm and a stick, which to me is a most useful weapon to lever off against my lack of balance.

We expected to climb a barbed wire fence when we came up from the tunnel, with a big drop on to the road, but that night luck was with us, for we found that a nearby gate had been left open conveniently and very unexpectedly.

As the last of us emerged, Hargest put in place a piece of wood made by Boyd and Ranfurly which exactly fitted our escape hole, covered it with earth and pine needles, stamped them in, and then joined the rest of us. We all went along the road for a very short way before we dived into the cover of the hillside.

The moment we were off the road I took a deep breath and suddenly felt myself to be three times my size ! We were free . . . and freedom is a precious thing and worth the highest price a man can pay, and that moment I tasted it in full.

At the bottom of the hillside Dick and I parted from the others, shook hands silently, and let the darkness swallow us up. Having reconnoitred the roads and paths so carefully during our walks, Dick and I knew exactly how to proceed, and all went swimmingly for five or six miles when my sense of direction failed me and I took a wrong turning. Dick quickly spotted my mistake, although this bit of country was new to him, and after this blunder we washed out instinct and took all our directions from a map, which Dick read with the utmost ease, though I personally dislike them intensely and have absolutely no flair for them. Suddenly the beam of a searchlight found us, hung on us, and then to our relief passed over us, giving a stray cursory glance round the countryside.

All through the night we walked on and on without one pause, and the next morning found us trying to seek our way through the intricacies of Borgo San Lorenzo and on to the main Bologna road, from where we climbed a small hillock to have our first feed and rest. Both our rucksacks were filled with tins of bully beef, hard biscuits, chocolate and Horlick's milk tablets, and we were rationing ourselves with a view to lasting out a fortnight, by which time we hoped we should be somewhere near the frontier, two hundred and fifty miles from our start.

I was already paying the penalty for not going out for walks, for notwithstanding the softness of my boots, I was suffering acutely from a painfully blistered toe.

All that afternoon on we went, up hill and down dale, through lovely country which we were beginning to enjoy, and through several villages we could have done without. We met no trouble and were continuing to taste the savour of our freedom when evening descended and we approached a farm and asked if we might spend the night. The farmer gave us accommodation with his cows and we were extremely glad to have it ; if we had but known it, then, it was far and away the pleasantest and most welcoming night we were to spend !

The farmer was very hospitable, and invited us to the family dinner and gave us an excellent meal, thereby allowing us to preserve our rations for a rainy day. In the middle of the meal the door opened and in came one of the sons of the house, dressed in uniform, and my heart sank, but Dick rose magnificently to the occasion, broke into voluble Italian and jabbered away to the whole family as to the manner born, whilst I confined myself to eating and inwardly blessing the more studious Dick. After feeding we retired to the cows and found them most delightful sleeping companions. We had walked thirty-two miles carrying over twenty-five pounds and were probably very tired, though we were too exhilarated either to admit or notice it. My blistered toe was agony, but it was no good taking any notice of it as we had no time for maladies. The farmer insisted on giving us breakfast and would not take a penny in payment from us, and the only way we could think of repaying his kindness was by giving his daughter-in-law money to buy the grandchildren some presents. As usual in Italy, the family was prolific !

That day we had the most beautiful of all walks over wild mountainous country, carpeted by strongly scented violets, and we felt it desecration to stamp them down with our heavy hobnailed boots. The sun shone and we gloried in our escape

Mr Smythe Utd Ltd FUSION

TRAIN TICKET COLLECTOR
L M S EXCESS FARE TICKET

B.R. 3250

AL 094349

Date *11 Mch* 19 *56*

Ticket held* _____ No. _____

Excessed from *Perth*

To *Euston*

Train _____ Available until _____

Cause of Excess	Class	No. of Passengers		£	s.	d.
		Single	Return			
Without Tickets:— (a)*	*3rd*	*Two*				
(b) Workman						
Ticket short of destination						
Ticket out of date						
Difference between	*keeper*			*40/-*		
Third Class to First						
* Give description						

NOT TRANSFERABLE _____ Collector

Issued subject to the Bye-Laws, Regulations, Notices and
Conditions published in the Company's Bills and Notices.

from prison bars. By that evening the charm was lessened as we found ourselves in much more populated country with recurring villages. Our appearance was scruffy in the extreme and must have been very putting off, for we suffered two or three rebuffs and had great difficulty in finding a willing host. At last we found a lady, tender-hearted enough to allow us the freedom of her shed, complete with a stack of straw for our bones to lie on. Our involuntary hostess had first of all suggested that we should accommodate ourselves with some soldiers in the neighbourhood, and it took all Dick's flattery to persuade her that the charms of her shed were infinite! Dick and I passed a warm night in the closest proximity with his feet resting happily upon my face.

The next day was far from pleasant, the country stiff with soldiers and no wild mountains for friendly cover and poetic rhapsodies. As a last obstacle we came to a bridge stretching over a wide ravine, guarded by sentries at both ends of it, and from our point of view hopeless to try and cross. We had to retrace our steps and negotiate the ravine instead; it was steep and rough and as unpleasant as the day. Again poor Dick had to wheedle an ungracious lady into letting us tuck up with the cows, but judging from the expression on her face and her undisguised reluctance, she deemed it very hard luck on the cows.

Meals were, I suppose, on the monotonous side, but that did not worry either of us, as we are not enormous eaters and do not notice what we eat, and Italy is full of springs with drinking pumps all along the roads. For the first time I realized the life-giving properties of fresh water. A long, cool draught acted on us like champagne, and often now I think of that water and what it meant to us.

Another day of plodding along the hard high road. Although now we passed carabinieri without a tremor, we did not relish the publicity of the highway. That night we suffered a most inquisitive host who asked to see our papers. We palmed him off, saying we would show them to him in the morning, but we got up early before anyone was about and avoided that danger. After we had gone about two miles I found that I had lost my watch, which was a bitter loss to me as I am never happy unless I can gaze at the time every few minutes regardless of their importance! We did not feel inclined to face our nosey host again, so I had to cut my loss, but I missed my very old friend.

That afternoon we were pulled up by an officious individual, who claimed official status and demanded to see our papers. This was Gambier-Parry's moment, when his skill was put to its first rigid test. He emerged with flying colours, and O'Connor rose to further heights of Italian fancy and poured out answers to the volley of questions put by this unattractive man. I turned on my deaf-mute act, and soon the creature was satisfied and allowed us to pass on. Our relief was enormous, but the incident gave us tremendous confidence in Gambier-Parry's handiwork, especially to me, as I had been loath to have any papers at all and had been forcibly persuaded by O'Connor and Gambier-Parry, who, of course, were proved entirely right.

After our success it was only natural that we should meet with a setback, and that night not even Dick's fluency could get us a roof for the night. We had been anxious to get through the town of Vignola, but we were divided from it by a wide bridge, which we thought was heavily guarded in the way of all bridges. We resigned ourselves to spending the night inconspicuously underneath a farm cart standing in a farmyard, and we crossed the bridge in the early hours of the morning before anyone was stirring. A few miles beyond we found a nice field with a stream running through it, and we had our first shave and an extensive wash not one second before it was necessary. Various passers-by saluted us and occasionally insisted on a chat; our remarkable caps had led one inquisitor to ask if we were Yugoslavs. At least I think it was because of our caps, though Dick rather rudely suggested that it was more likely to be my fly buttons. Having sewn my money into the seams of my trousers, I was having great difficulty in doing them up.

Daily life was getting more and more difficult, for the country was far too open and thickly populated. We felt that we should move only by night, and try and find cover by day. That night we had a horrible walk through towns full of troops, and when we did dare to sit for a few minutes it was on a luxurious heap of uncut stones.

Again we found a field with a stream, and were about to repair our faces when we were inflicted with a covey of curious peasants, far too friendly and inquisitive for our liking, and we were glad to move on in the later afternoon and get rid of them.

Nothwithstanding Dick's aptitude and penchant for map-reading, the route was getting very difficult to find. We were in the Po valley, more or less due south of Verona, and the country in front of us was depressingly flat with villages one after another and some largish towns we had to try to avoid.

Feeling we might be wasting precious time, we stopped a passing peasant to ask him the way, and he gave us the startling information that if we went straight on we should come to a British P.O.W. camp. He had hardly got the words out before we whipped round and retreated down a nearby lane to re-study the map and consider the situation. The move was fatal, for as we were studying the map up rode two carabinieri on bicycles, gave us one look and dismounted, came up to us and asked for our papers. They scrutinized them and could find no fault with them, but, unfortunately, they proved to be that rare thing, men with an instinct. Our unsavoury appearance may have had a good deal to do with it, but these two carabinieri were devoured by a suspicion which could not be calmed, and my infirmities intrigued them so much that they insisted on peering at my stump, thinking I must be doing a conjuring trick with my left hand.

We knew the game was up, but when we informed our two captors of our identity they nearly embraced us and were so overcome with joy that they insisted we should finish the journey to their carabinieri post in a cart, making a triumphant entry. Obviously there was a price on our heads and our two friends kept telling us to be sure to tell the high authorities who it was who had captured us, as they felt sure the head carabinieri of their post would try and take the kudos, as well as the prize.

On arriving at the post there were some abortive attempts at interrogating us, but when that failed we all got down to abusing the Germans with wholehearted zeal, and were soon on excellent terms with our captors. We gave them all our left-over provisions, as we did not want to return with our rucksacks full of food, considering all the trouble the Italians had taken to see we had not got any.

The authorities at Bologna had been notified that we were in the bag, and two senior carabinieri officers came and fetched us and took us to their headquarters, where we were locked up for the night.

The next morning we were taken by train to Florence, where we caused a tremendous stir on the platform, and as we were being marched down bristling with guards we met one of our ex-warders who promptly cut us. He had been obsequiously friendly to us at Vincigliati and now we considered him a very poor thing.

We were handed over to the Vincigliati guards, who gave us a chilly reception, having been severely rated for letting us escape. On arriving back at the *castello* we were received with great chivalry by Major Guillaume, a most charming man, who bore us no ill-will for causing him a lot of trouble for which later he paid a heavy price by being imprisoned in a fortress.

We were subjected to a thorough search, but in the interval we had either got rid of or concealed anything incriminating. Dick had one serious loss, his shaving-stick, which must have given the searcher a pleasant and profitable surprise, as there was a certain amount of paper money hidden in it. I was deprived of a pipe, an innocent one, but my rather flamboyant flies were left discreetly alone ! When they had finished searching us we were taken to our rooms and placed under guard.

Though it was disappointing to have been caught, I felt so invigorated and exhilarated after our eight days of liberty that it saved me from any feeling of depression. Dick and I had covered one hundred and fifty miles with good loads on our backs, and with our united ages making one hundred and sixteen (mine took sixty-three of them) we had nothing to be ashamed of and, beyond my now completely skinned toe, we were twice the men we had been when we started. I personally never felt fitter in my life.

My biggest consolation that evening was a bath. Whenever I have one I lie back, revel in it, and deem it absolutely essential to my everyday existence, and yet whenever it is impossible to have one I don't miss it at all and wonder why I spend so much of life bothering with it ! During this first precious bath I had a row with my sentry, who insisted on opening the door and popping his head round to see if I had gone down the plug, and when my curses proved unavailing I sent for a carabinieri of more exalted rank, who allowed me to splash in peace.

I cannot remember how I was told of what had happened to our fellow escapers, but soon after getting back I had heard all their stories. Hargest and Miles had made a clean getaway and had not been heard of since. Combe had been recaptured in Milan the next morning when he was gazing intently into a shop window. He was arrested and told that he would be treated as a spy, but he ignored the threats and very courageously refused to make any revealing statement.

Boyd had been very near success, for he had boarded a goods train which had arrived at the Swiss frontier, but had tactlessly shunted into a goods yard. Boyd's patience having run out, he climbed out of his truck and was captured on the edge of freedom.

I learned also that twenty-four hours elapsed before our exit hole had been discovered, and then only by Gussie's dog. Gussie had left it behind when he had been sent away, but the dog proved too intimate a friend to us, and had unwittingly given away our secret. The guards then followed our trail backwards, and having fetched up in the disused chapel they proceeded to fill up the tunnel with concrete and frustrated anyone's efforts to pass that way again.

The morning after our return to the *castello* the area commander, General Chiappe, came up and we were taken before him. His greeting was typical of the man, a good soldier and a great gentleman, for the first thing he said was : " *Mes félicitations et mes condoléances.*" Then he sentenced us to the regulation punishment—one month's solitary confinement. This time we were not to be banished to a rival fortress, but were to be allowed to stay in our rooms, probably because the authorities did not want the fact broadcast that so many senior officers had managed to escape.

Under such conditions solitary confinement was not a hardship ; it was a privilege. When a dozen men have been bottled up together for a couple of years, it is only some ethical idea of manners which forces them to utter, and I found that if speech is silver, then silence was the purest of gold.

We were allowed out in pairs for an hour in the morning

and an hour in the afternoons for exercise in the grounds, but escorted by sentries to see we did not get within speaking distance of each other.

The batmen who had been with us the whole time and to whom we owed so much were sent away, but before they left they were allowed to come and say good-bye to us, and I had Prewett and Baxter in to see me, and I felt very sad to see them go.

Notwithstanding the very fair treatment meted out to us by most of our commandants, there were occasional curious instances of a different set of values. O'Connor had asked permission to attend the church service and had given his parole that he would not speak to anyone. The Italians saw fit to send an officer to that service to see that Dick kept his word, and could hardly understand when Dick, on seeing his escort, promptly returned to his room. Perhaps " parole " had no equivalent in Italian.

Our month's confinement ended, the daily routine seemed dull to deadly, and the guarding was so strict as to wipe out for the time being any more ideas of escaping.

A ripple of excitement broke over us when news came from the outside world that Mussolini, the Bullfrog of the Pontine Marshes, had blown himself up to such inflated size that he had burst.

We hoped this would mean Italy would sue for peace, and daily we waited for the news, but weeks passed and nothing happened and gradually our hopes subsided.

The supervisor of the camps, Colonel Bacci, had been replaced by a most despicable individual called Viviani, who descended to the pettiest of annoying restrictions for the sheer love of trying to irritate us, and I long to meet the gentleman again in more equal circumstances.

CHAPTER XVII

WINGS OF A DOVE

ONE night in the middle of August, I was having one of my backgammon duels with Neame, when an Italian officer entered and said that I was wanted in the next room. I found our commandant waiting to tell me that I was to go to Rome next morning. My news caused a buzz of excitement among the rest of the prisoners, for we knew enough to be aware that things were going badly with the Italians, and we wondered if my journey to Rome might have anything to do with an armistice. On the other hand, the Italians might be simply sick of me and intending to have me shot.

Dick came to help me pack and we argued the possibilities round in circles, arranging that if it proved to be that armistice was in the air I should send him back a book by hand of Yellow-Belly, who was to escort me. I hated the idea of leaving Dick still sitting in prison, after all our adventures together ; glad as I was to go, it took a lot of the gilt off the gingerbread when I realized he was not coming too. Dick got up early in the morning to see me off. On arriving at the front door my optimism rose at the sight of two very " posh " cars. I inquired who was to come in the second car, and when I heard the startling information that it was for my luggage, my spirits rose still higher. The Italians must have been well aware that my luggage consisted of some dirty socks and a few holey shirts and nothing more, so this grandiose procession seemed to augur well. I was bowed into the car by two very deferential officers and the whole atmosphere bore no resemblance to a firing squad.

On arriving in Rome I was taken to a voluptuous apartment in a private palace, reserved only for Most Important People. I went into luncheon immediately and sat down to a first course of a lobster mayonnaise that touched the very heights of civilization, and my humility dropped from me as I guzzled.

In the evening I was visited by the Italian Deputy Chief of Staff, General Zanussi, who circled warily round the truth, and told me that in view of my age and disabilities his government wished to repatriate me. Considering they had already had two years in which to achieve this noble desire, I waited for more. Then Zanussi broached the information that the Italian Government wished him to accompany me to England to discuss certain questions dealing with P.O.W.s, to which I replied it was a point for my government to decide. Zanussi asked me if I would mind getting into plain clothes, which brought forth the rejoinder that not only had I no clothes whatever, but that the Italians having taken all my money I had not the wherewithal to buy any. The General said that if I had no objection the Italian Government would be delighted to provide me with an adequate wardrobe. I felt quite faint at the thought of myself in a bright green suit with padded shoulders and a wasp waist, and replied nervously that I had no objection provided I did not resemble a gigolo. As I agreed, a tailor shot into the room with such precipitation that he must have been waiting outside with his ear clapped to the keyhole, and produced several patterns for the suit, and a selection of shirts and ties. I chose two white silk shirts of excellent quality and an unassuming dark reddish tie, and I awaited the suit with bated breath. It was ready for me next morning, completed in twelve hours without a fitting and was as good as anything that ever came out of Savile Row before the war, and greatly superior to anything that I can get now. With my nice clean shirt and quiet tie I put on a layer of *amour propre* with my suit.

Presently in came General Zanussi to ask if I was satisfied, and to tell me that a car was at my disposal to drive anywhere I liked, so long as I was accompanied by an Italian officer also in plain clothes. Zanussi then admitted that his government did not want the Germans to know that I had been let out, and at this admission I guessed that I was to be used for some form of negotiation.

I had a delightful surprise, for suddenly my jewellery, which had been confiscated at Vincigliati, was returned to me intact. Somehow I had never expected to see it again, and when I was handed my key chain with all my lucky charms attached I felt my luck had come back with it—their janglings in my pocket seemed so pleased and friendly as if they were glad to come home.

Zanussi took me to see his chief, General Roatta, who had been Military Attaché in Warsaw just after my mission there had come to an end in 1924. We had never met before, but had heard so much of each other that we felt ourselves to be old acquaintances, and had a very cordial meeting. He did not beat about the bush, but told me frankly that the Italians wished to ask for an armistice, and had already sent an Italian general to Lisbon to negotiate. Their anxieties were growing, and as they had heard no news of him they wished this time to send me as a token of their good faith with General Zanussi. We spoke in French; he had a delightful turn of phrase and remarked: *"J'ai envoyé une colombe, mais comme elle n'est pas retournée, je vais envoyer une seconde."* I have been called many things in my life before, but never, never a dove.

General Roatta told me that after we had made our escape from Vincigliati, descriptions were sent out to help our arrest. Not content with the fact that I was missing in one eye and one hand already, the description took off a leg as well, and General Roatta was rather surprised to see me walk into the room with two. He was most amiable, and asked me if I had everything I needed to make me comfortable. I hope that one day I shall see him to thank him for his kindness to me. I believe he was tried as a war criminal for having ill-treated the Yugoslavs, and was found guilty, though I heard that he managed to escape.

I was to stay in Rome until all arrangements for our journey were complete, and meantime was given a nice escort called Conti, who had been a restaurateur in London before the war. We went for drives and Conti showed me a number of the German positions and their headquarters, all of which would have interested me enormously had it not been for Conti's mania for airing his English, especially when we were surrounded by Germans, which kept me on tenterhooks, waiting for us to be arrested. I had been to Rome as a small boy with my father and must have endured a surfeit of sightseeing from which I have never recovered. I can endure the outsides of buildings, but not the insides, and mural paintings and headless, armless and almost pointless sculptures leave me quite unmoved. I was avoiding the Vatican City, not only because it was neutral, but because the British Minister at that time had shown himself to be unfriendly to me, and I had no wish to see him. Frascati with its innumerable fountains was much more to my taste, and as we strolled around the gardens in the sunshine, Conti regaled me with some very amusing but unrepeatable stories about a bishop.

My new passport told the world that I was an Italian born and educated in Algeria, which would account for my speaking French, and when all the papers were in order I started off with Zanussi and a staff officer for Lisbon.

Our arrival at the aerodrome near Rome was not encouraging, for it was swarming with German officers, but they eventually departed in planes bound for Germany, and we climbed into ours bound for Seville first stop.

General Zanussi was a charming man and a most delightful companion. He was slim and short and very well turned out, with an immovable monocle and the quick movements of a friendly bird. He was a fervent patriot and wanted the best for Italy, but was a realist and knew that she must work hard and straight to see that she gets it, and he himself did all he could to help her. He told me many things, and one item concerned him greatly, though I must admit it left me quite cold. Zanussi was most disquieted by the disappearance of Grandi, who at the outbreak of war had been Ambassador in London and on returning to Italy had joined the Fascist Cabinet and wielded great power. He disappeared the day of my release and had not shown sign anywhere.

Beyond a few Italian A.A. guns loosing off at us, the journey was quite uneventful and on landing at Seville we put up at an excellent hotel for the night. We were to go to Lisbon early next morning.

On reaching the aerodrome the first person we saw was Grandi. It was evident that he was no more anxious to see us than we were to see him, and we all discreetly looked in opposite directions. He was on our plane to Lisbon, and I had a splendid view of the back of his head for the whole of the journey.

I was not allowed to notify our embassy of my impending arrival, so that there was no flourish of trumpets to greet my arrival, and no one to meet Zanussi. In fact the only person to have official recognition at the airport was Signor Grandi, who was met by a car. A professional exile seems to be a very paying job ! In our more humble station we hired a taxi and I dropped General Zanussi and the extremely nice staff officer at the Italian Embassy and drove on to the British Embassy.

Sir Ronald Campbell, a former Ambassador in Paris, was British Ambassador to Portugal : he showed no great pleasure at seeing me, and obviously found me an embarrassing visitor. He told me that the first Italian general had been in Lisbon in conference with General Eisenhower's chief of staff and was already on his way to Italy with armistice terms, though no news had been heard of his arrival in Rome.

The Ambassador wired to London to tell the Foreign Office that I had arrived in Lisbon with General Zanussi, who wished to come on to London to discuss armistice terms. A reply came to say that I might come home, but that General Zanussi must go and see General Eisenhower in North Africa.

In the course of that afternoon General Zanussi came to see me at the embassy, and I told him that our people wished him to go and see General Eisenhower and that as I had only been allowed out of prison on the understanding that he was to come to England with me, I was now quite prepared to return to prison again. Zanussi at once said that he would not hear of my returning to Italy, adding he knew that I had done all that was possible to get him to England, and that he would go and see General Eisenhower as suggested. Returning to Italy would have been a terrible anti-climax after the excitement of the last few days, and I was not relishing the idea ; Zanussi's insistence was a great relief to me and a generous gesture on his part, in view of his disappointment at not coming to London.

Zanussi and I then went in to see the Ambassador, and to hear from him that the first Italian general had returned to Rome by train. This news came as a great shock to Zanussi, for he knew that the Germans were already deeply suspicious of their allies, and that the Italian general's diplomatic status would be a matter of complete indifference to them. If they ransacked his papers, which they were more than likely to do, negotiations would be compromised.

Whilst we were talking to the Ambassador a message was brought in from one of the embassy sleuth-hounds to report that two suspicious-looking individuals had arrived by plane that morning from Rome. Perhaps for once they were right.

General Zanussi said that he was quite prepared to return to Italy after seeing General Eisenhower in North Africa, but he would not consent to going overland, and insisted on either air or submarine as means of transport. In the end I think he went by air to Sicily, where he was picked up by an Italian plane after prearranged recognition signals. I bid Zanussi a very friendly adieu, and I hear from him often and have had the pleasure of seeing him in Italy in happier circumstances.

Lisbon was full of spies and seething with the intrigue peculiar to neutral capitals in war time, and I was not allowed out for fear of my being recognized. The Assistant Military Attaché kindly lodged me in his flat, where I stayed concealed for the next two days. The embassy thought it unwise for me to travel home on an English plane, and had booked a passage for me on a Dutch plane. Then someone got cold feet and thought I had better not travel at all, and I might be in Lisbon still if it had not been for the intervention of the British Minister, Henry Hopkinson, who very sensibly pooh-poohed the old wives' fears, and arranged for me to leave at midnight on August 27th, in the Dutch plane.

We had barely started when up came the Dutch pilot and said : " General, won't you come and sit in front with me ?" So much for secrecy ! As we were on our way home I did not feel it mattered very much, but when we landed at Bristol I reported the incident to the security officers, but as they knew the pilot well and were confident of his discretion, they were not concerned.

At Bristol I was met by the head of M.I.5, Brigadier Crockatt, who drove me to Beaconsfield to an Intelligence camp, where he told me I was to stay put, without setting foot outside, and forbidden to communicate with the outside world until I was given leave to. It all seemed very hard to me, having been shut up for two and a half years in Italy, to return home and virtually be imprisoned again.

That night, and for the first time in my life, I felt really important, like the chief character in one of Buchan's stories. I was taken up under cover of the black-out to see Mr. Attlee, who was deputizing for Mr. Winston Churchill as Prime Minister, Mr. Churchill having gone to the Three-Power Conference at Quebec. I had a long talk to Mr. Attlee, who asked me many questions, but I had been so long out of the world that I did not feel my answers could have been enlightening.

When my interview was over I was taken to the War Office to be interrogated by the Director of Military Intelligence. One of his first questions was, who had taken me to Lisbon ? When I told him General Zanussi he informed me that Zanussi had a very bad dossier. I told the D.M.I. that I know nothing about his record, but that I had seen the General under conditions which very soon reveal a man's character, and I had only good to tell of him. A few days later I was informed by the War Office that they had made a mistake about General Zanussi, so the fact that I stuck up for him may have saved him from eternal damnation.

Brigadier Crockatt did all he could for me at Beaconsfield to make life agreeable, and as he had been practically in charge of all escape plans from this end he was most interesting, and from my side I could tell him of our difficulties and weaknesses.

There was a large house in the park where our camp was situated, and a number of high-ranking Italian officers were imprisoned there. I should have enjoyed going to see them in our changed roles, and should also have liked to have seen how the conditions of their lives compared with ours in Italy, but I was not allowed in.

I knew that my friend and ex-A.D.C. Arthur Fitzgerald was living not far away at Buckland, and as he had been looking after my things whilst I had been abroad, I asked Crockatt if he would allow me to go and retrieve some clothes to wear. He gave me leave, and I had my first taste of freedom, though it was only comparative, as I was not allowed to move outside the grounds at Buckland.

The Italian armistice was announced on the night of September 7th, and the next morning I was a free man.

For some extraordinary reason, totally unmerited, it was assumed by the world that I had manipulated the armistice with Italy, and for a few days I achieved a cheap notoriety as embarrassing as it was inconvenient.

The chief inconvenience was the letters I received in their hundreds, many from relations and friends of prisoners in Italy asking for news of them which I could not give, as I had none. I had not met more than twenty prisoners during the whole of my time there, and we had no knowledge of anything outside our own small world. Eventually I answered everyone, and first of all I communicated with the relatives of my fellow prisoners at Vincigliati, but very diffidently, as I felt they must resent my coming home ahead of the rest. I met Lady O'Connor for the first time and had much to tell her, as Dick and I had founded and cemented a friendship which will stand the test of time.

I found a flat within a few hours of arriving in London, where I hoped to hide myself for a little, but within half an hour the first newspaper men arrived and I spent most of my time dodging them. One of my first calls was on the Red Cross to try and thank them for all they had done for us. I had been very lucky, for I had been classed as an invalid and as well as the ordinary prisoner's parcels, received many extras that had helped to give us a great variety of food, and really by the end we were feeding better than the Italians themselves. Mrs. Bromley Davenport was in charge of this depot. There are no ex-prisoners who are not firm admirers and devotees of the Red Cross. They gave us their time and their money, and saw to it that both were well spent.

After two or three days of freedom the fête-ings and the clamour and the social round began to pall on me, and I was soon chafing and wondering if the authorities would ever employ me again, or whether they were writing finis after my name. I half hoped I might still be sent to Yugoslavia, where the guerrillas seemed to be very active, and I could not think of anywhere else very suited to me.

Three weeks passed. I had answered all the letters, I had wined and dined *ad nauseam*, I had seen all the people I had wanted to see, and a great many that I hadn't, and into the middle of rapidly-advancing boredom came a ray of light. A message from Mr. Winston Churchill to go and stay the night at Chequers. . . .

CHAPTER XVIII

MR. CHURCHILL SENDS ME TO CHINA

Soon after I arrived at Chequers, Mr. Churchill took me up to his room to tell me that he wished to send me as his personal representative to Generalissimo Chiang Kai-shek. I felt very flattered but a little diffident, realizing my knowledge of world affairs to be a trifle distorted by the Italian version of them, but nevertheless I accepted the post on principle.

General Herbert Lumsden was also staying at Chequers,

and Mr. Churchill was sending him in the same capacity as his personal representative, but to General MacArthur in the Pacific.

China had never figured in my book of reckonings, and I imagined it as a long way off, full of whimsical little people with quaint customs who carved lovely jade ornaments and worshipped their grandmothers. I felt intrigued with the idea of setting foot in the Far East, and although reluctant to leave the war in the West, I felt I was lucky to be re-employed at all.

Lumsden and I spent the next three weeks being put in the picture of our respective theatres, finding staffs and collecting our kit. We were each to have two staff officers, but my personal difficulty was to find men suitable for China, as I felt it a necessity for them to have some knowledge of the Far East. I had a tremendous stroke of luck; out of several candidates I picked Major Dowler. Dowler was reasoned, unassuming, and equable and he had a knowledge of China without thinking he knew all there was to know about it. He turned out to be invaluable, worked himself to the bone, and exercised a most restraining influence on me, discreetly modifying my telegrams when they became a little strong.

A wire came from General Auchinleck at Delhi to say he had found a suitable A.D.C. for me, and on October 18th, 1943, Lumsden and his staff, Dowler and myself left by air from Hendon to fly to India. Our start was not propitious, for we arrived at Portreath in Cornwall, where we were held up for four days by bad weather. Finally we got off and proceeded by Gibraltar, Cairo, Karachi to New Delhi, where we were met by some of the staff of Lord Mountbatten, Commander-in-Chief, S.E.A.C., and taken to his headquarters mess at Faridkot House. This house had been lent him by the Maharajah of Faridkot, and was a most luxurious establishment run with great efficiency.

This was my first trip to India since my soldiering days in 1904, and though there had been many changes, both political and physical, it seemed to me that they were all for the worse, and I disliked the place as much as I had before. The native was coming into his own, but it did not succeed in making him look any happier, and he is the most wretched, down-trodden-looking creature in the Middle or Far East. New Delhi had sprung up like a mushroom, and although a sumptuous enterprise it did not appeal to me.

I was anxious to go on to China at once to take up my post, but learned in Delhi that there was no house ready for me in Chungking. As personal representative of the Prime Minister, I could not risk starting off on the wrong foot, and it was impossible for me to go to China and find myself homeless, for in Chinese eyes it would have entailed the biggest humiliation for me—" loss of face."

Delhi was full of interesting people, and meeting them after having been shut up for two and a half years went a little way to reconciling me to doing nothing.

Lord Wavell was our Viceroy; I met him for the first time, and did not suspect how often I should enjoy his hospitality on my many future trips to India. I feel that no man has done more for England than Wavell. He had the most difficult job with overburdening responsibilities, but he met them without flinching. He had great reserves of power, and whatever the crisis he could draw on them, and is the personification of " Unto thy day so shall thy strength be."

Wavell was a man who wasted very few words, and he was often silent, but when he did speak it was invariably to say something worth hearing and not for the pleasure of hearing his own voice. When asked for advice he gave it readily, and as he was interested in China I often sought his opinion, and always left him wiser than when I arrived.

General Sir Claude Auchinleck, the Commander-in-Chief in India, had had a very hard war, but his prestige among the Indians has never been surpassed.

One of the most interesting characters I met there was Orde Wingate, whose name and fame had become legendary. He was laid up with enteric at Viceroy's House, and a more intractable patient could not be imagined. He was being nursed with great care and infinite tact by Sister McGeary, who had been brought from Imphal specially to nurse him. A man of Wingate's forceful character and energy does not submit to sickness easily, and I have seldom met a man who gave me such an impression of determination. He was full of original ideas, and believed in them to a point of fanaticism, but they were always of a practical nature, and I doubt if there was another man alive who could have achieved what he had in Burma. The opposition to him was strong, and came not only from the Japs, as his unorthodox methods of soldiering did not meet with universal approval. That he succeeded as he did before his untimely death was due to his own determination and the personal support he received from Mr. Churchill, who believed in Wingate and saw to it that his beliefs were upheld.

I was feeling around trying to get as much information as I could on the subject of China, and I found one member of Mountbatten's staff of the greatest help to me. He was John Keswick, Mountbatten's political officer, and in private life the head of Jardine Matheson's in China. He was very knowledgeable and gave me much valuable advice, stressing the importance of making friends with the Chinese. He seemed to have a different attitude from that of the others, who knew China intimately, for they all appeared to shrug their shoulders, content to explain that : " East is East and West is West and never the twain shall meet ! " John Keswick implied quite differently, and I felt interested and pricked up my ears.

There seemed no prospect of my house being ready, and I continued to sit in Delhi, chafing at the bit, until it was decided to hold the Mena Conference and I was ordered to attend it. It was a pleasant break in the monotony, and as the Generalissimo and Madame Chiang Kai-shek were to go to the conference, I was excited at the idea of meeting them. They were to pass through Agra on their way to Cairo and I flew down there to meet them.

On arrival at the airfield I could not help noticing the behaviour of the Generalissimo's staff. Frankly they were terrified in case anything should go wrong with their arrangements, and as I had heard it said that the Generalissimo was a man of violent temper, I gathered there might be some truth in the accusation. We waited and a message came through that the plane was delayed and could not come in that night, so I left the airfield. Just after I had departed their plane landed, and having missed them at the airfield I followed them to the hotel. Madame had already retired after the long flight, but the Generalissimo received me.

I had made up my mind that I would not form an opinion of him at our first meeting. I have never met a Chinese, and all I knew of them was from the romantic novels of Lin Yutang, Daniele Varè and Pearl Buck. In spite of my resolutions to retain an unbiased outlook, I could not help but be tremendously impressed with the Generalissimo. Although he was a small man he had a great deal of simple dignity without any form of show, most unusual in dictators, who need an ornate façade to help to build them up to their worshipping public. The Generalissimo speaks no English and I speak no Chinese, so we had to depend on the efforts of an interpreter. The next morning I returned to Delhi, and soon after we left for Cairo.

The Mena Conference was the first and last of the Big Three meetings which I attended, and though I cannot profess to have profited much from the experience, it did give me an insight into things I knew nothing about.

Mena produced such a galaxy of star names that it made it difficult for anyone to stand out, but of all the great personalities gathered together those that impressed me most were President Roosevelt, General Marshall, Admiral King, Admiral Cunningham and General Alanbrooke. I placed General Marshall at the top of my list, for rarely have I seen a man who gave out such a feeling of mental strength and straightforwardness, which was accentuated by his physical appearance.

I have left Mr. Winston Churchill out of my list, for I put him in a class by himself, as do many other people of the world, regardless of nationality.

I met Madame Chiang Kai-shek for the first time, and was struck forcibly by her attractive appearance and obvious cleverness.

Out of a sea of faces I picked out one of remarkable strength and pugnacity, and on asking who it was, found it was General Chennault of Flying Tiger fame. It was an extraordinary face, engraven with a million lines of character, and I was told that Mr. Churchill was supposed to have seen him at a conference in the U.S.A. and asked who he was. On hearing it was Chennault, Mr. Churchill said : " I'm so glad he's on our side." Chennault had collected a crowd of hard-fighting American airmen to fight against the Japs, after they had attacked China, long before 1939. China owes Chennault and his volunteer group a large debt of gratitude, and she knows it, and never hesitates to acclaim them.

General Stilwell, Chief of Staff to the Generalissimo, was also at Mena, and though undoubtedly a personality, it was that of the fighting soldier and no more, and he was an extremely hard man to deal with. He had strong and definite ideas of what he wanted, but no facility in putting them forward. He was very friendly to me and offered to put me up in Chungking until my house was ready for me, but I declined, as I did not think this would prove satisfactory to either of us, and I preferred to wait for my own abode.

Six weeks after I had arrived in Delhi word came through that all was ready for me, and the R.A.F. provided me with a plane for my first flight over the famous " Hump."

I left Delhi with my two staff officers, a clerk, a batman and a vast quantity of stores. Strangely enough, I was seen off by the same man who had sped me on my unlucky trip to Yugoslavia, Air-Marshal Sir John Baldwin, and I am afraid the very sight of him brought on a rush of superstitious qualms.

The first stop was at Dinjaan, where we were to get the latest weather reports for our " Hump " flight. Within half an hour of our leaving Dinjaan, Jap bombers raided it, but by that time we were fourteen thousand feet up in the air, dodging in and out of the mountain peaks in brilliant sunshine. My qualms proved quite unjustified, for my first flight over the dreaded " Hump " was made under the most perfect conditions, and remains one of the very few times that I ever saw it, for usually we had to fly high above it lost in cloud. At times we were flying level with the peaks, and I could not help feeling a thrill of fear at their sharp unfriendliness, with an occasional mountain top towering high above us, silhouetted against the clear blue sky.

Jap planes were very active in those days, and we flew much farther north than we did subsequently when Chennault got the measure of the Jap Air Force and drove them out of those skies.

Once over the mountains I waited eagerly for my first sight of China. When it came it was the most unsurprising thing in the world, exactly as I had imagined it ; the picture books all come to life. The country was under heavy cultivation, with every little piece of earth showing and growing something. The fields are a curious sight from the air, for they follow the contours of the hills, and in miniature they have an exaggerated and odd perspective.

Our first stop in China was Kunming; as we circled above it preparing to land, we saw it sitting near a large lake, surrounded by high mountains, and making a wonderful picture in the crystal-clear air and dazzling sun.

We lunched and refuelled and were about to continue when word came from Stilwell that weather conditions were not suitable for our flight, and that he was not keen for me to fly to Chungking with a British pilot, as he felt the American pilots had a better knowledge of the intricacies of the flight, and especially of the landing. I had every confidence in my pilot's ability to fly anything anywhere, for he was Flight-Lieutenant Vlasto and one of our best British pilots. I spent the night at Kunming, and Stilwell agreed to Vlasto flying me on to Chungking provided that an American pilot came with us. When I had my first glimpse of the Chungking aerodrome I did not wonder at Stilwell's insistence, for after a tricky three-hour flight I saw a small patch of baked earth surrounded by menacing mountains. I was told I was lucky to see it : usually the whole field was invisible owing to cloud and mist.

I was met at the airfield by General Chen Cheng, the head of the Foreign Affairs Bureau, and he took me to the house which the Generalissimo had kindly put at my disposal. The house was at Hua Ling Chiao, a new quarter just outside the town, and sitting on the Chialing river, which is a tributary of its big brother, the Yangtze. The house was delightful, fully equipped with a staff and a motor-car. Chungking was very picturesque, situated on the sides of the mountains overlooking both the Yangtze and the Chialing. It is a city of steps, stone steps about three feet wide and eight or nine inches in height ; innumerable flights of them bear witness to the toil of the Chinese. There were very few good houses left standing, for the Japs had been very free with their bombs, and the Chinese had practically no defence against air attacks. The climate is bad, extremely hot and with a high humidity in summer, and in winter, although not severely cold, it is perpetually damp, and for a great part of the year the place is shrouded in mist.

My house, at the bottom of a hill, was going to be hot and airless in the summer, and as I saw another house standing empty some hundred feet above, I asked General Chen Cheng if I might have it. He told me that they had thought of giving it to me, but as there were one hundred and twenty steps to be climbed to get to it they had been chary of suggesting it. They did not know of my Italian training, nor that I consider steps or stairs essential to keep my figure under control.

The steps were rather trying in hot weather, but otherwise the house had every advantage, and as it was half-way into the country we could walk straight out into the hills clad only in shorts and native sandals and be sure of not meeting any other official. The house had a nice garden which flourished under Dowler's care, and the view from my bedroom window right over the river and up to the hills beyond remained a daily delight.

In the shops of the town colours were of a deep and rich intensity that made the most ordinary fruit and vegetables remarkable; the luscious redness of oranges and tomatoes was unforgettable. I loved to go through the streets at night on my way out to dinner; they were lined with vendors, whose little stalls were lit by tiny flaming torches which imbued their wares with a mysterious attraction they did not have by day. Again oranges won the prize for colour; the primitive floodlighting made them look like food for the gods.

There were always crowds around the stalls, buying, buying, and the chop-houses were full of Chinese eating their weird but delicious fairy-tale food at all hours of the day and night. In this part of China neither men nor women are attractive. The men have tremendous muscular development, and they carry loads which I could not lift from the ground, swinging them up easily to their shoulders. Many coolies wear enormous hats which act as umbrellas or sunshades according to the needs of the moment. When I saw Chinese carrying their funny little umbrellas I imagined they were ornaments, until I saw Chinese soldiers carrying them too, not as a badge of respectability as I do, but for good practical use when it rained.

The language sounded strange and full of nasal intonations; accustomed though I was to foreign languages, I could make nothing of it. Most of the upper classes speak English and, knowing that to master Chinese was quite beyond me, I made no attempt to learn the language, although I realized that I would be missing a great deal without it.

The visiting-card habit is deeply ingrained in the Chinese soul. I was continually having visiting cards thrust into my hand by whomever I happened to be speaking to; the trouble was that when I got home and started to try to sort them out I could never manage to fit faces to the names.

Two things struck me forcibly: the first was the amount of sheer hard work the people were doing, and the second their cheerfulness in doing it. Coming from a country where hard work is unpopular and usually indulged in by voluntary workers only, I found this impressive. Their smiling faces were in complete contrast to those of the depressed Indians, although they had much less to smile about, after years of war, bombardment and hunger.

The cheerfulness of the Chinese had more than a touch of embarrassment for me; in the beginning I kept feeling that they were laughing at me, and were being deliberately rude. Soon I realized that laughter is their normal reaction to people and to life, and I envied them their philosophy; they had desperate need of it. All the same, they often made me feel self-conscious.

The upper classes were not quite so obviously cheerful, but they were delightful. The Chinese women must be the most attractive in the world: they have enchanting manners and a confiding charm calculated to enhance the vanity of a man by making him feel twice his size and tremendously important—most soothing after the frankness of the English.

When they are young they seem artless and gaily inconsequential, but very soon after marriage they take a firm grip on their husbands and family, although they always retain their charming femininity. By the time they reach forty years of age they are a great power in the household, and I am told that then they are allowed to grow fat, but I must say I never noticed it.

Their dress is very becoming and of an almost uniform

simplicity, varying only in materials and embroidery. Many women have adopted European styles of hairdressing.

The men no longer wear their Chinese gowns, except occasionally in their own houses ; they wear ordinary European dress, with the exception of the Generalissimo, who, standing as the symbol of China, prefers to wear Chinese dress when not in uniform. To my regret the traditional pigtail of my imaginary excursions in China was no longer to be seen.

Prices seemed to me fantastic, and the value of the Chinese dollar changed as quickly as the tides ; after buying a flat-iron for £8 and a box of matches for half a crown, I gave up shopping and asked General Cheng if he would get it done for me instead. It seems to be my fate to live in countries where inflation rules the day and where money is almost valueless and has to be carried round in suit-cases as in Poland or Germany after the 1914–18 War.

Domestically I lived in real comfort, bordering on luxury, considering the times of stress. I had a most excellent staff, with a wonderful Chinese cook who cooked European food as skilfully as Chinese. I served European food at all my parties, and as I dislike cocktail and lunch parties I made it a practice to give frequent dinners to ten or twelve guests. I liked the custom in China of a lengthy gathering before dinner, drinking cocktails or tea, followed by a delicious dinner of seven or eight courses after which one could go home without being accused of bad manners. It suited me to the ground, as I hate sitting up late, and always got up in the morning at 5.30 a.m. I used chopsticks ; although I never became an expert, they had the unique effect of making me eat slowly which nothing had achieved before. Rice wine, not a teetotal drink by any means, is drunk throughout the meal. The Chinese art of absorption is large and their hospitality larger. Luckily, the serious drinking of healths known as " Gambe " which means " no heel-taps," takes place during the meal ; I personally have no capacity for drink on an empty stomach. Incidentally, an empty stomach would have been an achievement in China, where eating is so much a part of official jobs, but although a great deal of food is served, it is light and never gives one that awful feeling of having over-eaten.

Sir Horace Seymour was our Ambassador in China, but he

was on leave when I arrived and Lady Seymour kindly gave a large cocktail party for me where I met all the prominent Chinese and the various diplomats. Almost at once I felt the warmth and friendliness given out by this far country and her people; I felt that they accepted me as a person, irrespective of my job or my nationality. If the spirit of that small community could be infused into the world, U.N.O. would be out of a job.

After I had been in China a few weeks and had realized the enormous distances I had to contend with, I felt that it was essential to the success of my job to have my own plane. The British had none in China, and though the Americans were most generous and offered me a plane on every occasion, I felt it was bad for British prestige to behave like a poor relation waiting for crumbs from the rich man's table. I asked Lord Mountbatten if he could provide me with a plane; he passed on the request to the R.A.F., who said they would try and get me one, but it would be some months before delivery. My need was almost desperate, for China is a continent more than a country, and I could not carry out my duties sitting in Chungking writing letters. I wired to Mr. Churchill for his help in the matter, and he at once sent a most characteristic wire to the R.A.F. worded as follows :

" You will provide General Carton de Wiart with a plane and report to me weekly until he gets it." Needless to say I got it very soon.

The R.A.F. were anxious for me to fly a British plane in China, showing that our machines could compete with the extreme weather conditions which prevail, and they sent me out a Wellington. As it was a Wellington that had deposited me in the sea *en route* for Yugoslavia, I was not particularly keen, but felt beggars could not be choosers. I made two trips to Ceylon in it, three thousand miles each way, and it behaved quite nicely, but on the third journey blotted its copy-book. We were returning from India loaded with stores and with the bomb chambers filled to the brim with liquid propaganda, which was unprocurable in Chungking. We were about to land on our aerodrome at Chungking when my pilot sent me word that we were going to crash. I felt this was a pity in view of our precious cargo, but prepared myself for a bump. It came; the plane was completely flattened out and although none of us was hurt I had great fears for our liquor. The usual crowd of people collected round us, busy gaping, and among them I saw an American mechanic. I suggested that he should help us jack up the plane to get at the bomb-chambers and look at the remains. He said it was not possible, but when I told him that if he managed it he would get a bottle of whisky, he took a more hopeful view of the situation. Whisky at that moment in China was worth £130 a bottle, so it was a good tip. I left my competent A.D.C., Captain Donald Eckford, in charge of the salvaging party and he returned a few hours later with our entire cargo intact.

Another Wellington turned up to replace the first casualty, but crashed owing to a burst tyre. Again none of us was hurt, but the plane was a total wreck and our Wellington skeletons were dotted round China. The third one crashed on its test flight in India, and that was the end of my Wellingtons. I was given a Dakota C.47, which in two years of constant flying never failed me. It was ably piloted, first by Paddy Noble and then by Ralph Shaw. I had absolute confidence in its flying powers and capacity to compete with the tricky conditions in China.

CHAPTER XIX

CHINESE CHARIVARI

My house on the hill was possessed of delightful neighbours, who added considerably to its charm. On one side of me were Mr. and Mrs. R. C. Chen, who became my greatest friends, and from the first made me realize the rare charm and quality of the Chinese.

R. C. Chen was a Director of the Bank of China and Mrs. R. C. was one of the smartest and most attractive women in society. My other neighbour was Mr. T. V. Soong, a brother of Madame Chiang Kai-shek. He had been Prime Minister and Foreign Minister of China, was a renowned financier and very Westernized in his ideas and manners.

At that time Mr. K. C. Wu was the vice-Minister of Foreign

Affairs, an exceptional man who allowed nothing to floor him and got through an incredible amount of work. Now he is Mayor of Shanghai, and it is hard to imagine a more difficult job, but he will have brought to it all the courage and energy discoverable in man. Mrs. K. C. Wu is like a lovely little piece of porcelain, and one of the prettiest women in a land of pretty women. A devoted and wonderful couple, they became great friends of mine.

The Yangtze is a fascinating and turbulent river crammed with river craft of every size and shape and with a life of its own. Some of the summer residences were on the opposite side of the river to my house and parties entailed most adventurous journeys by boat and steps. One day I was crossing to the south bank on a very crowded steamer and there was a man on board selling something to a seething and enthusiastic crowd. He held forth without pausing for breath, extolling the virtues of his wares, and even though I could not understand a word of what he was saying, I could sense the tender praise in his voice. His success was electrical. He did a roaring trade with both men and women, and, my curiosity having been aroused, I asked my interpreter what the man was selling. His answer was: " Only aphrodisiacs, sir." They seem extremely popular in the East, and no doubt in the West, too, but in the West there is more secretiveness and feigned ignorance of such matters. One night I was dining with a Chinese of some importance; he told me with undisguised relish that for one course of our dinner we were to eat bear's paws. Apparently this delicacy answered the same requirements as our ferry-boat friend's popular snack, but I can only think that this little bear had been born without ambition, for I could perceive no change coming over the company.

In spite of these two incidents I saw and heard less on the subject of love in China than in any other country of my acquaintance. I am sure their reticence is not for hypocritical reasons, but simply from feelings of delicacy and reserving the right topic for the right place. I saw no courting couples in dark lanes or side alleys, and in public their behaviour was most decorous ; I have no knowledge of what goes on indoors.

Acres and acres of the countryside were taken up by cemeteries, so much so that one could not help thinking that the Chinese die more often than anyone else. There were very few places which did not hold coffins, and when my garden was being made in Chungking we found that several people had been buried in it. Funerals were incessant and made a curious sight with the procession of mourners all dressed in white. After a cholera epidemic there were never enough coffins to go round, or else the poor could not afford them, and one would see the corpse being carried through the streets with a cock sitting on its chest. The idea of the cock was nourishment for the corpse on his journey to the other world ; as a rule the cock was a dead one, but some-times I saw a live one sitting on the chest of the corpse, which would have proved a pretty tough meal.

In addition to being the Prime Minister's personal repre-sentative, I was also acting as Lord Mountbatten's liaison officer with the Generalissimo. Although we had some dif-ferences of opinion, I have a great affection for Mountbatten, and a high regard for his abilities and attractive personality. Dicky Mountbatten is a curious mixture of royal-democracy; he can mix equally well on a high or low level and be exactly right in each. There is a story of him that is utterly character-istic. He was inspecting some American posts, and it was obvious that the Americans had been well primed beforehand as to their behaviour. All went swimmingly until Mount-batten came up to a certain sentry who immediately stretched out his hand and said : " I'm Brown from Texas." Mount-batten, not the least taken aback, shook the outstretched hand and answered: " There are a lot of you Texans out here." Whereupon the soldier replied : " Yes, that's why the war's going so well."

Chief of staff to Lord Mountbatten was Lieutenant-General Sir Frederick Browning, who had succeeded Sir Henry Pownall, after Pownall had gone home for a badly-needed rest. Pownall had had a very hard war and had been carrying on for months suffering from ill-health. Boy Browning came out soon after his Arnhem epic, which had shown him as a man of great fighting qualities and a fine leader. He was one of the few officers of high rank who had never been to staff college, but I have never known a better staff officer. Nothing was too much trouble for him and he was ready to help over anything, whether great or small.

Early in 1944 General Wingate came up to Chungking to stay with me as he wanted to see the Generalissimo and try to get help for his forces in Burma. Wingate offered to take a number of Chinese to train them in guerrilla warfare, and I could see that the Generalissimo was very impressed with him. I enjoyed his visit enormously, for he was an invigorating companion with his tremendous enthusiasm for whatever he had on hand. Soon after he left me I heard the tragic news that he had been killed in an air crash, and could not help wondering what would happen to his force now that the main inspiration of it had gone. That it continued on its glorious career was another proof of Wingate's greatness, for he had imbued the officers and men with his own spirit, and they continued their gruelling war in a manner which would have made him very proud.

After Wingate's death I felt that I should like to go down and see his force in Burma, now commanded by General Lentaigne. Several times before I had suggested to Stilwell that I should come down, but he had always put me off as he was not at all anxious to have outsiders putting their noses in, which I could well understand.

Major Louis Kung, a nephew of Madame Chiang Kai-shek, who was serving in the Scots Guards, was in China on six months' leave, and he came with me on this trip as an extra A.D.C. I took him on many trips and found him an expert organizer, always seeing that we were met by cars sent by the Bank of China. If we had been left to the mercies of our British organization, often we should have had to walk !

On this trip to Burma I left my own plane at an Indian airfield and was flown down by the ever-helpful American Air Force in one of their transport planes. As we were about to land I saw below us a small area cut out of a forest and entirely submerged by water, and was informed that that was the airfield. My feelings were that if we managed to land I still did not see how any plane could take off again, but I did not know the American Air Force. My admiration grew hourly when I saw the country they had to operate in and found that they carved airfields out of jungle, which was often impenetrable forest, in a matter of days. Their losses were heavy and an American officer in charge of the airfield from which I took off told me that they had had eleven crashes that day, but nothing could shake or deter them.

We went on to General Slim's headquarters to spend the night. I had seen General Slim before, but I had never met him on his own ground, and when I saw him here with his staff and his troops, I realized what an outstanding man he was. Like Wingate, he inspired keenness and confidence, and what he achieved, considering the difficulties he had to contend with, was nothing short of miraculous.

I went down to Arakan and had an interesting day there with General Festing, who took me over some of his positions. He was commanding the 36th Division and he earned the highest praise for his work even from General Stilwell, who did not give praise easily. Festing drove us himself in a jeep, and in that country it was an exciting experience.

I was very keen to go to Imphal, but the Jap Air Force were too active for me to be provided with an escort, and I had to give up the idea. I had seen enough to make me realize what the 14th Army were up against, with nature proving as bitter an enemy as the Japs. I came away feeling that I should have been a proud man if I could have served with them, and it does not say much for the world that they were ever known as " The Forgotten Army." Posterity will be better informed.

Although the Generalissimo and Madame Chiang Kai-shek were the most important factors of my life in China, I have left it until now to describe them. Mr. Churchill in making me his personal representative had given me a position and a natural asset which were almost unassailable, and from the beginning the Generalissimo's and Madame's treatment of me had been most kind and amazingly friendly. I think that they both felt that I was absolutely frank with them, and that I personally was there to help them, although during my stay there were many difficult situations when England was not always helpful to China.

My first impressions of the Generalissimo's calm and dignity were fully confirmed, and I never saw a sign of the violent temper of which he was accused. In actual fact I have never seen a man with such self-control ; in spite of the continual crises and difficulties which swept over him, he never showed an outward sign of feeling. As a man he was head and shoulders above any other man in China, a fact even admitted by the Communists. He holds very decided views, and they are difficult to alter, yet in direct contradiction to that statement I found him most reasonable on many occasions when I had to approach him, and sometimes when the reason for my approach was distasteful to us both. He is intensely loyal to his supporters, often to his disadvantage, for to reward them for their services he had to raise them to positions they were not fitted to hold. Undoubtedly this is one of the weaknesses of dictatorships. That the Generalissimo should have held his position in China for so many years in the face of the intrigues round him is proof of his real greatness.

Unfortunately the Generalissimo speaks no European language and only Madame could interpret successfully for him, giving the true meaning of his thoughts and wishes. The other interpreters were far too frightened of the Generalissimo, and their terror made them practically unintelligible as interpreters.

Madame is bi-lingual in Chinese and English, having been brought up in America, and when she interpreted I found conversation very easy, and I was far happier whenever she was present. Madame is a most attractive and brilliant woman, of very youthful appearance and the best-dressed woman in China. She has many friends in the world, but like all people with a vibrant personality, she has some enemies, and one or two of them used to say that when Madame interpreted she did it to suit her own views and wishes. I can only believe that Madame's wishes were identical with the Generalissimo's, for at heart they both had one thought, one pursuit, and one happiness—China.

Behind me I had Mr. Winston Churchill. I found him the ideal master to serve, for in a crisis I knew that he would back me in the face of the entire world, even if I were wrong. I knew, equally, that in private he would tell me exactly what he thought of me.

General Wedemeyer of the U.S. Army, deputy chief of staff to Mountbatten, came to Chungking in 1944 and spent several days with me, as he wanted to make a tour of the American airfields and have a thorough look round. He came to the conclusion that although he found the airfields themselves to be excellent, he could not see how they were to be defended if the Japs advanced. I was very struck with Wedemeyer ; he was a charming man, tall, well-built, with a young face and white hair, and he was a perfect staff officer, with quick wits and sound judgment.

Some time after his visit the Japs started to attack in Burma, and succeeded in driving our forces back towards India, and then began the most awkward series of conferences.

Mountbatten wanted the Generalissimo to send him Chinese troops immediately to help to divert the Jap advance. The Generalissimo was, not suprisingly, very unwilling, for he was afraid that the Japs would take advantage and start an attack on China. Finally the Generalissimo consented to send five divisions to Burma, which I considered a generous action.

This situation had entailed so many conferences that I never quite recovered from conference sickness after it, and heartily agreed with the gentleman who described a conference as " The taking of minutes and wasting of hours."

Before the Chinese troops could be of much assistance in Burma the tide turned in our favour in that theatre, and the Japs switched their overtures to China and started a big attack.

I thought I would like to go down to Kweilin to see what was happening, and General Chennault kindly lent me a plane for the trip. On getting into the plane I found it smelled appallingly ; when I asked the pilot what was the cause he said he had been plying backwards and forwards filled with corpses from Kweilin, and had no time to disinfect the plane !

The approach to Kweilin affords the most wonderful view from the air, for the country around is one mass of sugar-loaf hills, the kind of shape I had imagined existed only in the eye of an artist.

We had a mission at Kweilin, the British Army Aid Group under Colonel Ride, who had made a great reputation for himself. He had been a professor at the Hong Kong University, and had been taken prisoner by the Japs when Hong Kong had fallen. He had escaped from his prison camp, and was now proving the most useful source of intelligence to us. He got on admirably both with the Americans and the Chinese, and no Britisher did better work than Ride in China.

The day after my arrival Ride took me up to the front, and we saw the Chinese G.O.C., who struck me as very over-confident. I asked him if he anticipated a Jap attack, and by his answer he gave me the impression that he thought me a fool to imagine such a possibility. He suggested that I should stay and have lunch with him, but my hackles were up and I smelled an attack in the air and declined his invitation. Within two or three hours the Japs attacked and took the town, and although the confident General escaped, he was later shot by order of the Generalissimo.

The people of Kweilin had a better appreciation of the situation than the unfortunate general, for they were evacuating the place as fast as they could. The city was in a state of utter panic, the refugees streaming along the roads with all their worldly goods on their backs, the trains crammed to suffocation point inside, with as many hanging like monkeys from the roofs, and all with that look of hurt bewilderment typical of the refugee in any country. Many months later they returned in the hope of finding their homes still standing, but the whole town had been razed to the ground.

General Wedemeyer's prediction about the impossibility of defending the airfields proved absolutely correct, for when the Japs attacked, all the main airfields had to be destroyed or evacuated. Both the beautiful airfields of Kweilin and Luchan were abandoned, and Chennault's Air Force had to operate from behind the Jap lines, where they had managed to cling on to one or two airfields. Their indefatigable work deserved the highest praise, for they were continually up in the air, only landing to refuel and off up in the air again.

The Japs now turned westwards as the Generalissimo had feared, and as we were not capable of stopping their advance anywhere they were soon threatening Chungking.

General Stilwell's relations with the Generalissimo had never been good, and at this tense moment they snapped finally, and Stilwell returned to America. He was replaced by General Wedemeyer, who could hardly have chosen a more awkward and unenviable time to succeed to the job.

Already there was talk of evacuating Chungking, but I felt sure that the Generalissimo would never agree to such an evacuation. The fall of Chungking would have been a big moral blow to the prestige of the Chinese, but for practical reasons I, personally, was much more afraid of the Japs going for Kunming. Every single thing that entered came in over the " Hump " to land at Kunming, and at this time the planes were landing there every two minutes of the day and night, bringing about 50,000 tons of supplies a month. By the end of the war the supplies brought over had risen from a mere 6,000 tons to 75,000 tons a month. Kunming was our lifeline, and nothing will persuade me that if it had fallen China could have gone on fighting seriously.

The Generalissimo wished to bring back the five divisions of troops he had lent to Mountbatten in Burma, but Mountbatten was very unwilling to part with any troops as he wished to make quite sure of his pursuit of the Japs. Wedemeyer, with innate tact and good management, arranged to get the troops back, and finally stemmed the Jap advance.

From this successful beginning Wedemeyer never looked back for he gained the Generalissimo's confidence and, incidentally, relieved him of an enormous amount of work. Like many other great men, the Generalissimo found it difficult to delegate work to his subordinates, preferring to rely on his own efficiency, but he had been imposing a strain on himself too great for one human being, and now he was content to allow Wedemeyer to share the strain. Wedemeyer was the right man for the job, and although his duties were unending, he was always within his remarkable capacities.

At that time we had various missions in China all working under their own orders, but from the moment of Wedemeyer's taking over he insisted that every mission came under his sole authority and worked into his overall plan. He was very much criticized for his insistence, but personally I think his plan of co-operation was the right one. There is a nice story about Wedemeyer. A British general took great exception to Wedemeyer's pronunciation of the word " schedule," which, as all Americans do, he pronounced " skedule." " Where did you learn to speak like that ? " he asked. Wedemeyer replied : " I must have learned it at ' shool ' ! "

By December, 1944, the Jap threat to Chungking had subsided and I was ordered home to report to the Prime Minister. Mr. Churchill did me the signal honour of taking me before the Cabinet to make my report, which was an interesting and important experience for me.

General Sir Hastings Ismay, now Lord Ismay, was Secretary to the War Cabinet. I had not seen him since we had soldiered together in Somaliland, and I was delighted to find that he was the man with whom I had most dealings. He was fulfilling his arduous job with brilliance and he had one of the most difficult jobs of the whole war. First of all he had to keep up with his chief, Mr. Churchill, in itself an achievement; he had to handle almost every class and nationality with tact and firmness; in addition, he dealt with an ever-changing situation on all fronts. He was one of those rare men who always have time—and he was invaluable to me with his sound advice and understanding and often helped me to overcome my shortcomings.

I stayed at home three weeks, found London battered but unbowed and arranged to report home every six months to enable me to keep in touch with the situations on both sides of the world.

Calcutta was still loathsome to my eyes, but owing to the delightful people whom I found there, I came to regard it with greater lenience. When I first arrived Mr. Casey was Governor of Bengal, and the empire never produced a finer representative. Mr. and Mrs. Casey were the kindest of hosts and hostesses. By a strange coincidence Mrs. Casey had been a V.A.D. at 17 Park Lane in the 1914–18 War, when I had been the home's most recurring inhabitant. Mrs. Casey said she was sure that I could not have remembered her as she had spent her entire war under the beds cleaning the floor. I did remember her, so she must have come up for air occasionally.

Another piece of luck was that my co-prison friend, Dick O'Connor, was given Eastern Command in India, with his headquarters in Calcutta. Thanks to my aeroplane, I became contemptuous of distance, and regarded Dick, 1,800 miles away from Chungking, as my neighbour.

General Douglas Stuart commanded The Fort at Calcutta. Having started life in the Canadian Mounted Police, he fought in the 1914–18 War in France, and then joined the Indian Army. In my opinion to say that a man has been in the Canadian Mounted Police is tantamount to describing him as the finest type of man, and General Douglas Stuart was no exception.

Besides performing my official duties in Calcutta, I used it as an excellent centre for my shopping. Prices were still soaring in China.

Lord Mountbatten moved his headquarters from New Delhi to Kandy in Ceylon, a very charming spot consisting of many white bungalows surrounding a small lake. Ceylon, with its high hills and varied tropical climate, has a fresh green appearance, blazing with tropical flowers, but it is all so small and pretty-pretty that I have no love for it.

On one of my trips to Kandy I had the luck to meet Admiral Sir James Somerville, Commander-in-Chief of the East Indies Fleet, and he kindly offered to take me for a sea journey as he was about to bombard Sabang. The Admiral flew his flag in the *Queen Elizabeth* and I was delighted to accept his invitation.

I cannot remember exactly what the force consisted of, but there was a French cruiser, two British cruisers, a British aircraft-carrier, and a number of destroyers, including a Dutch destroyer. The greatest secrecy was to be observed over this operation, for the success of it depended on our arriving off Sabang in the very early morning unsuspected. I sat comfortably on the bridge of the *Queen Elizabeth* in a deck-chair and prepared to watch the proceedings.

The destroyers tore into Sabang Harbour and in my land-trained mind I compared their attack with a cavalry charge. The noise was hell let loose, and as I had never been in a ship firing anything heavier than ack-ack guns the difference was somewhat marked. I had been expecting a good deal of noise and vibration, for everything had been removed from the walls of the ship, but it was nothing to what I heard and felt.

Aeroplanes from the aircraft-carrier were taking an active part in the bombardment, and without doubt they were the masters of the Jap planes and shot down a number of them. We lost only one plane, and the pilot baled out into the sea and was safely picked up by us. The Jap reply to our shelling was very feeble, and although I believe they did put two shells through one of our destroyers, neither of them exploded. Our casualties numbered two, both war correspondents.

The bombardment over, we started back and late in the afternoon some Jap fighters came after us. Up went our planes from the carrier and drove off the Japs quickly and decisively, with enough time to spare to enable them to land on the carrier before dark. When they landed safely in the nick of time, I could sense the relief of Admiral Somerville and I marvelled at the enthusiasm of the pilots for their very dangerous game.

A curious fact was that this was the first occasion on which the *Queen Elizabeth* had fired her guns in anger since the Dardanelles operation in 1915, and my ears could testify as to her might.

Admiral Somerville was a fine sailor and a great character with a robust sense of humour, and I defy anyone to have a dull moment in his convivial company.

In Chungking my household was continuing to run on oiled wheels, guided by the efficient hand of Colonel Yang. I had no idea how many staff were employed in my house, but I knew that my slightest wish was attended to, and that I was the most fortunate of men to be so well served. One day during an outbreak of cholera it became necessary for my household to be inoculated against the scourge. When the medical officer came to tell me that he had done all the required inoculations, I asked him how many people he had performed on in my house. His answer was forty-eight. Probably the total included some wives and children, but even so I felt that I was not exactly pigging it.

The servants were delightfully practical and unfussy. The chimney was smoking in the drawing-room, and I told my Number One boy to send for the sweep. There was no sweep in Chungking, and without bothering to put out the fire or cover up the furniture, the boy sent a coolie up on to the roof armed with a brick covered in straw. The coolie proceeded to drop the brick down the chimney, clearing it most effectively, but his success was not appreciated by my two staff officers who were standing in the room. Like the coolie, they were black with soot. They entirely failed to see the ingenuity of the entertainment.

My Chinese cook was due to have an operation for goitre, and I was surprised to find him still in the house when I thought he had gone to hospital. I asked him what had happened and he told me that he had decided not to have the operation after all, as the doctor could not guarantee that he would not die. This in a land where life is held very cheaply seemed a contradiction in terms.

By now I felt that I was really getting to know, like and understand the Chinese. The foreigners who had been in China for some time, known as "China Hands," thought me absolutely useless, for they felt that I had no background or knowledge of either the country or her people. Personally, I found my own judgment no worse than the opinions of the so-called experts, who seemed to me to be too full of prejudices, and apt to make out the Chinese to be quite unlike any other living mortals. To me there was no difference; they had the same loves, the same hates, the same tragedies, hopes and despairs, and I found it was only their customs which were different, not their characters.

In China the family comes first and they regard a bad relation as better than a good friend, which is in direct opposition to us in the West, where relations seem only sent to try us. Their religion I never discussed with them, and although many of them are converted to Christianity, the majority live by the Analects of Confucius, who seems to me to have been a most sane and sensible man. Confucius gave his attention to the world in which he lived, believed in the infectious power of good, and the importance of setting an example. On being asked his advice on good government he gave a nice piece of advice that might well be digested by many of our governments to-day. He said to the Minister Chi K'ang Tzu : "If your aspirations are for good, sir, the people will be good. The moral character of those in high positions is the breeze, the character of those below is the grass. When the grass has the breeze on it, it assuredly bends." One of his definitions of virtue seems to have been faithfully remembered by the majority of Chinese, for he said : "In private life be courteous, in handling public business be serious, with all men be conscientious. Even though you go among barbarians, you may not relinquish these virtues."

The predominating trait of the Chinese is their humour, which makes them more merry than witty, and full of laughter. Like the French, they are highly civilized and love the good things of life. They neither eat to live, like the English, nor live to eat like the Teutons. They eat and drink because it breeds friendliness and good manners, and promotes a pleasant *bonhomie* even in matters of business. It is not easy to disagree when the palate has been mollified with delicious food and warm rice wine, a fact not sufficiently appreciated by certain Foreign Ministers.

The " China Hands ", to my mind, were apt to resemble the Chinese only in their weaker characteristics. They confused themselves, talked in circles, apeing the Chinese and thinking to deceive them. On the contrary their motives were transparent to the subtle comprehension of the Chinese, and they were invariably out-manœuvred on favourable ground. Remembering the warnings John Keswick had given me when I met him in Delhi, I came to see more and more clearly how right he was, and how much he had moved with the times. The attitude of the Chinese to the foreigners who inhabited their country had changed. They were no longer grateful dependants of rich exploitation ; they were the hosts in a country where both sides could reap a mutual benefit.

Of the diplomatic coterie in Chungking my chief friends were Sir Horace and Lady Seymour, the British Ambassador and his wife, General Pechkoff, the French Ambassador, and Mr. Keith Officer, the Australian Chargé d'Affaires. Sir Horace was a reasoned, broadminded and charming man, with none of the pettinesses and jealousies often prominent in official life. I owed a great deal to his co-operation and friendship, for with a lesser man our interests might have clashed. Lady Seymour was the perfect ambassador's wife, a brilliant hostess full of vitality and with a kind and generous heart.

General Pechkoff and I felt that we had a very great bond, for we had both lost an arm on May 9th, 1915, Pechkoff his right arm, and I my left. General Pechkoff had had a distinguished career as a soldier, starting in the Foreign Legion, and he had a smart military appearance combined with a shy, quiet manner of deference, which had earned him a host of friends of every nationality. There can have been no *diplomat de carrière* who possessed more innate tact and sensibility and his undeniable qualities must be recognized by the French nation as a whole, for irrespective of what Government or party is in power, he remains one of France's greatest ambassadors, and is now in Tokio.

Mr. (now Sir) Keith Officer, the Australian Chargé d'Affaires, was born in Australia and brought up in the tradition of Oxford and retained the best qualities of both. He had the fresh vigour of the young country mellowed with the wisdom of the old. He was back in China as Ambassador, 1948–49.

CHAPTER XX

THE END OF IT ALL

My flights over the " Hump " continued, but never again did I see it in the perfect conditions of my first flight. Often it was a most unpleasant experience ; our worst flight over it was made at 25,000 feet with a hundred-mile-an-hour gale against us, when it took us five and a half hours to get over, instead of the usual three. The plane was unheated, and my A.D.C. got his toes frostbitten, and when at last we were about to land at Delhi the wheels would not lock. We were all strapped in our seats, and the pilot said he would try to touch the ground with his wheels to lock them. He succeeded, much to the disappointment of all the ambulances which had collected below hurriedly to pick up the bits.

These " Hump " pilots were a wonderful lot, for whatever their innermost feelings they always gave the impression they were off on a joy ride. There were many accidents to planes flying the " Hump ". A large number of the occupants parachuted out and the Americans had wisely arranged to reward the natives who guided them to safety. The results of this arrangement had been very satisfactory.

I found the flight from Kunming to Chungking consistently bumpy and unpleasant, and the landings on the miserable little airfield wreathed in mist most chancy affairs.

How Paddy Noble and Ralph Shaw managed to shoehorn us off and on continually, and without mishap, remains a mystery to me.

The R.A.F. mission was commanded by Air Marshal Sir Lawrence Pattinson at Chengtu, and the mission ran the Chinese Air Force Staff College and did admirable work. Air Marshal Pattinson earned the respect of everyone including the Generalissimo, who had the greatest confidence in him. He was succeeded by Air Vice-Marshal MacNeece Foster, who carried on until the Americans took over the mission, for not unnaturally they wanted to keep all missions in their own hands.

When I first arrived in China the Communist question was not much talked about, and at that time the Central Government took a firm line and would not allow any press correspondents to go into the Communist area. This restriction was a very sore point with both the Communists and the press correspondents, and it finally provoked such feeling that the Central Government had to yield and give their very reluctant consent. Once the correspondent set foot inside Communist territory, the Communists seized their opportunity and went all out to show how ably they were running their own show. Their insidious propaganda was flagrantly successful, and when the press correspondents returned they were lyrical in their praise for both the organization and the fighting powers of the Communists. Foreign countries almost invariably incline in their sympathies towards a minority and, true to form, Communist shares soared on the world market until the question loomed large and ominous on the political horizon.

Undoubtedly, the organization of the Communists was good, but their forces were concentrated into a specific area, which made matters very much easier for them. The Central Government suffered from the drawbacks of geography, with their forces sprawling awkwardly over vast areas both unmanaged and unmanageable, with a transport problem which was insoluble.

The Communist policy of giving to the peasant his own piece of earth was largely responsible for their success, for to the agricultural Chinese a plot of ground was of infinitely more worth to them than a handful of gold. As to the fighting qualities of the Communists, I do not consider that they contributed much towards defeating the Japs. They excelled in guerrilla warfare, which had a nuisance value but no more, and their refusal to co-operate with the Central Government's Forces at the time of the Jap advance in 1944 put those forces in a serious position by compelling them to leave troops on the Communist front when every soldier was needed against the Japs. This refusal showed the Communists in their true light; that they were Communists before they were patriots, and that they put a political creed above their country.

Taken as a whole, the Central Government treated the Communists very correctly and quite well enough considering their continual loud-voiced demands. They allowed the Communists to send a few representatives to the San Francisco Conference, but it only resulted in their asking for more.

The Americans tried to remedy the situation, but mistakenly they insisted on treating the Communists as a government, which succeeded in investing them with still more " face ". Mao Tse Tung, the Communist leader, came to Chunking and Mr. Roosevelt's personal representative, General Hurley, sent his own car to meet him at the airfield. It was a tactical error, for these small points add up to large totals in the East and attain a significance not understood in the West.

Personally I had nothing to do with the Communists, for I felt it was no business of mine to mix myself up with them. I met Mao Tse Tung at dinner during one of his visits to Chunking and I knew him already by reputation. He was a fanatic, Moscow-trained and completely unco-operative, and during dinner he treated me to a discourse of praise on the qualities of the Communist organization. When he got on to how hard they were fighting against the Japs, he tried my credulity a little too far, and I cut short any further fabrications. I told him that what they were really doing was to keep looking over their shoulders to see what the Generalissimo was doing first. To my surprise, Mao Tse Tung took no offence and merely laughed. Another of their leaders asked me why I had never been to Yenan to see their set-up. I answered quite frankly that I hated Communism and that if I went up there it might be taken as a sign that I was interested in them, and besides that they would bombard me with their propaganda. Communism must knock sensitiveness completely on the head, for they continued to invite me into their lair, but needless to say I never went.

Chou-en-Lai, the second in command of the Communists, is a far better man than Mao Tse Tung, extremely clever and with a nice personality, and personally I have always hoped that through him, one day, a compromise might be reached.

Russia has, of course, helped the Communists in China, and at certain times more than others, but it was my impression that although she might be ready to help them, she was by no means anxious or prepared to burn her fingers over them. The Russian Military Attaché told me once that if the Generalissimo attacked the Communists then Russia would certainly take a hand, but when in June 1945 the Generalissimo did attack them, Russia did not see fit to join in the fight.

The United Kingdom and the United States were both against the Generalissimo attacking the Communists, and I was asked by several eminent people to try and persuade the Generalissimo that an attack would be bad policy. I went straight to the Generalissimo and told him frankly the opinion of these knowledgeable people. The Generalissimo was aware that my own personal feelings were different, and that I felt that there was only one answer to the Communists and that was defeat. To me the right time for negotiations is after a victory when, backed by force, words seem to attain a meaning not so well understood before.

In June 1945 the Generalissimo did attack the Communists and gained a few victories, but they were not decisive, because although he had the men, he had not the materials. Perhaps if he had had full backing then the situation might have been different now. Governments may think and say what they like, but force cannot be eliminated, and it is the only real and unanswerable power. We are told that the pen is mightier than the sword, but I know which of these two weapons I would choose.

The war in the West had ended, which made the war in the East a foregone conclusion, and atom bomb or no it would have petered out very soon. The end came suddenly and caused a small stir of excitement for a few days, but it soon wore off and gave way to the difficulties of peace which spring up so quickly and die down so slowly.

On the British side we had considerable difficulty over the Jap surrender of Hong Kong. Hong Kong had been included in the Generalissimo's theatre of operations, and when the time came for the surrender to take place, the Generalissimo delegated the power to accept it to the British. Immediately the storm broke : we would not admit the Generalissimo's right to delegate power to us over one of our own possessions. The Generalissimo maintained that Hong Kong had been placed in his theatre by directive of the Big Powers, thereby constituting his right. What the people of England did not seem to realize was that if the war had continued for another few weeks, the Chinese would have taken Hong Kong from the Japs by themselves, and then there would have been something to wrangle about.

Naturally this squabbling did not improve our relations with the Chinese. The long and exhausting war against the Japs had welded the Chinese together in an intense national feeling, and the return of Hong Kong to China was one of the major issues of the Nationalists.

British diplomacy may have been questionable at this time, but the choice of personnel was inspired and the situation was saved by two men, Admiral Harcourt who took the surrender and became the first post-war Governor of Hong Kong, and General Frankie Festing, G.O.C. Troops, Hong Kong. These two men by their tact and integrity smoothed away every difficulty as it arose and what is more, prevented other difficulties from arising. The Chinese held them both in affection and respect, and it is to their credit almost alone that we own avoidance of most serious trouble.

A few weeks later I flew down to Singapore to assist at the formal surrender of the Japs. In a way the ceremony was impressive, but the Japs looked such insignificant little objects, that I could not help wondering how they had kept us occupied for so long.

From Singapore I flew straight on home, feeling full of a strange and awkward diffidence. In the interim our great war leader, the world's most loved and admired man, and my particular boss, had been ousted as Premier, and Britain was now a Socialist country. Being so far away I had had no inkling of the overwhelming change which had swept over the face of Britain. It was the same old story as in Poland, ingratitude walking hand in hand with politics. The aftermath of war breeds discontent, the people are no longer buoyed up to danger, *camaraderie* disappears with the last bomb, and they desire change at any price whether for better or for worse. But, in the case of Mr. Churchill, it was a cataclysmic blow, for he was rooted in the heart of England as no one man had ever been before.

The shock to me was purely personal, for I have no politics and am utterly uninterested as to what party is in power. I imagined that my job as personal representative of the Prime Minister would cease, and I was surprised and pleased when Mr. Attlee asked me to stay on as his representative. He was very nice to me, and I left him feeling very satisfied but realizing that inevitably the tenor of my job would change with the personality behind it. Then I went to see Mr. Ernest Bevin, the Foreign Secretary, and felt instinctively that here was a man who was sound, practical and wise, and I liked him enormously. People are apt to ask for one's views on a subject quite mechanically, and without any desire to hear them before rushing on to bombard one with their own opinions. Not so Mr. Bevin. He asked me to tell him what I knew of China, listened patiently to all I had to say, and then quietly proceeded to give me his side of the picture, and I felt that I knew exactly where I stood.

I returned to Chungking and found that with the Labour Party in power my work had rather changed in character. In Mr. Churchill's time, when something critical occurred, he took everything into his own hands, whereas his successor delegated responsibility to the War Office and the Foreign Office. This considerably lessened my contacts with the Generalissimo, although he generally discussed matters with me as a friend rather than as the representative of the Prime Minister.

Major Dowler had returned to England after a serious

operation in China and was replaced by Colonel Chapman Walker who came to me from a staff appointment with General " Jumbo " Wilson, who quite rightly had a high opinion of his abilities. Chungking released from war was a centre of sociability; my staff had a very good time, and were out on the tiles every night. Chapman Walker and Eckford went to a dance one night in my " Jeep " and proceeded to lose it. Later it was found abandoned; I had it painted scarlet, and it was never lost sight of again. In the two years that Eckford was with me he never failed to be up in the morning before me, with all my papers sorted, whatever time he went to bed. It says a great deal for his stamina.

In December came the prospect of a visit to Peking, which had not been possible in war time as it had been occupied by the Japs. Enthusiasts had told me that it was the most beautiful city in the world, and I was prepared to be bitterly disappointed, knowing how people spoil things by over-exaggeration. Also I imagined that the Japs were no respecters of fine buildings and that I should find the whole place desecrated, with the population wallowing in hunger, poverty and despair.

My first view of Peking was from the air, and I saw it below me in a countryside all under snow, with many little frozen lakes dotted around and shining like diamonds in the clear, frosty, sunny air. When we landed I found my fears melting rapidly, for the city was intact; the people gay and laughing and the whole scene was one of riotous colour. It was the most undisappointing place I have ever seen, and I could well understand the many people I have met who have told me that they would rather live in Peking than in any other city in the world, for it was beguiling, fascinating and lovable. We were feasted and fêted for several wonderful days by delightful officials who did us great honour, and for the first time in my life I was led willingly to see the sights. I should have been a very churlish and ungracious man not to fall for the loveliness of the Forbidden City with its yellow-tiled roof, or for the Temple of Heaven and the Summer Palace, and I kept feeling so thankful that there was one exquisite spot in the world which man had not seen fit to destroy. When I got back to Chungking I received a letter from the Lord Mayor of Peking which I shall treasure all my life. It went as follows :

> For favour of perusal by General Carton de Wiart.
>
> The recent gracious visit of the Mighty Chariot added lustre to the appearance of the City. How sad, how regrettable that it was not possible to stay long and that the feelings of the host could not adequately be expressed.
>
> It was heard with deep relief that the Mighty Chariot had returned in safety to Chungking. Many exposures were taken by attendants of the places visited while in Peking; one print of each has been respectfully made and is sent herein, presented with both hands, to form ' the imprint of the wild swan on the snow and mud ' and a souvenir of former travels. It is respectfully hoped that they may be accepted with a smile (of benevolent condescension); this is my earnest prayer.
>
> Respectful wishes for the Sage's birthday.
> Respectfully written by
>
> Hsuing Pin
>
> December 20th

The Jap war over, the Central Government moved back to their former capital of Nanking, more conveniently placed geographically about two hundred miles from Shanghai, the commercial pulse of the country. The climate of Nanking was pleasanter than Chungking, being far less extreme, and I was given another charming house in the compound of the University, which had belonged to Professor Buck, husband of the authoress Pearl Buck. From my bedroom window I gazed on to Purple Mountain towering 2,000 feet above us, the only height in an otherwise nearly flat countryside.

In spite of my nice house and the agreeable climate I never liked Nanking, nor did I feel as happy there as I had in Chungking. I missed the hurly-burly of that overcrowded city and its cheerful informality bred by war ; the little shopkeepers and the ordinary citizens going about their business were of infinitely more interest than the State officials. Nanking had a permanent atmosphere of white kid gloves ; the *tempo* of life had slackened and I felt my *raison d'être* departing. My chief consolation lay in a daily walk up Purple Mountain, but even that was a more civilized outing, for I could no longer walk in my shorts and native sandals and burn myself black with the sun. I had to motor out to the foot of Purple Mountain, take the steepest path up and climb as fast as I could for an hour and a half, discreetly divesting myself of my shirt when out of sight. There were many pilgrims and sightseers to the mountain, for on it stands the tomb of Sun Yat Sen built in magnificent white stone, an impressive monument to the first great leader of Nationalist China, who died in 1925, and whose mantle was to fall on Generalissimo Chiang Kai-shek.

I went down to Calcutta again, and found the new Governor of Bengal, Sir Frederick Burrows, who had been appointed by the Labour Government. He was one of the most delightful men I have ever met, with a very fine presence and natural dignity. He had endeared himself to the " Burra Sahibs " of Calcutta with one of his first speeches when, alluding to his modest beginning on the railway, he said : " When you gentlemen were huntin' and shootin ", I was shuntin' and hootin '." He seemed to me to be far more proud of having been a sergeant-major in the Grenadier Guards in the First World War than he was of being Governor of Bengal !

The summer in Nanking grew oppressive and stifling. The Generalissimo with his usual thoughtfulness offered me a house in the mountains at Kuling, where I could go whenever I felt that I needed some fresh air. My staff had been reduced to one A.D.C., Bobbie McMullan, and he and I flew to Kukiang at the foot of the mountain, where we found there was a climb of 3,500 feet to Kuling. It was the custom to be carried up the mountain in a chair borne by two coolies, but as I disliked the idea of being carried, we elected to walk up. We could see flights of stone steps (so beloved by the Chinese) stretching way up to the top of the mountain, but our daily assault on Purple Mountain filled us with a false pride, and we overrated our training and arrived at the top virtually in a state of collapse. I found a nice little chalet earmarked for me with all the comfort I had come to expect in China, and yet the place did not strike me as typically Chinese. The houses might have belonged anywhere ; they were mostly one-storeyed stone bungalows mainly frequented by missionaries of all nationalities. The Chinese have a mature civilization and a passion for Nature, especially in her wildest moods, and in their deeply rooted love of mountains they find spiritual refreshment and an escape from man. Kuling was a little village at the top of a mountain dominating the vast plains stretching below. The walks were wonderful in their infinite variety, for one moment I found myself wandering through wooded green-land, and the next I was gasping on the raw edge of a crag with a 3,500 foot drop. The air was like champagne and revived us rapidly and, a few days after, we prepared to descend the mountain on our return journey. Bobbie and I found it a far tougher proposition than the ascent, and arrived at the bottom with our knees jangling and our tummies in our toes.

Once again I went back to England to report, and this time I was given a British plane to take back to China. It was a Lancastrian, a very wonderful machine, and we only made four stops between London and Nanking, practically eliminating the feeling of distance. This plane made a great impression on everyone who saw it, and did much to raise British prestige. I took any opportunity I could to give lifts to other people, and especially to the Chinese.

Soon after I got back I arranged to go to Tokio, and I must admit that it was with much more desire to see Mac-Arthur than any wish to see Japan. Being on the fringe of General MacArthur's theatre of operations, I had followed his campaign with interest and wholehearted admiration. Personally I had thought his campaign in the Pacific the biggest military achievement of the war, for it was of a type which had never been attempted before. His planning had covered many thousands of miles and included combined naval, military and amphibious operations ; although he had magnificent troops in the U.S. Marines, it had needed a supreme commander to make the best use of them in such a vast scheme.

General Lumsden, who had been my opposite number in Japan, was killed very tragically in a battleship bombarded by the Japs. He had been succeeded by General Charles Gairdner, with whom I was to stay.

General MacArthur invited me to lunch, and I felt interested at the prospect of meeting him. I had half expected to find a dynamic swashbuckler, but instead I found a tremendous personality and a charming man. He is accused by his critics of being a *poseur*, but certainly he had something to pose about, and there is no doubt that a little " pantomime " can be very effective in the right man.

MacArthur pleased me enormously by the nice things he said about Lumsden. He said that when Lumsden was killed he had lost the most popular man in his force, and I knew that he meant what he said. Armies in all countries are conservative and prejudiced, and there are not many commanders who would have paid such generous tribute to a foreigner.

I did not see very much of Japan, although I flew over Hiroshima, which from the air looked much like any other bombed-out city. The whole country was pretty without being magnificent, and I noticed that the women looked far more attractive and pleasing than the nasty little men.

The country was being run admirably and efficiently by the Americans, who left no one in any doubt as to who were the masters in Japan. MacArthur's administration in peace seemed as ruthlessly efficient as in war, for he was a conqueror, and he looked it, and I left with my admiration for him intensified.

In July, 1946, Sir Horace Seymour's time as Ambassador came to an end, and it was with real sadness that the Chinese saw him depart. Both Sir Horace and Lady Seymour had succeeded beyond all praise in the art of true diplomacy, and they left behind them the nicest memories of two charming people. They were succeeded by Sir Ralph and Lady Stevenson, who are immensely popular also. They are now facing the difficulties of a China torn apart.

One more trip to Peking filled me with more enthusiasm for that enchanting city, but by now I was getting fidgety, felt that I had outgrown my usefulness and my thoughts turned to home.

At this psychological moment the Generalissimo gave me me one of the biggest surprises of my life, for he asked me to stay on in China as his personal adviser. My persistent diffidence is one of my worst enemies in life, for I am apt to imagine myself a failure, even without any reason, and the Generalissimo's offer did more to raise my morale than anything else could have done. At least I felt that I must have achieved something, if only a feeling of trust, and I was immensely gratified and extremely proud.

I was going home to relinquish my post officially, and I reserved my answer to the Generalissimo until I got back. I was not quite sure about it, as I am not keen on officialdom in peace time, but I knew that I should be blown one way or another at the dictates of Fate, and was prepared to leave it to her as usual. I had no plans, no home, no job, and with Poland out of reach China might take her place in my interest. War had given me no opportunity or time to see this vast country or indulge in any sport, but I knew the opportunities for shooting were limitless, and I wanted to explore them.

CHAPTER XXI

AND SO TO BED

ON my way home I called in for my first visit to Indo-China at Saigon, and found it in a most unsettled state. The French had had a difficult time there during the war, and although the British had done what they could by para-chuting agents and supplies into the country, they were like drops in the ocean in that vast territory. Now no one could go outside Saigon without fear of being attacked, and the atmosphere was anxious and unpleasant. I spent a day there, and in spite of the difficulties I was given a warm welcome by our Representative and his wife, Mr. and Mrs. Meiklereid. We were all invited to dinner by the French Governor of Indo-China, Admiral d'Argenlieu, a remarkable man, who had had an extraordinary career. The Admiral had been a naval officer in the 1914–18 War, but shortly after it his wife had died, and he left the Navy and became a Carmelite monk. In 1939, when France entered the war, he rejoined the Navy and became an admiral, fighting with the Free French, who elected him Governor of Indo-China. Later he was recalled and he returned to his monastery.

From Saigon I flew to Rangoon to stay with Brigadier C. L. Duke, who had been with me in the 61st Division at Oxford and Ballymena. We lunched modestly, and I went up to my room. Coming down again, I slipped on the coco-nut matting in my leather-soled shoes and crashed to the bottom of the stairs. I hit my head on the wall, knocking myself almost unconscious, broke my back, crushing a vertebra, and was very lucky not to break my neck. When I came to and realized what had happened to me it seemed to ring the death-knell to every hope, enjoyment or job, and in my heart I never thought I should walk again.

Once again my luck held, for at Rangoon Hospital there was an orthopædic surgeon of a high order, Colonel Bonnin. He clapped me into plaster of Paris, insisted on my doing exercises after a few very days, and restored both my interest and my confidence in myself. The plaster held me together and I was able to creep about in a fashion, and after a month he sent me back to England in my own plane. He sent an excellent nurse with me, and with the wonderful efforts of the crew and my own batman, Pritchard, I had a remarkable journey home. Tied up in knots, I proceeded to do my farewell tour of the world like a prima donna, but unlike most prima donnas, I did feel that this was to be my final trip.

Again I stayed with the Wavells at Delhi. They feted me on champagne and I tried not to compare my journey home with my journey out. Two nights with General Allfrey in Cairo, and with Sir Clifford and Lady Norton in Athens, did much to cheer me up, but I was not sure of my destination in England. Colonel Bonnin had wired home to try and get me accommodation in the Royal Masonic Hospital, which he told me was one of the finest hospitals in London. In spite of its being closed as a military hospital, the Freemasons kindly consented to my going there, although I do not belong to their fraternity. For seven months they operated on me, nursed me, housed me and fed me, and all with unremitting kindness and skill ; and no man has more reason to be grateful to them. Not only did they mend my back, but they tidied me up inside and outside, excavated all sorts of old bits of scrap-iron, and sent me away a fitter if no wiser man. I must give my thanks again to Mr. Buxton, the orthopædic surgeon, to Mr. Pannet of St. Mary's and to the matron, medical and nursing staff who looked after me and performed their separate miracles.

I had been laid up too long to be able to accept the General-issimo's appointment as personal adviser, but I think that both he and Madame knew how sad it was for me to refuse.

They wired me, offering to keep the job open for me indefinitely, but I felt that I was a crock and might prove to be a useless one. I loved China, her people and her country, and had found great happiness there, and I could not have wished for a pleasanter fate than to go back and be of some use to the Generalissimo and Madame, but it was not to be.

My recovery was in slow motion, and *au fond*, I still wondered whether my future lay in a bath chair at Brighton. Gradually I discovered that I did not snap in half when I bent down, and it dawned on me that if my legs could walk me down a passage, they might, in time, be induced to walk me up a hill. Whereupon I renounced invalidism, white grapes and the insidious sympathy of my friends, and decided to get well, resorting hastily to those hateful but regrettably beneficial morning exercises! I relinquish them on one pretext only — a journey. Then I put on what is known as my " journey face " and become a bane to my household and fellow travellers, and arrive at the station in time to catch the train the day before.

My first journey after emerging from hospital was to the land of my forbears, Belgium, where my childhood's friend and cousin, Count Henri Carton de Wiart and his wife, were celebrating their golden wedding anniversary. I stayed with my other cousin, Baron Edmond Carton de Wiart, and although it was fifty years since we had been boys together, the years between felt very short. I stood there surrounded by the succeeding generations, and I felt a strange feeling that the circle was closing and I was back at the beginning again. *Plus ça change, plus c'est la même chose.*

Other PAN Books of True War Adventure

Enemy Coast Ahead GUY GIBSON, V.C., D.S.O., D.F.C.

Heroic bomber pilot tells of his adventures in the early days of the War, leading to a wonderful account of the raid on the dams, which he led. *Illustrated.* (2/6)

The Dam Busters PAUL BRICKHILL

Reveals certain details of the attack on the dams which were secret when Gibson wrote *Enemy Coast Ahead*, and tells how 617 Squadron later smashed Hitler's most alarming secret weapon, and destroyed the battleship *Tirpitz*. Now filmed. *Illustrated.* (2/6)

Escape—or Die PAUL BRICKHILL

Narratives of eight daring escapes by R.A.F. men. Introduction by H. E. Bates. (2/-)

They Have Their Exits AIREY NEAVE, D.S.O., O.B.E., M.C.

Captured in 1940, the author was sent to Colditz Castle, from which he was the first to make a successful ' home-run '. Later he worked with the French Resistance rescuing Allied airmen grounded in enemy territory. In 1945 he was appointed to serve the indictment for war crimes on the Nazi leaders in their prison-cells. Foreword by Lord Justice Birkett (one of the judges at the Nuremberg Tribunal). (2/-).

The White Rabbit BRUCE MARSHALL

The story of Wing-Commander Yeo-Thomas, G.C., M.C., British secret agent who was captured by the Gestapo in Paris, and suffered torture in prison-camps. *Illustrated.* (2/6)

Unbroken ALASTAIR MARS, D.S.O., D.S.C.

Inspiring record of a British submarine's adventures in the Mediterranean in 1942, by her commander. *Illustrated.* (2/-)

The Colditz Story P. R. REID, M.B.E., M.C.

The author was in charge of escape-planning at Colditz Castle, which the Germans believed to be escape-proof. He tells how he organised many daring exploits and how he himself got away to Switzerland. Now filmed. (2/-)

The Latter Days at Colditz P. R. REID, M.B.E., M.C.

Sequel to *The Colditz Story*, telling of daring exploits of Allied prisoners in Colditz Castle 1942-5 (including the building of a glider in an attic room). 2/6)

Dare to Be Free
W. B. THOMAS, D.S.O., M.C.

New Zealand officer's story of his escape in Greece to the Mount Athos monasteries, where he was hidden for many months. Finally he reached Turkey in a stolen boat. (2/-)

Two Eggs on My Plate
OLUF REED OLSEN

Having escaped from Norway in a small boat in 1940, the author returned as an Allied agent, establishing radio stations and sabotaging enemy installations. *Illustrated.* (2/6)

Odette: the Story of a British Agent
JERRARD TICKELL

The story of Odette Churchill, G.C., M.B.E. No war book surpasses this as a record of a woman's superb courage. *Illustrated.* (2/6)

The Road to En-dor
E. H. JONES

First World War's most famous escape book, telling how two British officers pretended to be receiving 'spirit' messages, and completely deceived their Turkish captors. With new Foreword by Eric Williams, M.C., author of *The Wooden Horse.* (*September*, 1955.) (2/-)

The Naked Island
RUSSELL BRADDON

Famous book by an Australian captured by the Japanese in Malaya —a narrative of appalling suffering but also of indomitable courage on the part of Commonwealth soldiers. *Illustrated.* (2/6)

The Last Days of Hitler
H. R. TREVOR-ROPER

Oxford historian tells how he tracked down the truth of the fantastic events that culminated in the suicide of the Führer and of Eva Braun in the Berlin Bunker and the secret burning of their bodies. (2/6)

The Diary of a Young Girl
ANNE FRANK

In 1942 Anne Frank and her family went into hiding in the sealed-off back rooms of an Amsterdam office building. For two years they remained undiscovered. Then they were betrayed to the Gestapo; Anne died in the concentration camp at Belsen. This diary—astonishingly intimate and gay—was found in a heap of rubbish. (2/-)

Boldness Be My Friend
RICHARD PAPE, M.M.

" I shall not forget it," says Marshal of the R.A.F. Lord Tedder in his Foreword to this narrative of a British prisoner-of-war's astonishing adventures and escapes. *Illustrated.* (*October*, 1955.) (2/6)

Adventures in the World's Largest Forest

JULIAN DUGUID'S
Green Hell

This is the record of an expedition into the almost unknown Gran Chaco regions of South America, by the route taken by a Spanish Conquistador in 1557. The author, bored by office life in London, collected a Bolivian diplomat and a cinematographer, and was joined by a Russian jaguar-hunter nicknamed "Tiger-Man." Soon the latter became their leader, for the others were so inexperienced that without him they would have died. They met man-eating fish, alligators, and tarantulas the size of a kitten; the author wrestled with a 15-foot snake while his friend took a cine-film of the struggle; they trailed a wounded jaguar; vampires attacked their animals. For three weeks they had to cut a way for the mules through "Green Hell", while they suffered agonies from thirst and clouds of biting insects. Savage Indians stalked them and killed a boy in a party ahead of them. Mr. Duguid recounts all these adventures with great gusto and humour. A distinguished writer, he has in recent years become known to a new public through his broadcast talks, for the B.B.C. sent him as their special correspondent on trips to Pakistan, the Middle East, South Africa and Brazil.　　　　　　　(2/-)

Pioneers in the Art of Healing

DR. HARLEY WILLIAMS'
Masters of Medicine

An account of great discoveries in the field of medicine and surgery during the last 150 years, told through the life-stories of some famous pioneers. The chapters are: Conquerors of the Germ (Edward Jenner, Louis Pasteur, Paul Ehrlich), The Painful Birth of Anæsthesia (Crawford Long, Horace Wells, William Morton, Sir James Young Simpson), The Beginnings and Growth of Modern Surgery (Lord Lister, the Mayo brothers, W. S. Halsted, Harvey Cushing, Lord Moynihan), The Control of Tropical Disease (Patrick Manson, Sir Ronald Ross, Hideyo Noguchi), The Fight against Tuberculosis (Robert Koch, Sir Robert Philip, Edward Livingstone Trudeau). Directly or indirectly, almost every reader of this book enjoys the benefits these great men have passed on.　　　　　　　(2/6)

"A magnificent series of clear, living, vital 'pictures'. Interest never flags; there is nothing drab or stodgy. The reader is made to feel some of the author's enthusiasm. . . . We found it difficult to put down the book until we had finished the whole at one sitting."—*Medical Press.*

ALAN VILLIERS'

The Set of the Sails

The autobiography of a seaman whose experiences in sailing-ships is unrivalled and whose fame as a writer of books on ships and the sea is worldwide. From his boyhood days in Melbourne, Australia, he was determined not only to go to sea in sailing-ships but also to command one. When he was fifteen he shipped as a cadet in an ancient barque. For some time he lived in a large drain-pipe on the waterfront at Bordeaux; then he boarded the *Lawhill* for Australia and when she collided with a buoy he was pitched off the yard, striking the rigging all the way in his fall to the deck. He joined a whaling expedition to the Antarctic; he sailed with a film camera in the 'killer' ship *Grace Harwar*; he was in the famous Cape Horn grain-racer *Herzogin Cecilie* and was part-owner of the record-breaking *Parma*; he put in a spell with Arab deep-sea dhows; and to crown his life's ambition he bought a Danish training ship which he renamed *Joseph Conrad* and sailed her three times round the world. *With 8 pages of photogravure illustrations.* (2/6)

" Alan Villiers is one of those rare men of action who can *write*, simply and compellingly."—JACK MCLAREN in B.B.C. talk.

"An excellent tale of seafaring adventure. It offers unusual entertainment, it provokes thought."—ERIC LINKLATER in *Observer*.

A Paradise Beneath the Waves

PHILIPPE DIOLÉ'S

The Undersea Adventure

This remarkable book reveals a new world of boundless practical possibilities. Using the 'aqualung' (compressed air diving equipment), the author has swum beneath the Mediterranean waves amid a wonderland of vegetation, fish and other creatures decked in the most brilliant colours. He tells of such curiosities as vast floating fields of seaweed and pink eel-larvæ that take three years to drift across the Atlantic. He describes the spectacular mating habits of eels, lampreys and octopuses; octopus-charmers who stroke these many-tentacled creatures as if they were cats made of flannel; the exquisite mating-dance of the sea-horse; the boisterous conjugal life of the whale; the thrill of discovering wrecks of Greek and Roman ships laden with wine-jars, statues, and other objects of profound interest to archæologists. *With 8 pages of photogravure plates (some in two colours).* (2/6)

" A new and strange world, teeming with its own life, is opened to one's most intimate gaze."—RICHARD GARNETT in *Spectator*.

" Will surely rank as an inspiring work of literature, a classic in its limited class."—DANIEL GEORGE in *Bookman*.